GREAT
MOMENTS IN
AUSTRALIAN
HISTORY

Other books (selected) by Jonathan King

The Other Side of the Coin (1976)
Stop Laughing, This is Serious! (1978)
Waltzing Materialism: Attitudes that shaped Australia (1978)
A Cartoon History of Australia (1980)
Governor Phillip Gidley King (with John King, 1982)
The First Fleet: Convict voyage that founded a nation (1982)
The First Settlement: Convict village that founded a nation (1985)
In the Beginning: The founding of Australia from the original documents (1986)
Voyage into History (1987)
Australia's First Fleet: The original voyage and the re-enactment (1988)
Battle for the Bicentenary (1989)
The Man from Snowy River (1995)
Australia's First Century: A pictorial history of Australia (2000)
Gallipoli Diaries: The Anzacs own story, day by day (2003)
Gallipoli: Our last man standing (2004)
Mary Bryant: Her life and escape from Botany Bay (2004)
Gallipoli's Untold Stories (2005)
Historica (2006)
Western Front Diaries: The Anzacs own story, battle by battle (2008)

GREAT
MOMENTS IN
AUSTRALIAN
HISTORY

JONATHAN KING

ALLEN&UNWIN

For Jane King (née Lewis),
my wife, who worked long and hard on this book,
as she did on all of my other books

First published in 2009

Allen & Unwin
83 Alexander Street
Crows Nest NSW 2065
Australia
Phone: (61 2) 8425 0100
Fax: (61 2) 9906 2218
Email: info@allenandunwin.com
Web: www.allenandunwin.com

Cataloguing-in-Publication details are available
from the National Library of Australia
www.librariesaustralia.nla.gov.au

ISBN 978 1 74237 127 6

Internal design by Simon Paterson, Bookhouse
Image restoration, retouching and pre-press by Bookhouse
Set in 12/15 pt Garamond Premier Pro by Bookhouse, Sydney
Printed in Australia by McPherson's Printing Group

10 9 8 7 6 5 4 3 2 1

FOREWORD

It is a bright idea to select the great moments in Australian history and breathe life into them.

This book presents over sixty of those moments or turning points: Governor Arthur Phillip sailing into Sydney harbour in 1788, the first Aboriginal reaching Britain, the exploring of the Blue Mountains and the vast dry interior, and the excitement of finding rich gold in an Australian creek. Here is a labourer winning the Victoria Cross at Gallipoli, the first woman—a West Australian—winning a seat in parliament, and some tense moments of World War II. I know of no other Australian book with this approach, though Justice Michael Kirby recently urged Canberra to devote a whole museum to the 'Defining Moments' in our history.

Jonathan King begins each episode with his version of the conversations and gestures that might have taken place between those who observed or created these moments. I must admit that I feel uneasy when I see, in history books, these conversations being plucked from the vanished airwaves. At the same time, many Australians now learn much of their history from films and television specials, and there the conversations are freely 'made up'. Significantly, in the last fifty years no single history book has been so powerful a teacher as the film *Gallipoli*.

Jonathan King has often tried to awaken Australians to their history, and believes that the awakening has far to go. His book sets out to reach 'people who do not normally buy history books'. Many historians—even those who might choose a different set of moments—hope that his book succeeds.

Geoffrey Blainey
Melbourne

CONTENTS

INTRODUCTION

This book highlights some of the great moments in Australian history—the key events that defined the nation.

Each moment and its historical background is reported in the style, and at roughly the length, of a newspaper feature story. Since the choice of events is bound to leave some readers dissatisfied, it's appropriate to explain the selection criteria. The main one was news value. All the events had to be headline-making—either 'front-page news' in its day or important enough in hindsight to have hit the front pages. They had to be of wide significance, affecting the whole nation rather than sectional interests. This approach generally favoured big-picture events over great achievements by individuals, though most stories are told from a single point of view. The story of Sydney's founding by Captain Arthur Phillip, for example, tells us a great deal about the first British settlement from the European point of view; the account of Bennelong's tragic life reflects the consequences of that settlement for indigenous Australians.

The events also had to be turning points, altering the course or character of the nation. Edward Hargraves's 1851 revelation that gold was to be found in New South Wales, for example, helped launch a gold rush that completed the transformation of the former penal colonies into thriving societies of free settlers.

Many of the stories, particularly those that cover the best-known events, are told from the perspective of the people involved. We see James Cook taking possession of the continent's east coast for Britain; Gregory Blaxland, William Lawson and William Wentworth crossing the Blue Mountains; the Australian Imperial Force landing at Gallipoli and establishing the Anzac legend; Prime Minister John Curtin transferring Australia's allegiance from Britain to the United States in the face of a seemingly imminent Japanese invasion; and Eddie Mabo winning recognition of title to his ancestral lands in 1993.

This Aboriginal rock painting of the Lightning Brothers, Yagjadbulu and Jabaringi, was traditionally associated with the arrival of rain—always celebrated when it finally came after the long dry periods that characterised life in northern Australia.

The events include significant firsts, such as Willem Jansz's becoming the first European to land on Australian soil; Edith Cowan's becoming the first woman elected to Parliament; and John Bertrand's 1983 America's Cup win, the first by a non-American challenger in 132 years. They also include colourful or dramatic events, such as the wreck of the *Batavia* in 1629 and William Buckley's return to European settlement in 1834 after more than thirty years living with Aboriginal tribes. Among the individual stories with national impact are those of New South Wales colonial Premier Sir Henry Parkes, who inspired Federation; Aboriginal activist Charlie Perkins, who helped break down discrimination; and environmentalist Bob Brown, who began his distinguished career in the fight to save the Franklin River.

Even with these guidelines, and the advice of many other historical scholars, deciding what to include and what to leave out was difficult. I have tried to achieve a balance between colonial and modern; between men and women; between Aboriginal and European; and between radical and conservative politics.

The great moments were not all good moments by any means. Some were very bad, at least for those involved. The sinking in 1941 of HMAS *Sydney* with the loss of all hands was a terrible moment, and it left Australians wondering for the next sixty-six years what had happened. That mystery added to the significance of the wreck's eventual discovery.

The stories embrace exploration, war, politics, industrial relations, crime, sporting achievements, natural disasters and even a little poetry. They are presented in chronological order and written in a style that first-time readers of history should find accessible and enjoyable. Since this is a popular book rather than a scholarly treatise, there are no footnotes or references.

Each story begins with a dramatised opening, in which the historical characters are imagined acting out or discussing the great moment as it unfolds. Wherever possible, these are individuals who were in a position to give an eyewitness account of the event in question, but the settings, action, and dialogue are fictionalised. In most cases, these dramatisations are based on contemporary accounts, journals, books, newspaper or magazine reports, or documentary films. I have also relied on imaginative empathy—on my *feel* for the subject matter. In some cases, the characters seemed to put words into their own mouths.

After the opening dialogue, I explain why this was a great moment and provide the historical background. Each story ends with a postscript that notes interesting facts, unforeseen consequences or surprising twists. Explorers Robert

O'Hara Burke and William Wills may have been first to cross the continent from south to north, but after four months away from their camp, they missed a rescue party by mere hours. After weeks trekking through the icy wastes of Antarctica, where his two companions died, explorer Douglas Mawson made it back to the Australian base just a few hours after the relief ship sailed for home. After hitting century after century, cricketer Don Bradman went out for a duck on his last innings.

But the 'beautiful lies' that visiting American writer Mark Twain noted in Australia's history are not in fact 'all true', as Twain claimed they were. Captain James Cook did not discover Australia; Matthew Flinders did not publish the first map of Australia; Edward Hargraves was not the first to find gold; and Blaxland, Wentworth and Lawson did not actually cross the Blue Mountains.

The whole is much greater than the sum of the parts. Together, these stories do more than note the big milestones and main events: they provide a potted history of Australia.

Some events and individuals also form narrative threads that run through several stories. Like runners in a relay race, social and political reformers pass the baton to like-minded souls in later generations. Edith Cowan, the first woman to sit in an Australian Parliament, was continuing work begun by women like Catherine Spence in the late nineteenth century. It was carried on by Dame Enid Lyons, the first female member of Federal Parliament; Julia Gillard, who became Deputy Prime Minister in 2007; and Anna Bligh, who was elected Premier of Queensland in 2009. Other relay runners also achieved great advances in Aboriginal affairs, industrial relations, the law, social welfare and environmental reform.

History does repeat itself, and these stories reveal some interesting patterns. One is the number of lost white men who have been helped by Aborigines— including escaped convict William Buckley and John King, the sole survivor of the Burke and Wills expedition.

Successive Labor leaders have pursued the idealistic 'light on the hill' via the path of social reform. John Watson, John Curtin, Ben Chifley, Gough Whitlam, Bob Hawke and Kevin Rudd have all done their best to improve the lot of the working classes. Working-class heroes have also played their part, from the gold miners who fought for democratic rights at Eureka in 1854 to the gold miners who persuaded Western Australia to join Federation in 1899, to Jack Mundey and the New South Wales builders' labourers who helped launch the environmental movement in the 1970s. The radical group Tocsin ('alarm bell') warned in the nineteenth century against the power the Constitution gave to governors-general, saying that such an official might one day dismiss a Labor government. That prophecy came true when Sir John Kerr dismissed Labor Prime Minister Gough Whitlam in 1975. New South Wales Premier Jack Lang, another Labor leader, was also dismissed by a representative of the Crown in 1932.

Some things never change. Australians have always loved sports heroes—all the more so if they are pretty. 'Golden Girl' Betty Cuthbert won the hearts of her sports-mad compatriots at the 1956 Olympics, where she won more gold medals than any Aussie athlete before her. Nearly half a century later, just before her Aboriginal successor Cathy Freeman also took gold at the next Games to be held in Australia, Cuthbert carried the torch with which Freeman lit the Olympic Flame.

The stories show that much has improved in Australia—thank heavens. Conditions have changed for the better for Aborigines, women, poor people, workers and the environment. While there is still much to do, life for Aboriginal people has come a long way since Captain Arthur Phillip captured and 'civilised' Bennelong, who, after drinking tea with King George III in London, returned to Sydney to a life of drunken misery and an early grave when his tribe refused to take him back. Aborigines whose ancestors were shot in 1788 are today appointed as governors, elected to Parliament and applauded as sporting heroes and artists; in 2008 they were formally apologised to by the Federal Parliament.

Life has also been transformed for women. In 1788, most white females in Australia were convicts and/or prostitutes. For at least the next century, they were overworked, underpaid and not allowed to work in professions such as law, let alone vote or sit in Parliament. Today women serve as premiers, deputy prime ministers and governors-general.

Life has been transformed for working people thanks to the trade unions that won them an eight-hour day, a five-day week, and conditions such as workers' compensation, sickness benefits and pensions.

The environment too has been transformed. For a time, trees were felled without thought, rivers became as polluted as sewers and species were hunted to the brink of extinction. Now the natural world is far better protected, though this remains an urgent work in progress upon which our very survival will depend.

Many of the figures and events that appear in this book have been floating around in my head for years. I sailed on a replica of Jansz's tiny ship *Duyfken* and on a replica of James Cook's *Endeavour*. I also worked with Aboriginal leader

Burnum Burnum (Harry Penrith) on the bicentenary and received advice from activist Charlie Perkins, who told me to pursue that 'whitefella's dream'. I wrote a book on convict escapee Mary Bryant, revived 'that Jolly Swagman' for the 'Waltzing Matilda' centennial celebration in Winton, Queensland, and re-enacted the 'Man from Snowy River' ride for its centennial celebrations in the Snowy Mountains. I interviewed the last ten Anzacs from Gallipoli, the final fifty from the Western Front, and 39th Battalion veterans of Kokoda. Both sides of the dismissal drama, Gough Whitlam and Malcolm Fraser, together launched my book *Australia's First Century* and I recently talked to bushfire survivor Gary Hughes after the Black Saturday bushfires early in 2009.

I apologise for leaving out many stories that deserved inclusion. They include those of explorers Hamilton Hume and William Hovel; Tasmanian colonial figure George Augustus Robinson; political giant William Charles Wentworth, who shaped early democratic institutions; Charles Todd, who built the overland telegraph; J.F. Archibald, who founded *The Bulletin*; colonial women's rights campaigner Catherine Spence; Captain Neville Howse, who won a Victoria Cross in the Boer War; adventure photographer and filmmaker Frank Hurley; Archbishop Daniel Mannix, who led the First World War campaign against conscription; John Flynn ('Flynn of the Inland'), who brought medical services to the Outback; pioneer aviator Nancy Bird-Walton; the Rats of Tobruk; Prime Minister Robert Menzies, who held power for eighteen years; the army of workers, most of them migrants, who beat formidable odds to build the great Snowy Mountains Hydro Electric Scheme; Fred Hollows, who treated the eye ailments of Aborigines and underprivileged people around the world; Truganini, 'the last Tasmanian', who was eventually buried at sea; High Court Judge Mary Gaudron and other great women in the legal profession; scientist Peter Doherty, who won the Nobel Prize; and medical-humanitarian giants like virologist Gustav Nossal, cardiologist Victor Chang and Graeme Clark, inventor of the cochlear implant; the boat people who have so enriched Australia since arriving after the Vietnam War; and Paul Hogan, who so successfully promoted Australia around the world, armed with little more than a very big knife. Theirs are all worthy stories, and perhaps they will appear in a later edition.

Australia's history has no shortage of great moments.

TIMELINE

General timeline—with the great moments in **bold**

c. 60,000 years ago Humans arrive on Australian continent

1606 Dutch navigator Willem Jansz is first European to land on Australian soil

1629 *Batavia* shipwreck off west coast becomes first major European event

1768 Captain James Cook sails for Tahiti to record transit of Venus

1770 Cook discovers fertile east coast of New Holland

1783 New Yorker James Matra proposes that British settle Australia

1787 First Fleet leaves England for Australia

1788 Lieutenant King makes first fully recorded contact with Aborigines

1788 Captain Arthur Phillip's First Fleet establishes European settlement

1789 French Revolution

1789 Mutiny on the *Bounty* off Tahiti

1790 'Floating brothel' *Lady Juliana* arrives in Sydney

1791 Convict Mary Bryant takes part in open-boat escape from Botany Bay

1793 Bennelong becomes first Aborigine to meet King George III

1804 **Matthew Flinders names Australia**

1805 **John Macarthur 'starts' wool industry, putting economy on sheep's back**

1808 **Rum Rebellion deposes and imprisons Governor Bligh**

1810 **Governor Macquarie lays structural foundation of the nation**

1813 **Blaxland, Lawson and Wentworth cross Blue Mountains, opening up land**

1834 **Convict William Buckley returns after thirty-one years with Aborigines**

1840 Convict transportation to New South Wales stops

1851 **Edward Hargraves announces his discovery of gold in New South Wales**

1854 **Peter Lalor leads Eureka rebellion demanding democracy on goldfields**

1856 **Trade union leaders win world's first eight-hour day**

1856 All colonies save Western Australia win self-government

1858 Population reaches one million

1860 **Burke and Wills cross continent for first time, opening up interior**

1868 Convict transportation to Australia ends

1880 **Ned Kelly, last of the big bushrangers, arrested**

1889 **Sir Henry Parkes delivers Tenterfield Oration, inspiring Federation**

1890 **Banjo Paterson writes 'The Man from Snowy River'**

1895 **Banjo Paterson and Christina Macpherson create 'Waltzing Matilda'**

1896 First modern Olympic Games held in Greece; Australia competes

1899 Boer War starts

1900 Referendums enabling Federation passed in all Australian colonies

1901 Australia become a nation, with Edmund Barton as Prime Minister

1901 Queen Victoria dies

1904 John Watson forms world's first Labour Government

1908 United States' 'Great White Fleet' visits Sydney

1911 *Yongala* sinks off Queensland, Australia's worst maritime loss

1911 Amundsen reaches South Pole, followed by Scott

1912 'Unsinkable' *Titanic* sinks, with greatest single loss of life at sea

1913 Mawson survives Antarctic ordeal to claim territory for Australia

1913 Australia's first naval fleet, including HMAS *Sydney,* arrives in Sydney

1914 First World War starts

1914 HMAS *Sydney* sinks German ship *Emden*

1915 Anzacs land at Gallipoli, accompanied by reporter Charles Bean

1915 Albert Jacka wins Australia's first Victoria Cross of First World War at Gallipoli

1916 Australians fight on Western Front, losing 2000 in battle of Fromelles alone

1917 Sir John Forrest rides first train linking east and west

1917 General Chauvel leads Light Horse in history's last successful cavalry charge

1918 General John Monash wins turning-point battle of Hamel

1918 Armistice ends First World War

1918 Start of worldwide influenza epidemic that kills 11,000 Australians

1919 Smith brothers become first to fly from England to Australia

1921 Edith Cowan, in Western Australia, becomes first woman elected to a parliament

1927 Dame Nellie Melba sings at opening of Federal Parliament by Duke of York

1929 Great Depression starts

1930 Don Bradman begins breaking records in world-class cricket

1930 Wonder horse Phar Lap wins Melbourne Cup—and nation's heart

1932 Having defied British banks to build Sydney Harbour Bridge, Jack Lang opens it—with unwanted help

1933 Recovery from Great Depression begins

1933 Bodyline bowling undermines traditions of Test Cricket

1934 Bradman scores 451 with Bill Ponsford in record Test partnership

1934 Charles Kingsford-Smith flies across Pacific Ocean

1936 Tasmanian Tiger becomes extinct

1939 Second World War starts; Australia declares war on Germany, later on Japan

1941 German raider *Kormoran* sinks HMAS *Sydney*

1941 Prime Minister John Curtin switches allegiance from UK to US

1941 Australian troops win honours as Rats of Tobruk, North Africa

1941 Japan attacks US by bombing Pearl Harbor

1942 Japanese bomb Darwin, then other towns in the north

1942 Sydney Harbour defenders repel Japanese mini-submarine attack

1942 39th Battalion 'Choco Soldiers' stop Japanese invaders at Kokoda

1943 Enid Lyons becomes first female Federal Member of Parliament

1945 Howard Florey wins Nobel Prize for developing method to isolate and manufacture penicillin

1945 Allies win war in Europe, then use atomic bombs to bring about Japan's surrender

1945 **The Dancing Man celebrates end of Second World War**

1949 Liberal leader Robert Menzies wins election, starting sixteen years as Prime Minister

1950 Korean War starts, runs until 1953

1951 Referendum confirms right of Communist Party to exist

1953 Queen Elizabeth II crowned

1954 **Queen Elizabeth II becomes first reigning monarch to visit Australia**

1954 Soviet Union defectors Vladimir and Evdokia Petrov win asylum in Australia

1956 **'Golden Girl' Betty Cuthbert dominates first Olympic Games in Australia**

1962 Australia sends advisers to Vietnam

1964 The Beatles visit Australia, establishing new concert attendance records

1965 **Charles 'Charlie' Perkins leads Freedom Rides, winning new rights for Aboriginal people**

1967 Prime Minister Harold Holt disappears while swimming near Portsea, Victoria

1968 Australian combat troops begin serving in Vietnam

1968 Anti-Vietnam War protests increase throughout Australia

1969 First man lands on the moon

1970 Vietnam protests peak with Moratorium

1971 **Jack Mundey defeats developers with green bans**

1971 **Neville Bonner becomes first Aboriginal Australian elected to Federal Parliament**

1972 **Aboriginal Tent Embassy established**

1972   **Gough Whitlam leads Labor to power with 'It's Time' campaign**

1973   Boat people start arriving from Asia in increasing numbers

1973   **Queen Elizabeth II opens Joern Utzon's controversial Opera House**

1974   Cyclone Tracy destroys many buildings in Darwin

1975   **Governor-General Sir John Kerr sacks Prime Minister
Gough Whitlam**

1976   Aboriginal Sir Doug Nicholls appointed Governor of South Australia

1976   Aboriginal woman Truganini's remains cremated and scattered off
Tasmania

1981   Pitjantjatjara people win land rights in South Australia

1983   **Green pioneer Bob Brown leads successful fight to save Gordon
below Franklin**

1983   Ash Wednesday bushfires claim seventy-three lives

1983   **John Bertrand wins America's Cup in Alan Bond's *Australia II***

1984   Greg Mortimer and Tim Macartney-Snape become first Australians to
reach summit of Mount Everest

1985   Uluru (Ayers Rock) is handed back to Aborigines

1988   **Triumphing against great odds, First Fleet of tall-ships sails
into Sydney**

1989   Newcastle earthquake claims thirteen lives

1993   **Eddie Mabo wins landmark Aboriginal land rights case**

1996   Liberal–National coalition led by John Howard wins election, governs
till 2007

1996   Port Arthur massacre claims thirty-five lives

1998   Andy Thomas becomes first Australian to live on a space station

1999   Republic referendum confirms that voters prefer constitutional monarchy

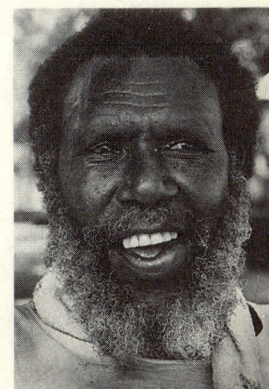

1999 Australia and the world celebrate the turn of the millennium

2000 Cathy Freeman wins gold in 400-metre race at Sydney Olympics

2002 Dr Fiona Wood's 'spray-on skin' helps save Bali bombings victims

2007 Labor leader Kevin Rudd wins election

2007 Julia Gillard becomes first female Deputy Prime Minister

2008 Prime Minister Rudd says 'Sorry' to Aborigines for 220 years of hurt

2008 Shipwreck hunter David Mearns finds watery grave of 645 *Sydney* sailors

2009 Australia's worst bushfires claim 173 lives

2009 Anna Bligh becomes first woman elected to head a State Government

Prelude

SIXTY THOUSAND YEARS AGO: ABORIGINAL ARRIVAL

'This looks like good hunting country, young fella,' the tribal elder said to the young warrior walking beside him. 'Plenty of fish, animals and birds.'

'Yes, father, this looks like a good place to bring our people,' said the young man, who held a spear in one hand. 'I don't see any trace of other humans, either—no old fires, no middens, no paintings on the cave walls. And certainly no gunyas or stone axes or spears.'

'We may be the first humans to come this far,' the elder replied. 'But we must find new hunting grounds. Back where we came from, too many tribes have been depending on the same ground for food. If there is no one else in this new land, perhaps we can stay without having to fight others.'

'Many of the animals are much bigger than any we've seen before,' the young warrior added. 'But they don't seem to be frightened of us at all. Even that big furry one hopping about—the one that looks like those small tree animals back home—isn't man shy.'

'True,' said the elder. 'That may be because they haven't been hunted before.'

'That will be good for our people,' the young man said with a laugh. 'We can eat well and grow fat.'

'Not too fat, young fella. You still need to be able to hunt. But yes, I think we should move here. Let us go back, tell all our tribespeople, and lead them to this land of good hunting.'

And the two men turned north to retrace their steps.

IT WAS A GREAT MOMENT because the first people had successfully walked south across the land bridge from New Guinea to the continent that would one day become Australia. After their new home became an island, these arrivals and their descendants would remain undiscovered for some 60,000 years, establishing the longest continuous culture on the planet. Their faraway continent had large expanses of harsh desert and dangerous giant animals, but unlike most of Europe and Asia, it was secure from invasion by marauding armies—and disease. The Aborigines escaped the plagues that repeatedly swept through other lands. For millennia they were also free to develop their own rich collection of stories about the Dreamtime in which humans and animals were created. They lived in harmony with their environment, which they treasured and tended with care. They remained largely undisturbed on this great and spacious southern continent until 1788.

Historical background

The first Aborigines probably walked to Australia across the land bridge that once linked the continent to New Guinea. Over millennia, *Homo sapiens* had spread from Africa's Rift Valley across the Middle East, into India and then Asia, and eventually to Australia. Meanwhile, the ancestors of the American Indians, who eventually reached the southernmost tip of South America, had moved north through Asia and across a land bridge to what is now Alaska. After their northern land bridge was submerged, about 12,000 years ago, Aborigines had the entire Australian continent to themselves.

The belief system that centres on the Dreamtime is far older than the monotheistic faiths of Judaism (5000 years) Christianity (2000 years) and Islam (1300 years). It contains explanatory stories about the creation of the land, people and animals. Among indigenous groups in Australia's north, those creation stories include references to earlier journeys of migration.

Postscript

Although the ancestral Aborigines chose their new home well, the submerging of the land bridge left them isolated from other peoples and their cultural and technological developments. Rising sea levels also left Aborigines in Tasmania cut off from those on the mainland.

In the north and west, the isolation was never total. Malay fishermen called in as they hunted for *trepang* (sea cucumbers). Much later, Portuguese and Dutch navigators sighted the coast or landed, but none ever stayed. Chinese and Egyptian sailors may also have visited. In 1788, however, the British Government decided to settle this ancient land with 759 convicts. Now, without warning, Aboriginal life was interrupted by British marines, soldiers, explorers and farmers—armed with guns and disease.

The ancient way of life was undermined or destroyed. Aborigines were displaced or driven off from their traditional hunting and fishing grounds. Forests were cleared and farms and settlements established. Smallpox, measles and venereal diseases killed thousands of Aborigines. A population that might have numbered over a million in 1788 shrank drastically. Within a century, many Aboriginal groups survived only in shanty camps on the fringes of towns. Those that did best lived in remote places like deserts and tropical forests. They, at least, had a chance of hanging onto the way of life that had sustained their ancestors since the Dreamtime—which for most had become a nightmare in 1788.

1606

FIRST EUROPEAN LANDS IN AUSTRALIA, BY MISTAKE

'Let's try landing on this strange shore one more time,' Captain Willem Jansz shouted above the wind to his first mate as he pointed to a sandy beach on the horizon.

'Aye, aye, sir,' the mate replied, scanning the view ahead from his position at the helm. 'I'll look for a safe anchorage, but I can't guarantee a safe landing if the natives are as hostile as they were in New Guinea.'

'If any more of our crew are killed we won't have enough hands to sail our *Duyfken* home,' Jansz said, shielding his eyes from the sun as he searched the shore. 'But if we don't find gold at this next landfall, we're going to be in big trouble with the Dutch East India Company.'

'Surely it doesn't have to be gold, captain. I know we've been sailing a long time and they need us to come back with a profit, but we could still earn a good one if the natives have spices to trade,' said the first mate, giving the wheel a turn.

'They won't!' Jansz replied angrily. 'They aren't like the natives of Java. If they are anything like the savages we've been seeing for the past few weeks, these natives won't have any trade goods at all. But look, we'll try. Sail our little *Duyfken* in closer until we reach a safe anchorage.'

'There's a sheltered bay, let's make for that beach,' the mate suggested. He steered the *Duyfken* in closer, then ordered the crew to drop anchor.

'Put out the boat,' Jansz ordered, pointing towards the shore boat lashed to the deck amidships. 'Make fast, men,' he said as they lowered the boat. Then he and the first mate collected their muskets, swords and bags of gifts for trading with the natives, and climbed over the gunwales and into the little open boat.

When they moved down the land bridge from the north the first Aborigines discovered an uninhabited land mass into which they could spread out at will. Apart from Malayan fishermen, Jansz was the first outsider to visit Australia's shores.

When Captain Willem Jansz of the Dutch trader *Duyfken* (Little Dove) dropped anchor in a peaceful bay on the west coast of the Cape York Peninsula in 1606 he had no idea Aborigines would attack his crew as soon as they landed.

Once they were sitting on the thwarts, Jansz ordered his oarsmen to start pulling towards the beach.

'The natives would have seen us by now, so they should come down to the beach to trade any goods they have as soon as we've landed,' the first mate said.

The boat nosed in closer and closer. 'Beach the bow in front of those trees that come right down to the sea beside that stream,' Jansz said. 'We can tie the painter to that tree,' he added, pointing to a big mangrove as the bow scraped the sand.

'Right! Landing party, ashore with the trading gifts and set up for the natives' arrival. Bosun, stay with the boat and keep a look-out,' the captain ordered, clambering out of the boat and walking up the beach with the other crew. 'It's good to be on dry land again, but don't waste time—get the gifts out fast so they can see what we have to trade.'

'My God! Look out, captain!' the bosun screamed from the boat. 'There are natives with spears in those trees. Come back to the boat!'

But it was too late—at least for one of the crew. Spears whistled through the air, thrown with deadly accuracy by unseen hands.

'Aaah, I am hit!' one sailor screamed. He fell to the sand, a spear through his chest, blood spurting onto the beach. He turned back towards the boat and groaned: 'My God, do not forsake me, boys!'

'Run before they attack again,' Jansz yelled. 'Get back in the boat!' He dropped the bag of gifts and grabbed the wounded sailor, dragging him back down the beach and into the boat as the first mate—thigh bleeding from a spear wound—jumped in and the bosun shoved off.

'Row, men, row,' Jansz called, steering for the open sea towards the *Duyfken* riding at anchor. The 'savages' watched from the trees, seemingly satisfied with the success of their defence.

The Dutchmen might have got away from the beach, but it was too late for one. Seconds later the wounded sailor gasped, spluttered blood, then, with a final desperate groan, died.

Flying Dutchmen

After Jansz visited the Gulf of Carpentaria in 1606, a long string of Dutchmen visited New Holland's western coast: Dirk Hartog, captain of *Eendracht* (Harmony), nailed a pewter plate recording his visit to a tree when he landed in 1616 on an island near Shark Bay (later named Dirk Hartog Island); the ill-fated *Batavia* struck the Houtman Abrolhos Islands in 1629; and Willem de Vlamingh collected Hartog's plate, took it back to the Amsterdam Museum (where it is to this day) and nailed another plate to the tree. French navigator Louis de Freycinet on *l'Uranie* stole the replacement plate for a museum in France but after the Second World War the French Government gave it to the Western Australian Museum in Perth.

Despite the popular belief that Captain Cook discovered Australia, all these Dutchmen came and went many decades before he arrived on the other side of the continent in 1770. They visited the west coast of New Holland (Australia) as they turned north on their way to their lucrative trading port of Batavia (Jakarta) in Java and the Spice Islands. They were not interested in settling New Holland, which they saw as barren and unproductive, especially as the Aborigines did not have any goods they wished to trade for.

'The black men here are wild, cruel savages,' Jansz said angrily as the boat approached *Duyfken*. 'They do not have gold, they do not grow spices, they have nothing to trade—and they kill us for no reason.'

'Captain, we must give up,' the first mate said, bandaging his thigh. 'We may be empty-handed, but we must stop sailing east and turn for Java before we lose any more crew and can't sail our *Little Dove*.'

Jansz swore bitterly as he climbed up the chain plates and onto the *Duyfken*'s deck. Turning to glare at the blood-stained beach, he declared: 'I will call this bloody shore Cape Keerweer (turn about), and we will never visit this godforsaken land again.'

IT WAS A GREAT MOMENT in Australian history—albeit bloody—because Jansz (also known as Janszoon) and his crew had just made the first authenticated European landing on the continent that would become Australia. It was March 1606, some 164 years before Captain James Cook's discovery of the fertile east coast that led to British settlement. Jansz also bestowed the first place name on the Australian continent on his landing spot, now known as Pennefather River. Mind you, Jansz did not know he had landed on a new continent: he thought he was still on the southern coast of New Guinea. But today he is honoured for discovering the western shore of Cape York Peninsula.

Visitors from Asia had certainly landed before Jansz, including Malayan fishermen (Macassans) to harvest trepang (sea cucumbers), and explorers from China. But Jansz was the first in a long line of European visitors who would eventually change the history of this land, including Dutch, Portuguese, British, French and finally the British again as colonists.

Historical background

Willem Jansz had been sent by the Dutch East India Company in search of gold, spices and other trading goods to be brought back to Batavia (now Jakarta) and then Holland. He was ordered by Dutch authorities 'to discover the great land of Nova Guinea and other East and South lands'. He sailed his ship *Duyfken* (Little Dove), a small vessel—19.2 metres by about 5.5 metres, with a draught of just over two metres—with a crew of about twenty from Bantam in Java via Banda, the Kai Islands and then Aru Island to search for trading ports along the south coast of New Guinea. At one halt on this trip, eight members of his crew were killed by natives in an ambush.

'We will never visit this god-forsaken land again.'

Tiring of this dangerous coastline, Jansz sailed south. Guessing the New Guinea coast would stretch far to the east but then eventually curve southwestwards, he took a short cut, hoping to pick up the land again where it came back west. Sailing south out of sight of land, he unknowingly crossed Torres Strait; the next land he sighted was Australia. He then sailed more than 400 kilometres more or less south, parallel to the west coast of Cape York Peninsula. His first landing was opposed by Aborigines with daunting effect. For the moment, they had managed to keep Europeans off their soil.

Postscript

Jansz may have been the first European to land in Australia, but it meant nothing to him. In fact, after he landed on that bloody beach he was running so short of crew (by now about half had been killed by natives at different landings), he had to return to Bantam before it was too late. Back at the commercial headquarters, he was severely reprimanded by Dutch East India Company officials for a failed mission. The first European landing in Australia had been nothing but a disaster.

1629

BATAVIA SAVAGERY KICKSTARTS EUROPEAN HISTORY IN AUSTRALIA

'I have examined the hull, my dear passengers and crew, and our poor old *Batavia* is stuck fast—wrecked on this dreadful reef,' the ship's commander, Francisco Pelsaert, announced to fellow survivors clinging to handholds on the sloping foredeck. 'I'll have to get another ship so you can complete your journey.'

'Where on earth will you get another ship in this godforsaken part of the world?' demanded the portly cargo manager, Jeronimus Cornelisz, who was obviously used to getting his own way.

'I will sail our longboat to where we were bound, our Dutch port of Batavia, and charter a rescue ship,' Pelsaert answered. 'I can use the south-east trade winds to get me there.'

'But I have a precious cargo which I am responsible for delivering,' said Cornelisz, banging his fist on the railing. 'It is worth millions; the buyers are waiting. How long will you be gone?'

'Depends on the winds . . . perhaps only a few weeks,' Pelsaert said with the confidence of an experienced sailor.

'And where the hell are we anyway, O trusty commander?' Cornelisz spat out.

'Not far from the island discovered by our countryman Dirk Hartog just four years ago on the western coast of New Holland. And very near the Houtman Abrolhos islands, only 24 miles off that same coast,' Pelsaert said, holding up his rudimentary chart for all to see.

'Abrolhos?' Cornelisz said. 'What kind of word is that? It's not Dutch.'

'Cornelis de Houtman chose the name a dozen years ago. It means "keep a good look-out", I believe.'

After Francisco Pelseart, the captain of the shipwrecked *Batavia*, left his passengers on the Houtman Abrolhos islands off Western Australia while he went in search of a rescue ship, they formed rival groups and started killing each other.

'Well, that's something you didn't do, did you, when we hit the reef this morning,' Cornelisz said with a glare. 'Now look at us—half a world away from Holland, and never to be seen again.'

'Cornelisz, you know damn well that drunken fool of a skipper Ariaen Jacobz is in charge of handling the ship. It was on the useless rogue's own watch that we ran aground here!'

'Well, where do you expect me and the commercial passengers to wait while you sail over the horizon?'

'I will transfer everyone ashore to these islands,' Pelsaert said, motioning towards low-lying sandy strips not far from the wreck. 'I want you to establish a settlement there.'

'But is there any water there?' Cornelisz asked, as the survivors stared at the sparse sands and muttered in protest. 'Or food, for that matter?'

'We'll just have to hope there's a spring, and that all the supplies from our ship can be salvaged,' Pelsaert said. 'We can set up a store on the island to issue the food as rations till I return.'

'And what if there is no water, good captain?' Cornelisz asked, turning for support to the grumbling crowd of passengers.

'I will call in at the New Holland mainland and see if I can locate water for you before I head north,' Pelsaert said. 'If I find it, I will bring enough barrels back to keep you going.'

'My God,' Cornelisz said to the protesting survivors as he stamped his well-shod feet on the deck, 'it sounds like our great captain is making up this rescue plan as he goes along.'

'We have little alternative, Cornelisz. Now I order you to help me salvage all the food and as much timber as we can from the ship to use as building materials for the settlement before the ship founders any further. The sooner I leave, the sooner I'll return,' Pelsaert said. He picked up some loose timber and moved towards the longboat as crew members began loading supplies for the settlement.

'God bless you, captain,' a woman passenger called from the sloping deck. 'Fair winds and following seas.'

After many trips in the longboat carting the food and timber for the settlement, Pelsaert transported all the surviving passengers to the island, left Cornelisz still on the wreck in charge, and headed for the mainland. He searched in vain for water before turning north for Batavia. Against daunting odds at sea and on land, where he was forced to stop from time to time to replenish his own supplies of water while dodging native attack, Pelsaert made it to the Dutch colonial outpost. As soon as he'd recovered, he hired a small rescue ship, *Sardam*, which he sailed back to find the *Batavia*'s survivors.

But as he found to his horror, everything possible had gone wrong on the islands.

Not long after Pelsaert left, the disgruntled and resentful Cornelisz—who, it was later revealed, had been plotting mutiny with Jacobz and other malcontents even before the shipwreck—seized all the weapons and declared himself governor of the islands, organising his henchmen in gangs. They divided everyone else into two groups: useful slaves and disposable victims—including children—who would be killed to save food and water. Cornelisz and his gang enslaved the attractive women for their sexual pleasure and murdered any sailors or passengers who tried to stop them. There were many bloody battles, but Cornelisz's opponents lacked the numbers or weapons to do more than survive on other islands.

'Now look at us—half a world away from Holland, and never to be seen again.'

When the captain of the *Batavia* shipwreck returned to the Houtman Abrolhos islands he arrested, then tortured and/or hung the mutineers who had dared to seize power and murder weaker passengers while he was away.

Cornelisz had even planned to capture Pelsaert on his return with the rescue ship, but he committed a fatal error when, fuming at the failure of his henchmen to kill or capture a group on another island, he set off to do the dirty work himself.

The group's leader, Wiebbe Hayes, captured Cornelisz. Soon afterwards, *Sardam* was sighted. Hayes warned Pelsaert, who quickly put the rest of the gang in irons and meted out the justice of the times. Cornelisz and his followers had their right hands chopped off (Cornelisz lost his left as well) before being hanged. Two lesser offenders were abandoned on the mainland, and some others were taken back to Batavia, where the local governor promptly hanged them anyway.

IT WAS A GREAT MOMENT because it was the first fully recorded European event—and an infamous one at that—in Australia. It was also a fortunate moment because Francisco Pelsaert managed to stop Cornelisz and his mutineers from capturing the rescue ship. That success led to the punishment of the first European criminals on the first European structure in Australia: a gibbet.

Historical background

The *Batavia* was sailing from Holland to Batavia (now Jakarta) in the Dutch East Indies (now Indonesia), full of silver coins and dressed sandstone for official buildings, as well as soldiers and would-be colonists from all walks of life, some with wives and children. But the wild winds of the Roaring Forties pushed the *Batavia* too far east and onto the Abrolhos Islands. Navigators of the time could calculate latitude, but before the advent of reliable chronometers around the time of Captain James Cook, fixing longitude was just educated guesswork. As a result, ships often came to grief en route to the Dutch East Indies. The crowded *Batavia* is thought to have carried 326 people, of whom forty drowned trying to reach shore and 125 were killed in the violent mutiny following the wreck. Pelsaert rescued about 161 survivors.

Postscript

The iniquities that followed the *Batavia* mutiny contrasted strongly with the success of the Pilgrims who landed in North America that same decade and, thanks to the Indian tribes, established the continent's first viable European settlement. The *Batavia* story did not end with the departure of the *Sardam*. The two Dutch crew members, Wouter Loos and Jan de Bye (or Pelzroende), whose death sentences had been commuted to abandonment, were issued with limited supplies and gifts to barter with the Aborigines. Before long they were befriended by a local tribe and allocated women, with whom these first European settlers had families. Their genetic influence lasted for generations. Long after they died, other navigators and early explorers reported seeing blond, blue-eyed Aborigines along the Western Australian coast.

1770

CAPTAIN COOK DISCOVERS EAST COAST OF NEW HOLLAND

'Land ahoy!' a seaman shouted from the fore topgallant yard of His Majesty's Bark *Endeavour*—and, in case anybody had missed it, added an even louder 'Land ho!'

Looking up from his journal, Lieutenant James Cook paused. Quill in one hand, he steadied himself with the other as *Endeavour* rolled westward. The wind snapped his square-rigger's canvas as the 'continual squalls' he was writing about buffeted the little ship.

'That's earlier than I'd hoped for,' Cook thought, listening for a further call amid the creaking of the old oak timbers and wondering whether he should go up on deck. 'Yet we did see those porpoises swimming around the bow yesterday, not to mention a gannet and other land birds. Perhaps we really are nearing landfall.'

'Land ahoy—off the starboard beam!'

'There's no mistaking that,' Cook thought, getting to his feet in a rush of excitement. Placing his quill in its holder, he reached for his spyglass and tricorn hat, steadying himself on the bulkhead as he made for the cabin door.

'We are only 211 degrees 7 minutes west of Greenwich,' he mused, 'and 38 degrees south. We are already approaching the longitude of Van Diemen's Land that Mr Tasman charted last century. I wonder if this could be New Holland's east coast already?'

It was a fair question. No European knew exactly where the east coast of New Holland was or how—or even if—it connected to Van Diemen's Land. Cook had at least demonstrated that New Zealand, which Tasman had also

visited, was not attached to Van Diemen's Land; but the land to the north remained a mystery.

Bursting onto the deck into the dawn light, Cook walked briskly forward to join the seaman on bow watch. Taking up his position just aft of the bowsprit, he trained his spyglass to the north.

'Have you confirmed the sighting, bow watch?' he asked, searching the horizon.

'Nay, sir, I ain't seen nothin' meself,' the sailor on bow watch reported, peering across the sea. 'But Mr Hicks is aloft, Sir,' he said, looking up to the fore topgallant, 'and he seen somethin', orright.' The officer of the watch and Cook's second-in-command had climbed into the rigging after the first hail to see for himself.

'Mr Hicks,' Cook called up, 'report to the deck!'

Lieutenant Zachary Hickes (who rarely convinced anyone, even Cook, to spell his name with the 'e') scrambled down the shrouds. Skipping one or even two ratlines at a time, he was on the foredeck in seconds.

Although Aborigines threatened Captain Cook when he landed at Botany Bay he managed to appease them with presents and gestures until he sailed off again to explore the east coast of New Holland.

'Are you certain it is land, Hicks?' Cook asked his senior officer.

'Yes, Sir, I've been watchin' it for ten minutes, and I can see the green of the trees and even yellow, which must be beaches . . . I'm certain, Sir.'

'Good work, Hicks,' Cook said, tapping the officer on the shoulder. 'Once I have confirmed your sighting I will name that land Point Hicks—and who knows, it may even turn out to be New Holland.'

IT WAS A GREAT MOMENT in Australian history because Cook had indeed just discovered the uncharted east coast of New Holland—the continent that would become Australia. It was 6 a.m. on 19 April 1770, according to Cook's log (though in fact it was April 20, because at sea navigators did not change over to the new date until noon). The eastern coast was much more appealing than the western and far northern shores Dutch sailors first saw in the early seventeenth century. As Cook recorded in his journal, at first sight it had 'a very agreeable and promising aspect. The land is of moderate height, diversified with hills, ridges, plains, valleys, with some grass but for the most part the whole was covered with wood.' His botanist, Joseph Banks, also thought the new land attractive, and on his return to England he added his voice to those recommending that the British settle this coast of New Holland.

Historical background

Cook had sailed west to New Holland from New Zealand, which he had circumnavigated and charted. He had sailed to New Zealand after taking his scientific party to observe the transit of Venus across the sun for the Royal Society from the superior vantage point of Tahiti. His voyage from England, which he left in August 1768, was officially a scientific expedition, but after successfully completing that mission in June 1769 he opened sealed orders that instructed him to sail west in search of new lands. Willem Jansz (or Janszoon) had visited the north-west tip of Cape York in 1606, and other Dutch navigators had regularly sailed along the west coast ever since, but no European had yet charted the east coast.

From his first sighting, Point Hicks, Cook sailed north, mapping the coastline as he went. He recorded that 'we discovered a bay which appeared to be tolerably well sheltered from all winds, into which I resolved to go with the ship'. This was Botany Bay (initially named Stingray Bay), and on 28 April 1770, when *Endeavour* dropped anchor there, the crew could see Aborigines fishing from canoes and eating fish by a fire on the shore. Cook went ashore with his scientific party, Banks and Daniel Solander, and an interpreter named Tupia, whom they had brought from Tahiti hoping he could translate the language of the people of New Holland.

Most of the Aborigines fled into the bush as Cook's party approached, apart from two brave men who stood on the beach holding out long spears towards the newcomers. As Cook reported, 'they seem'd resolved to oppose our landing'. Tupia shouted that the new arrivals only wanted to collect water, but of course the Aborigines did not understand and shouted menacing words as the boat approached the shore. Nevertheless, Cook ordered a landing, and the first British party—led by Cook's wife's young nephew, Isaac Smith—set foot on the east coast of New Holland. The Aborigines fled, and Cook and his party collected water and wood, caught fish and raised the British flag to take possession of the continent for King George III.

This first known encounter with Aborigines on the east coast was hostile. Observing from *Endeavour*, the ship's artist, Sydney Parkinson, reported:

> Their countenance bespoke displeasure; they threatened us, and displayed hostile intentions, often crying to us *Warra Warra Wai*. We made signs to them to be peaceable, and threw them some trinkets; but they kept aloof and dared us to come ashore. We attempted to frighten them by firing off a gun loaded with small shot, but attempted it in vain. One of them repaired to a house immediately and brought out a shield, of an oval figure, painted white in the middle, with two holes in the middle to see through and also a wooden sword, and then they advanced boldly, gathering up stones as they came along, which they threw at us.

During their time at Botany Bay, when Cook caused 'the English colours to be displayed every day', he ordered shots fired over the Aborigines' heads on one occasion; when they would not retreat, a shot was fired into a warrior's leg.

But the key reports that inspired later settlement by the British included claims by Cook, Banks and an American midshipman, James Matra, that the natives did not appear to be numerous, to live in large bodies, or to present any threat. In fact, 'they had not so much as touched the things we had left in their

'"Are you certain it is land, Hicks?" Cook asked his senior officer.'

Two brave Aboriginal warriors 'seem'd resolved to oppose our landing' Captain Cook said as he approached Botany Bay. His ship's artist, Sydney Parkinson, who drew this sketch added, 'they threatened us and displayed hostile intentions, often crying to us Warra Warra Wai' forcing Cook's party 'to fire off a gun loaded with small shot'.

huts on purpose for them to take away'. Cook and his party also said the trees were at such a distance from one another that the whole country, or at least a great part of it, might be cultivated without the need to cut down a single one. They also spoke of a deep, black soil capable of producing any kind of grain, fine meadows and a variety of beautiful birds. Persuaded by these claims, and under various geopolitical pressures, within eighteen years the British Government would dispatch a fleet to settle Botany Bay.

With his mission accomplished, Cook sailed north for home and charted much of the east coast en route. Spotting the entrance to Port Jackson, he suggested it might be a safe anchorage for British ships in the future: this was where the First Fleet would settle, Sydney Harbour, after their disappointing start at Botany Bay.

Postscript

Despite Cook's vast experience and his success with natives of various lands, history's greatest navigator was killed in Hawaii during a squabble on a beach at Kealakakua Bay just nine years after he confronted the Aborigines at Botany Bay. He died after being clubbed on the head from behind as he escorted the Hawaiian king back to his ship, *Resolution*. The king had agreed to serve as a hostage in exchange for the ship's longboat, which had been stolen by a maverick member of his tribe. Unfortunately, another chief had just been killed by one of Cook's party in a skirmish on another part of the island. When this news reached the bay—just as Cook was leading his hostage down to the beach—the natives attacked some of the English. Cook remained aloof from the fighting until one warrior crept up behind him and struck him. Others then joined in, attacking him with daggers and causing him to fall into the water. Cook managed to get his head up again, but another warrior gave him a shattering blow—and he went down for the last time.

1783

A NEW YORKER 'INVENTS' AUSTRALIA

'I've got it! I know just the place,' James Matra exclaimed as he put down the newspaper in the London coffee house. 'New South Wales—that's it!'

'What do you mean, that's it?' asked his lady friend, taking a swig of her strong Jamaican brew. 'Sometimes you make no sense at all, especially since you got back from the long voyage to the south seas. It must be all that sun.'

'But that's it—the south seas. New South Wales, which used to be New Holland, is empty, so that's where we can settle my fellow Loyalists. The paper says they're being driven out of the American colonies by the victorious rebels,' Matra said. 'It's a great idea. Why didn't I think of it before?'

'But James, it's so far away,' his friend said. 'You were gone from England for three years on that voyage with Captain Cook, weren't you? Three years!'

'Yes, but *Endeavour* was on a long, slow voyage of discovery, my dearest, charting new lands,' Matra explained, pouring himself another coffee. 'A fleet of us Loyalists could sail straight there in a few months.'

'But what about those savages who killed Captain Cook?' she asked, grabbing his hand. 'You mightn't come back this time.'

'That was Hawaii, dear. The savages of New South Wales are not that hostile,' he said reassuringly. 'They don't have any towns, villages or even houses—in fact, they don't own land at all, since they just roam around all the time. So they wouldn't mind if we came.

'Anyway, we have already raised the British colours there and taken possession on behalf of King George,' he said. 'I will put the proposal to Joseph Banks, and if he likes it I'll take it to the government.'

'Would *the* Joseph Banks help somebody as little known as you, James?'

'Of course—we were shipmates for three years on *Endeavour*,' Matra said, finishing his coffee. 'And he loved New Holland. He'll want it settled.'

'But perhaps not by an American,' she warned, putting her cup down. 'Be careful, James, or they may steal your idea and cast you aside.'

'We'll see . . . I'm an honorary Englishman now, having served under Cook—or at least I should be,' Matra said, standing up and putting some coins on the table.

Back in his London lodgings, Matra gathered some paper, picked up his quill and, sitting at his desk by the window, wrote: 'A Proposal for Establishing a Settlement in New South Wales.'

Drawing a deep breath, he plunged straight into his vision: 'I am going to offer an Object for the consideration of our Government, which may in time atone for the loss of our American Colonies,' he wrote in his beautiful script.

By the Discoveries and Enterprise of our officers many new countries have been found which know no Sovereign and that hold out the most enticing allurements to European adventurers. None are more inviting than New South Wales. Capt. Cook first coasted and surveyed the Eastern side of that fine country from the 38th degree of south latitude north to the 10th where he found everything to induce him to give the most favourable account of it. In this immense tract of more than 2000 miles [3200 kilometres] there was every variety of soil, & great parts of it were extremely fertile, peopled only by a few black inhabitants who in the rudest state of Society knew no other arts than such as were necessary to their mere animal existence & which was almost entirely sustained by catching fish.

Having visited Botany Bay with Captain Cook in 1770 as the *Endeavour*'s botanist, the politically well-connected Joseph Banks was just the right person to help his little-known *Endeavour* shipmate James Matra in the early 1780s to persuade the British Government to settle Australia. Painting by Thomas Phillips (1815).

And so he wrote, on and on, listing reason after reason for a settlement, including the acquisition of raw materials and resources and the development of new products in New South Wales for the British and other markets. Matra's wide range of prospective trade goods included wool, flax, hemp, spices, sugar, tea, coffee, silk, cotton, indigo, tobacco, timber, furs and whaling—many of which would, eventually be produced in the colony. He also noted that New

17

South Wales could serve as a useful naval base and good defence outpost for an expanding Britain, which planned on ruling the high seas for a long time to come.

Finally he got to his main point:

This country besides may afford an Asylum to those unfortunate American Loyalists to whom Great Britain is bound by every tie of honour and gratitude to protect and support, where they may repair their broken fortunes and again enjoy their former domestick felicity.

In all, Matra wrote nine foolscap pages, scribbling on until daylight faded and he was struggling to see.

'You'll go blind, James, trying to write in the dark,' his companion said, putting a candle on his desk. 'Here, see if this is better.'

'Actually, I've just finished,' Matra said. 'But I'd love you to read it, dear, and tell me what you think.'

Matra persuaded the government to use criminals as a labour force growing produce in New South Wales rather than sending them to the gallows, which was the punishment for over two hundred crimes in eighteenth-century England.

IT WAS A GREAT MOMENT because a private citizen, James Mario Matra, had just created the blueprint for the founding of a British settlement in New South Wales. His plan was adapted by others, but it formed the basis for the settlement of the land that was to become Australia. Matra did discuss it with Banks, who 'highly approved of the settlement' and who also suggested 'we may draw any number of useful Inhabitants from China' to help establish it. Banks also helped Matra cost the project, enabling the American to conclude that 'a Sum not exceeding £3,000 will be more than adequate to the whole expence [*sic*] of Government'. For any bureaucrat reading the letter, Matra's proposal of a new country (and on an entire continent) for £3000 must have seemed a real bargain.

Historical background

Matra may have been an American—the son of a New York doctor—but having sailed with Cook on *Endeavour* as a midshipman, he was well placed to draft this practical and visionary proposal. He was, after all, a Loyalist who had supported King George III against the democratic revolutionaries of 1776. He had worked in such colonial outposts as Tenerife and Constantinople, had served in the Plantation Department of the Home Office, and, having visited New Holland, could speak from first-hand experience. He also consulted a wide range of authorities apart from Banks. His letter included opinions from other leading American Loyalists, 'who all agree that under the patronage & protection of government it offers the most favourable Prospects that have yet occurred to better the fortunes & to promote the happiness of their fellow sufferers and countrymen'.

The British Government set up a committee to examine the feasibility of the settlement plan. Statements from witnesses, including a very optimistic Banks, convinced officials to proceed with the settling of New South Wales. Banks even claimed 'there are very few inhabitants there and they did not appear at all to be feared'. This was the foundation of the British notion of *terra nullius*—a land that was empty of inhabitants claiming ownership. Banks also said it would be very easy to procure 'a supply of women' to serve the needs of settlers: 'they might be obtained from the South Sea Islands at no other expense than the charge of fetching them' and would prefer European men to fellow islanders.

But the basic idea became reality. An inspired 'memo' gave birth to a new settlement that would become a new set of colonies for Britain on the other

'This country besides may afford an Asylum to those unfortunate American Loyalists . . . where they may repair their broken fortunes.'

The government liked
Matra's plan because the old
prison hulks they had been
using since their prisons filled
up were now overflowing.

side of the globe. Less than three years after Matra submitted his proposal, the
Admiralty was ordered to begin organising a fleet to sail for New South Wales.
It announced the decision on 18 August 1786.

Postscript

Although the British Government accepted Matra's scheme in outline, American
Loyalists were replaced by convicts, whom the nation had a pressing need to
be rid of. Since transportation to the American colonies had ceased with the
British defeat in the War of Independence, jails and prison hulks in England
had filled with criminals. Matra the Loyalist was also dropped from the plan.
The Admiralty appointed the experienced naval officer Captain Arthur Phillip
to lead the expedition.

Although Matra had little to show for his vision of settling New South Wales,
many years later appreciative Sydney residents did at least name a suburb after
him: Matraville.

1788
LIEUTENANT KING BEFRIENDS BOTANY BAY ABORIGINES

'I was ordered with Lieutenant Dawes of the Marines, to explore all the south side of the Bay, & trace the two inlets on the South side as high as possible,' Second Lieutenant Philip Gidley King reported two days after arriving with the First Fleet in Botany Bay. On landing, he said, he had ascended a hill and

perceived a red fox dog, and soon after discovered a number of the natives who halloo'd & made signs for us to return to our boats. Having only three Marines with me and Lieutenant Dawes I advanced before them unarmed presenting some beads and ribbands, two of the Natives advanced armed but would not come close to me, I then dropped the beads & baize which I held out for them & retreated, they took it up & bound the baize about their head, they then in a very vociferous manner desired us to be gone & one of them threw a lance wide of us to show how far they could throw it and the distance it was thrown was as near as I could guess about 40 yards & when he took it out where it stuck, it required an exertion to pull it out.

As I took this for a menace that more could be thrown at us if we did not retreat & being unwilling to fire amongst them, there being twelve of them, I retreated walking backwards till I came to the brow of the hill, where I halted and again offered them presents which they refused, on descending the hill they showed themselves on the top of it & were ten times more vociferous & very soon after a lance was thrown amongst us, on which I ordered one of the marines to fire with powder only, when they ran off.

Although Botany Bay Aboriginals were initially hostile towards Lieutenant Philip Gidley King he was able to establish such a good rapport that they offered their women to the young officer, 'a mark of their hospitality' that he declined.

This demonstration of force by the natives—and the knowledge that a similar one had killed Captain Cook in Hawaii nine years earlier—meant King had good reason to embark, as he recorded, 'with great trepidation'. Governor Arthur Phillip, on the other hand, had been on 'the South side of the bay where he had found the Natives very sociable and friendly'. King, who was in his late twenties, now had the benefit of Phillip's experience: the naval officer was a master of managing relations with natives in foreign lands.

We relanded on Lance Point & the same body of Natives appeared brandishing their lances and defying us, however we rowed close in shore & the Governor disembarked with some presents which one of them came and received, thus peace was re-established much to the satisfaction of all parties; they came round the boats & many little things were given them, but what they wanted most was the great coats and Cloathing, but hats was most particularised by them, their admiration of which they expressed by very loud shouts, whenever one of us pulled our hats off. When they found us so very friendly they ran up to the man who had thrown the lance & made very significant signs of their displeasure at his conduct by pointing their lances at him & looking at us, intimating that they only waited our orders to kill him, however we made signs for them to desist & made the culprit a present of some beads etc, then Governor Phillip went up another branch.

Left alone again in charge of a small group of men, King now had more success in building rapport with the Aborigines—with unexpected rewards:

When they found we were not disposed to part with any more things, they entered into conversation with us, which was very fully interpreted by very plain Signs that they wanted to know of what sex we were which they explained by pointing to where it was distinguishable. As they took us for women, not having our beards grown, I ordered one of our people to undeceive them in this particular—when they made a great shout of Admiration, & pointed to the shore, which was but ten yards from us, where we saw a great number of Women and Girls with infant children on their shoulders, make their appearance on the beach, all *in puris naturalibus pas meme la feuille de figeur* [stark naked without even a figleaf] those natives who were around the boats made signs for us to go to these Women & made us understand

Aborigines of Botany Bay carried their spears, shields, fish hooks, latest catch and fire stick so they could hunt, fish or cook whenever they liked. Painted by Lieutenant Philip Gidley King (1788).

their persons were at our service; however I declined this mark of their hospitality but instead found a handkerchief which I offered to one of the Women, pointing her out. She immediately put her child down & came alongside the boat & suffered me to Apply the handkerchief where Eve did the Fig leaf, the Natives then set up another very great shout & my female visitor returned on shore.

Women or no women, the visitors' time was up: 'As the evening was coming on fast & we were twelve miles from the fleet it was time to return, we wished the natives, "God be with ye" which they repeated, we got on board about midnight.'

IT WAS A GREAT MOMENT because this was the first really meaningful contact between British settlers and Aborigines. After such a hostile initial reception, it seemed to augur well for the future. The two cultures were dramatically different, to be sure, but in this brief encounter they communicated well. The British gave the Aborigines many presents (they had offered wine on an earlier occasion, King reported, but the natives had spat this out in disgust) and the Aborigines offered the British men their women—truly, as King says, a warm welcome. The British may have looked down on the 'naked savages', but fortunately the key player at this meeting, King, could see things from both points of view. The Aborigines, he wrote, 'seemed quite astonished at the figure we cut in being fully cloathed & I think it is very easy to conceive the ridiculous figure we must appear to those poor creatures who were perfectly naked'.

Historical background

This meeting was on January 20, two days after Philip Gidley King had arrived with Governor Phillip at Botany Bay, the harbour Cook had recommended after his visit eighteen years earlier. King was also in a good position to record this great moment, being Phillip's right-hand man—his *aide de camp*—and Second Lieutenant on the flagship HMS *Sirius*. He had transferred to the fastest ship, *Supply*, for the final leg of the voyage, so he was in the first party to come ashore on 18 January 1788, when *Supply* arrived ahead of the fleet. The hard-working King would himself be Governor of New South Wales from 1800 to 1806.

Postscript

The meeting King recorded was, as history shows, a real 'honeymoon' moment. Before long, the relationship between natives and newcomers soured. The Aborigines realised that these visitors, unlike Cook, had come to stay, and the colonists began mistreating the Aborigines, monopolising their fishing spots and destroying the habitat they needed for hunting. Conflict broke out, and relations deteriorated even further when, in 1789, the British inadvertently introduced smallpox, killing thousands of unsuspecting Aborigines.

As Lieutenant Governor David Collins noted in his journal in April 1789:

The people whose business called them down the harbour daily reported, that they found, either in excavations of the rock, or lying upon the beaches and upon points of the different coves . . . the bodies of many . . . natives . . . The cause . . . remained unknown until a family was brought up, and the disorder pronounced to have been the smallpox. It was not a desirable circumstance to introduce a disorder into the colony which was raging with such fatal violence among the natives; but saving the lives of any of these people was an object of no small importance, as the knowledge of our humanity, would, it was hoped, do away with the evil impressions they had received of us.

According to Collins,

The number that it swept off, by their own account, was incredible. At that time a native was living with us, and on our taking him down the harbour to look for his former companions, those who witnessed his expression and agony can never forget either. He looked anxiously around him . . . not a vestige on the sand was to be found of human foot . . . not a living person was anywhere to be met with. It seemed as if, flying from the contagion, they had left the dead to bury the dead. He lifted up his hands and eyes in silent agony for some time; at last he exclaimed, 'All dead! All dead!' and then hung his head in mournful silence, which he preferred during the remainder of our excursion.

'They then in a very vociferous manner desired us to be gone and one of them threw a lance wide of us to show how far they could throw it.'

25

1788

CAPTAIN PHILLIP FOUNDS A EUROPEAN SETTLEMENT HALF A WORLD FROM EUROPE

'Look at that, Lieutenant King, just look at that!' Commodore Arthur Phillip exclaimed as HMS *Supply* rounded the southern headland of the unexplored bay named Port Jackson and glided into its calm waters. 'Much more accommodating than Botany Bay, wouldn't you agree?'

'Yes, Commodore. What a relief,' King said, looking around the sheltered waters. 'This is a far superior harbour.'

'Without question. I think we can say we have found the finest harbour in the world,' Phillip exclaimed, 'in which a thousand sail of the line may ride in the most perfect security.'

'Indeed, Commodore,' King replied, scanning the multitude of bays and coves. 'Where will you place the settlement?'

'Well, having examined many coves with all possible speed on my earlier visit, I have fixed on the one with the best spring of water,' Phillip said, pointing south-west towards a small, sandy inlet. 'The ships can anchor there so close to shore that at a very small expense quays may be made at which the largest may unload.'

'And far enough from the Heads, Commodore, to be safe from direct attack by the French or other enemies,' King observed, looking back towards the fast-disappearing headlands.

'That is indeed another reason I chose it,' Phillip said.

'So will you name it Spring Cove, Commodore?'

Governor Arthur Phillip had so much experience working around the world, he was able to establish the first settlement in Sydney despite the lack of support from England. Painted by Francis Wheatley (1786).

'No. This cove I have honoured with the name of the Home Secretary, Lord Sydney. After all, it was he who issued the charter authorising the establishment of this colony.'

Phillip ordered the ship's master to nose the First Fleet vessel into that semi-circular cove to moor alongside the tall, long-limbed trees that grew almost to the water's edge. The naval tender spent the night of 25 January 1788 riding at anchor, her officers and crew waiting for first light on what would prove a most auspicious day.

In those hours, Phillip could reflect on an outstanding success. He had led a fleet of eleven ships safely from England to New South Wales, a minor miracle. By contrast, in 1620 one of the two ships trying to establish a permanent settlement in America, *Speedwell*, had been forced to turn back, leaving the *Mayflower* on its own. That voyage was also far shorter—a little over nine weeks across the better-known north Atlantic Ocean, compared with the thirty-three-week voyage to New South Wales across some of the world's most treacherous seas. And while the *Mayflower* carried well-disciplined religious pilgrims, the First Fleet had to carry 759 unruly convicts.

But Phillip succeeded. Marine Captain Watkin Tench described the entry to Botany Bay of his ship, *Charlotte*:

The wind was now fair, the sky serene, though a little hazy, and the temperature of the air delightfully pleasant; joy sparkled in every countenance, and congratulations issued from every mouth. Ithaca itself was scarcely more longed for by Ulysses than Botany Bay by the adventurers who had traversed so many thousands of miles to take possession of it. To us it was a great and important day and we hoped the foundation and not the fall of an empire would be dated from it.

As Commodore, Phillip had to command eleven ships of very different shapes, sizes and qualities, and make them all sail at least within sight of each other—something that had never been achieved by such a large fleet over such a distance. It was history's greatest voyage of migration. The ships included his naval flagship, HMS *Sirius*, 540 tons; her naval tender, HMS *Supply*, 170 tons; six transports—*Alexander* (for male convicts), 450 tons; *Scarborough* (males), 430 tons; *Prince of Wales* (females), 350 tons; *Friendship* (males and females), 275 tons; *Charlotte* (males), 335 tons; and *Lady Penrhyn* (females), 335 tons.

There were also three store ships: *Borrowdale*, 275 tons; *Golden Grove*, 375 tons; and *Fishburn*, 378 tons.

They started in dribs and drabs from London before all gathered at Portsmouth, where they waited for months for orders and final supplies—some of which—including criminal records of the convicts, female clothing and ammunition—never arrived. After settling a strike by the sailors, who had not been paid during this waiting period, Phillip sailed the First Fleet to Botany Bay as instructed, via Tenerife, Rio de Janeiro and Cape Town. Unhappy with the harbour Captain James Cook had recommended in 1770, Phillip explored Port Jackson, which Cook had also logged. Finding it superior, he led the fleet there to establish the settlement in Sydney Cove. As Lieutenant Governor David Collins observed:

> Thus, under the blessing of God, the voyage was happily completed in eight months and one week, a voyage which before it was undertaken, the mind hardly dared venture to contemplate. Its successful completion afforded great satisfaction, for in that space of time with a fleet of eleven sail we had travelled five thousand and twenty-one leagues; had touched at the American and African continents and had at last rested without meeting any accident in that distant and imperfectly explored ocean.

On 26 January 1788 (Australia Day) Governor Arthur Phillip rowed ashore in Sydney Cove with the official party, raised the flag and 'founded a state' which he said 'we hope will not only occupy and rule this great country, but also will become a shining light among all the nations of the southern hemisphere'. Painting by Algernon Talmage (1938).

Next morning, 26 January 1788, Phillip, King and the rest of the official party were rowed ashore and the flag was raised, as had been done at Botany Bay eighteen years earlier. This time, however, the British were there to stay, as Phillip's far-sighted speech confirmed:

I do not doubt that this country will prove the most valuable acquisition Great Britain has ever made. We have come here today to take possession of this fifth great continental division of the Earth, on behalf of the British people and have founded here a state which we hope will not only occupy and rule this great country, but also will become a shining light among all the nations of the South Hemisphere. How grand is the prospect which lies before this youthful nation.

IT WAS A GREAT MOMENT because Phillip and his First Fleet founded the settlement that became the basis of the nation of Australia. Charged with transporting 1350 people, more than half of them convicts, on square-rigged sailing ships to the other side of the world, Phillip had led one of history's great voyages of migration. It was an epic beginning for the European story that was about to unfold in the ancient land.

Historical background

The voyage remains unparalleled. Those eleven small ships sailed 15,063 miles from England without serious loss in 252 days, of which sixty-eight were spent in ports en route. The forty-two souls who died on the voyage were either old or sick to begin with and, thanks to Phillip's enlightened approach to nutrition, the remaining convicts arrived in good health. It was a magnificent feat of navigation and seamanship. The daily average run was eighty-two nautical miles and the average speed was slightly over three knots, very good sailing in the circumstances, especially for bluff-bowed vessels.

The speech-making over, the founding of the settlement that would become Australia then began in earnest. As Lieutenant Governor David Collins pondered: 'If only it were possible that on taking possession of Nature, as we had thus done, in her simplest, purest garb, we might not sully that purity by the introduction of vice, profaneness and immorality. But this thought, much to be wished, was little to be expected.'

Sydney grew to serve as the mother colony for others around this 'new' continent: Van Diemen's Land (Tasmania), settled in 1803; Queensland, 1824; Western Australia, 1829; Victoria, 1834 (after a false start in 1803); South Australia, 1836; and finally the Northern Territory in 1869, where the settlement that would become Darwin was established after some earlier failed attempts.

Postscript

Despite his hard work, Governor Arthur Phillip was abandoned for the first couple of years by the British Government, which did not commit enough resources to the settlement, and became embroiled in the Napoleonic Wars with France just eighteen months after the First Fleet landed. The promised food supplies and support fleets with more convicts to provide labour never arrived, so Phillip had to fend for himself. The only additional supply ship, HMS *Guardian*, sent in late 1789 with more convict labourers and cattle, was wrecked on an iceberg off the Cape of Good Hope. Later, instead of strong male labourers, the British Government sent the *Lady Juliana*, full of women. So Phillip was forced to send his only spare ship, *Sirius*, to get supplies from Cape Town, where the *Guardian* had been towed. When the Second Fleet did arrive in 1790, most of the convicts were sick or dying because the private contractors who had taken over from an uninterested navy had cut the rations, starving 267 convicts to death. The First Fleet's arrival may have been a brilliant start, but it did not take long for things at Sydney Cove to deteriorate.

'I think we can say we have found the finest harbour in the world, in which a thousand sail of the line may ride in the most perfect security.'

1791

MARY BRYANT MAKES THE GREATEST CONVICT ESCAPE

'I'll get in the boat first, William,' Mary whispered, creeping up to the edge of the wharf in Sydney Cove. In the dim moonlight she could see the Governor's cutter tied alongside. 'Then you pass me the children. Here, take Emanuel,' she said, passing the sleeping infant to her husband.

'Mind you don't fall in—it's bloody dark even by a smuggler's reckoning,' Will Bryant muttered, taking Emanuel in his arms and patting the head of their three-year-old, Charlotte, who was quietly holding onto his leg. 'And for Christ's sake don't make a sound, woman, or the sentry will come running.'

'You'd better tell your drunken mates when they get here to be quiet too,' Mary whispered back, lowering herself over the side of the wharf and gingerly into the boat. 'The oars are all here,' she murmured with relief, 'and the sails. William, it's all going according to plan.'

'Come on! Don't waste time looking over the boat. I paid our mates in the Marines plenty of rum to leave it shipshape,' William said, handing Emanuel over. 'Take the baby, then I'll pass you Charlotte.'

'But where's the supplies?' Mary abruptly asked, as she laid the children in the bow of the open cutter. 'We can't go without food. It's a long way to Timor, William.'

'The crew are bringing the supplies . . . they must be running late, damn their souls. Here, take the gun—mind, it's loaded,' William said, passing a musket down to Mary. 'Everything's fine. God, we've been planning it long enough. Put the gun up for'ard near the wee ones.'

'Behind you, William! Look!' Mary hissed. She pointed at dark shapes approaching the wharf.

'Who goes there? Give me your name, for Christ's sake!' William said, suspecting a nosy sentry and wishing he had kept hold of the gun.

'Easy, Will—it's just me, Jimmy Martyn, and the lads,' a reassuring voice whispered. 'Creepin' up in our socks.' Martyn emerged from the gloom, his sunburnt face barely visible against the backdrop of The Rocks.

'You'd better have the supplies,' Will said, motioning Martyn across the wharf towards the boat.

'Of course. That stingy bastard Governor Phillip might have put us on half rations months ago, but we've still saved most of 'em.'

'All right, everyone?' Bryant whispered to the dark figures queuing up behind Martyn. 'It's so bloody dark I can't see you, so say your names as you get into the cutter so I know you're all here.'

'I thought an old Cornish smuggler like you would be used to the dark,' the next voice joked.

'For God's sake keep it quiet till we get out past the Heads. Who's that?' the nervous skipper asked.

'Jimmy "Chips" Cox, you bloody fool. Yer a bit jumpy there, Bryant,' said the man carrying a carpenter's bag.

'Sam "Birdy" Bird, able seaman, at your service,' another fellow introduced himself, stepping into the boat with his dilly bag.

'Bill Moreton, navigator—and yeah, Will, I've brought the bloody compass and quadrant that cost all that rum.'

'Old "Silly Willy" Allen, your *senior* deck-hand,' a fifty-one-year-old sailor joked softly, jumping into the cutter.

'Nat Lilly, sometime highwayman, going back home to the wife and kids in the Old Dart,' said the Jewish member of the crew. 'And hopin' me missus ain't shacked up with a younger man.'

'Last but not least, Long John Butcher, soldier, reportin' for duty, sir,' whispered a man brandishing a musket. 'Look at this little beauty—I just pinched it tonight. We may need it against them savages.'

'Good work, Johnny boy,' the relieved Bryant said, patting Butcher on the back. 'That's it, Mary,' he hissed to the wife who had persuaded him to try this escape in the first place. 'Good thing she's a thirty-footer, eh?'

'And balanced beautifully,' his wife replied excitedly. 'Now let her go fore and aft and get to the helm.' Having grown up helping her father, a fisherman, the Cornishwoman was in her element. 'When you're in we'll hoist the sails.'

'Thank God for a fair wind,' Bryant said. Untying the lines from the bollards, he leaped into the crowded boat and silently pushed it away from the wharf. Once it was clear, he turned the bow towards Sydney Heads as a westerly night wind filled the hastily run-up sails. Nobody said a word. The crew of nine hardly dared breathe as the cutter slid silently out of Sydney Cove between the shadowy promontories of The Rocks and Bennelong Point.

As the two children slept, they sailed silently past the grim punishment island of Pinchgut and Camp Cove, where Governor Phillip had camped that first night in January 1788. Then, feeling the swell rising under the bows at last, they slipped through the Heads and into the open sea. Immediately a south-east breeze filled the sails, enabling Bryant to turn the cutter north.

Mary broke the silence: 'We're free! We're free! We've escaped! We're not going to rot in that hell-hole till we die of starvation or from the cat o' nine tails.'

Although escapee Mary Bryant and her fellow convicts criticised Governor Arthur Phillip for reducing their food rations, the careful Governor had no option because the British Government had failed to send him enough supplies to feed the struggling settlement and without capable farmers he had been unable to grow crops locally.

IT WAS A GREAT MOMENT because a gang of convicts had just pulled off a great escape from the heavily guarded Sydney penal colony. Led by the Cornish couple Mary Bryant, a convicted highway robber, and her husband William, a convicted smuggler, the nine convicts and two children had just sailed to freedom. They knew they had an excellent chance of success because Governor Phillip had no spare ships to chase them: HMS *Sirius* had been wrecked at Norfolk Island and his one remaining ship, HMS *Supply*, had been sent there to collect rations for the starving colonists.

Historical background

The Bryants had been planning to escape since they arrived in 1788 with the First Fleet (they met on board the transport *Charlotte*). Mary, who had been raped by a jailer, gave birth to her first child, Charlotte, during a storm en route to Botany Bay. They had both grown up on boats and knew the cutter well because William used it—he was the colony's official head fisherman. They had stolen supplies and guns, along with a chart, compass and quadrant bought from the captain of a visiting Dutch trading ship, who had no love for the British.

They recruited essential crew from the First and Second Fleets, including the indispensable William Moreton, a merchant navigator. They were also inspired by the story of Captain William Bligh, who in 1789 sailed an open boat from near Tahiti to Timor after being cast adrift from his ship *Bounty* by Fletcher Christian and his fellow mutineers.

Against the odds, they successfully sailed the little cutter north up the east coast of Australia, then west to the island of Timor in the Dutch East Indies. They survived repeated Aboriginal attacks from shore and constant shortages of water and food—they had to swim ashore through dangerous surf to get supplies. Their boat nearly sank many times, and they were scorched by the sun. But thanks to the great seamanship of the Bryants and the navigation of Will Moreton, they reached their goal.

Claiming they were shipwrecked sailors, they were well treated by the Dutch colonial administrators who agreed to house, clothe and feed them until they could find a ship back to England. One night, however, Will Bryant got drunk and told the truth to impress some drinking mates. The Dutch authorities promptly imprisoned the escapees until an English naval captain, Edward Edwards, arrived from Tahiti with some captured mutineers from the *Bounty*. He set off with the Bryants and their crew, along with his mutineer prisoners, via Batavia (Jakarta) to London.

'We're free! We've escaped! We're not going to rot in that hell-hole till we die of starvation or from the cat o' nine tails.'

Postscript

The little band may have escaped the penal colony, but at a high price: many never saw England again. William Bryant, aged twenty-seven, died of fever in Batavia on 22 December 1791. Mary Bryant, twenty-five, survived the voyage back to England, but was tried and sentenced to be hanged for escaping. Fortunately the kind-hearted lawyer James Boswell read her story in the London newspapers and defended her. He won her a pardon and permission to return to her home village, where she remarried and lived for the rest of her life. Her daughter Charlotte died at sea on the way back to London; her son Emanuel had not survived the voyage in the cutter.

James Martyn, forty, a stonemason convicted of stealing metal, was granted a pardon in London. He kept the only journal of the escape: *Memorandums*, now in the British Museum. John Butcher, forty-seven, transported for stealing three pigs, was also pardoned in London. Awarded a block of land, he returned

Mary and William Bryant escaped from the penal colony at night with their two children and seven other convicts, stealing a government cutter and sailing towards Timor, where they planned to pass themselves off as shipwrecked sailors. Illustration by John Curtis.

to Sydney as a farmer. Willy Allen, fifty-one, convicted of stealing linen handkerchiefs, was also pardoned, and returned to the sea as a sailor. Nat Lilly, thirty-five, sent to the penal colony for stealing a silver-cased watch, two silver tablespoons and a fishing net, was pardoned and reunited with his (faithful) wife and two children in London.

The brilliant navigator who guided the open boat to Timor, William Moreton, thirty-one, died en route between Batavia and Cape Town. Jimmy Cox, the thirty-five-year-old carpenter, who'd been transported for burglary, jumped overboard in the Straits of Sunda, presumably trying to swim ashore. And Samuel Bird, thirty-two, a convicted thief, died at sea between Batavia and Cape Town.

1793
BENNELONG BECOMES FIRST ABORIGINE TO MEET THE KING

'How do you do, Your Majesty,' Bennelong said, kneeling on a cushion at the feet of King George III. He was dressed for his visit to the palace in a fine suit and waistcoat.

'Ah, my loyal subject from Botany Bay, I believe,' King George said. 'Arise, dear man, arise and let me look at you.'

'I am very pleased to meet Your Gracious Majesty,' said Bennelong, standing before the King and holding out his white-gloved hand.

'The pleasure is all mine,' replied the King, taking Bennelong's hand. 'I can assure you I have longed to meet one of you noble savages ever since the late Captain Cook first discovered your existence,' he added, walking around Bennelong. 'What a fine, upstanding specimen of a man you are, Mr Noble Savage, and as black as I am white. You would be a wonderful addition to the labouring force on my farm—tall, straight and strong.'

'Thank you, Your Majesty,' Bennelong answered, looking mad King George straight in the eye.

'Pray tell me, big strong man,' the King said, continuing to size up his visitor, 'do you have a name?'

'Bennelong, Your Majesty. Bennelong of the Eora people,' said the first native of New Holland to visit England.

'Thank you, Mr Bennelong. Tell me, my good man, was Captain Cook correct when he wrote in his journal that you noble savages are "far happier than we Europeans" and "not interested in acquiring any of the possessions of modern life we value so highly"?'

'Your Majesty, since the Dreamtime the Eora have survived comfortably by hunting, fishing and carefully looking after our land,' Bennelong said. 'We have never needed nor wanted any more than that.'

'Lucky man, Mr Bennelong. Very fortunate indeed. How I would love to live like that instead of having my life cluttered with all the trappings of modern life,' the King said wistfully, nodding to his equerry to show Bennelong out. 'Thank you for sailing from Botany Bay to meet me. You are a loyal subject indeed, and it was a pleasure to meet you.'

'The pleasure, Your Majesty,' Bennelong said, bowing gracefully, 'was all mine.'

Despite sailing to England to meet King George III, the 'civilised' warrior Bennelong from the Eora tribe died as a poverty-stricken alcoholic after his return in 1795 because he was ostracised by both black and white cultures.

IT WAS A GREAT MOMENT because this was the first time an Aborigine had travelled so far from Australia, and because he went as an ambassador for his people, to meet a king. It was a meeting of contrasting cultures, giving the King of Great Britain the chance to see and speak with a member of the ancient race who inhabited the land his Navy had just settled. Since the King was the head of the state and could influence government decisions, his attitude to Bennelong could inform colonial policies towards New South Wales. It may also have been a great moment for Bennelong, but travelling to the glittering power centre of a conquering nation was also a great ordeal that contributed to his early death.

Historical background

This epic meeting took place on 24 May 1793, while Britain was locked in struggle with revolutionary France across the channel. There was also strife in the palace, for King George had suffered bouts of insanity for years. Captain Arthur Phillip had captured Bennelong in 1789, when he was about twenty-six, to train him, along with fellow warrior Arabanoo, as an ambassador for his people to London. Bennelong was housed in Sydney, taught English and introduced to the lifestyle, clothing, eating and sleeping habits of the British. A highly intelligent man, he quickly learned to speak English and adopted the settlers' lifestyle—including, unfortunately, a taste for alcohol. Although he

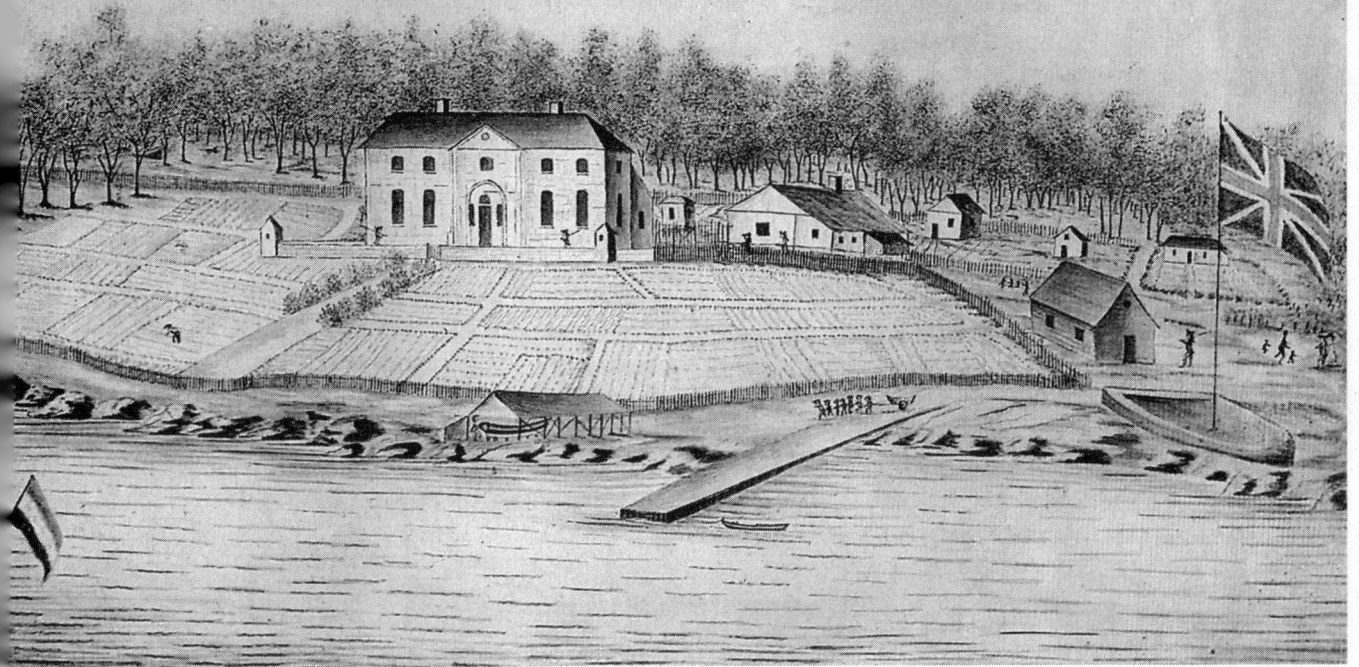

escaped back to his people in May 1790, Bennelong later returned to Phillip in Sydney. While Phillip was searching what is now Manly for Bennelong, another Eora warrior, Wil-ee-ma-rin, had speared him in the shoulder. Bennelong told Phillip he had punished Wil-ee-ma-rin for the spearing, and persuaded the Governor that the attack was caused by a misunderstanding. This stopped further bloodshed. Bennelong then stayed in Sydney, where he and other Eora tribesmen learned more about British ways and taught the settlers about their own culture, telling them stories and performing corroborees.

Phillip built Bennelong a brick hut on Bennelong Point and issued him with a red Marine uniform, whose jacket Bennelong wore much of the time. Phillip also asked Bennelong to help negotiate with Aborigines who were resisting occupation of their land by attacking settlers in outlying areas. Bennelong taught explorer George Bass the language of the Sydney Aborigines, and later gave Phillip the Aboriginal name Wolawaree to establish kinship between them.

Late in 1792, Phillip took Bennelong and another Eora warrior, Yemmerrawanie, to England. He wanted to show them off in London, partly to demonstrate his success in civilising the 'noble savages'. Yemmerrawanie fell ill and died, becoming the first Aborigine to be buried in England. After his tour of English society, Bennelong returned to Sydney with Phillip's successor, Governor John Hunter, in 1795.

Government House, where Governor Arthur Phillip entertained his Aboriginal guest, Bennelong, was so different to the Eora warrior's tribal camps that he never felt at home.

'Since the
Dreamtime
the Eora have
survived
comfortably
by hunting,
fishing and
carefully
looking after
our land.'

Postscript

Yemmerrawanie paid the highest price for travelling to England, but Bennelong suffered too. He might as well have died, for in the couple of years he was away his wife, Barangaroo, left him for a younger man. He defeated his rival in a duel, but his wife refused to take him back—as did the Eora, even though he discarded his clothes and returned to bush life. He was trapped between two cultures, truly accepted in neither.

Devastated by the rejection, he tried to steal a friend's wife, but was attacked by other warriors and badly beaten, suffering severe wounds that disfigured his face and impaired his speech. Not surprisingly, the lonely misfit consoled himself with alcohol, surviving on British handouts till he died at Kissing Point on 3 January 1813. Bennelong's name lives on in Bennelong Point, now the site of the Sydney Opera House.

King George III also met with misfortune. He spent his last years blind, deaf and crippled by rheumatism, and by the time he died was completely insane.

Nearly 200 years later the great Aboriginal activist and author Burnum Burnum, born Harry Penrith, also travelled to England. On 26 January 1988, he unfurled the Aboriginal flag on the cliffs of Dover, not far from the spot where Yemmerrawanie was buried, and 'claimed' England for the Aborigines.

Aboriginal people created a detailed record of everyday life during their 60,000 years in Australia before Europeans arrived, with such images as these Aboriginal rock carvings of humans and animals created by Eora artists (Ku-ring-gai Chase, NSW). Photo by Carmen Ky

When the captain and crew of the first ship to visit Australia—the Dutch trader *Duyfken*—went ashore on the west coast of the Cape York Peninsula in 1606, local Aborigines killed one of the crew. Painting by Dennis Adams (1974)

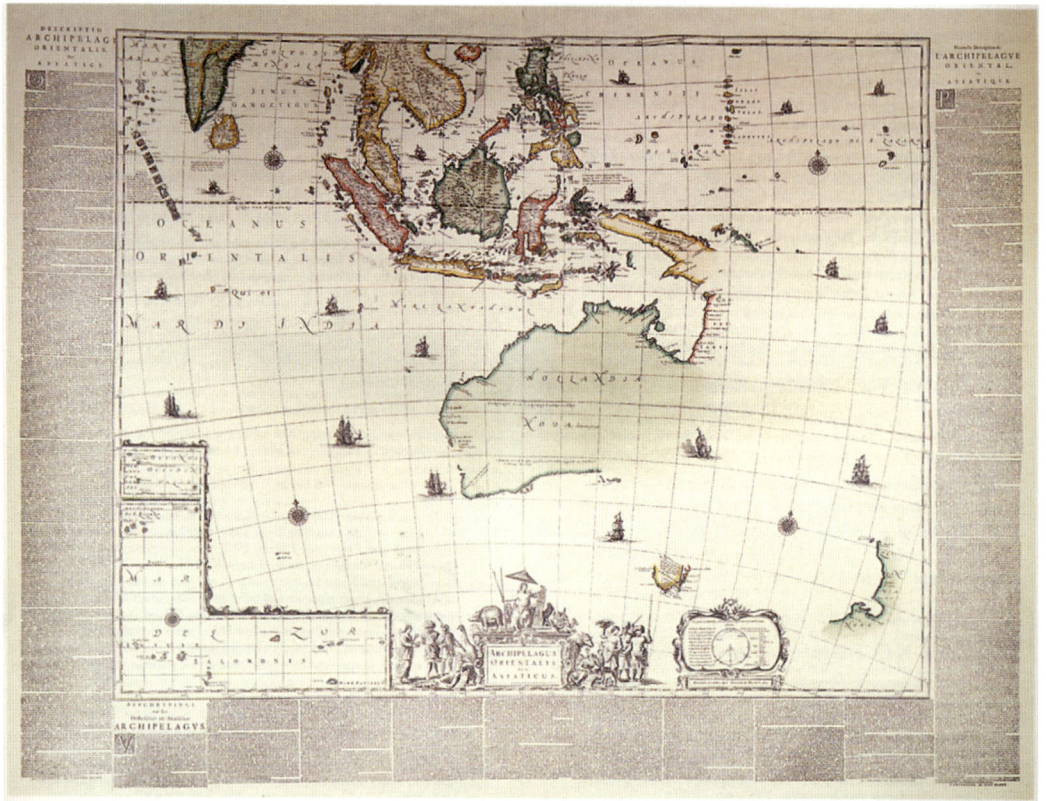

Little was known of the east coast of Australia, or the shape of New Zealand (or even whether New Zealand, Australia and New Guinea were connected to each other) before Captain Cook charted both New Zealand then the east coast of Australia in 1770, confirming it was separated from New Guinea. Joan Blaeu, *Atlas des Grossen Kurfursten (Atlas of the Great Elector)* (c. 1661)

When he returned to England after charting the fertile east coast of Australia, Captain Cook spoke well of the new land he had discovered and pointed out the advantages of settling it. 'To the South There is a Great Land', attributed to John Hamilton Mortimer (c. 1777)

It was a great feat of seamanship that all eleven ships of the First Fleet arrived safely in Botany Bay from England; the voyage across the world had taken eight months and one week. 'Botany Bay' by William Bradley (1788), State Library of NSW

Because the womanising Prince of Wales led such a debauched life, this cartoonist believed he and other public figures who were misbehaving at the time should have been sent to Botany Bay along with the convicts.
James Gilray (1786)

In an attempt to bridge the two cultures Governor Phillip captured the Eora warrior Bennelong and kept him at Government House where he taught him to speak English and live like an Englishman.
'Taking of Colbee and Benalon', by William Bradley (1789), State Library of NSW

Convicts worked like beasts of burden in the penal colony, especially for farmers like John Macarthur whose overseers used a lash to drive them as they pulled ploughs to till the fields for crops. Painted by an early unknown colonial artist (c. 1810)

When the officers and men of the New South Wales Corps, better known as the Rum Corps, broke into Government House to arrest Governor William Bligh they claimed they found him hiding under his bed upstairs and produced this unsigned cartoon. Attributed to William Minchin

As the first military officer appointed to govern New South Wales, after a long string of struggling naval officers, Governor Lachlan Macquarie found it easier to impose law and order, especially as he brought his own loyal force—the 73rd regiment. Attributed to John Opie or J. Graham Gilbert (early nineteenth century), Mitchell Library, State Library of NSW

Known as the 'Wild White Man', the escaped convict William Buckley caused quite a stir when he gave himself up after more than thirty years living with Aboriginal tribes around Port Phillip Bay. 'The First Settlers Discover Buckley', by Frederick Woodhouse (1861), State Library of Victoria

As there were so few of them, and they were so poorly armed, the miners at the Eureka Stockade did not stand a chance against the disciplined government troops, who easily overran their defences to defeat them. 'Eureka Stockade Riot, Ballarat' by J.B. Henderson (1854), Mitchell Library, State Library of NSW

Robert O'Hara Burke who led the Burke and Wills expedition, which was the first to cross the continent of Australia from south to north, may have been brave and strong but he made a series of mistakes that cost him his life and the life of his deputy leader William Wills. Painting by William Strutt (c. 1860), National Library of Australia

Apart from outwitting the police with his clever tactics the notorious bushranger Ned Kelly wore thick armour that made him appear especially fierce and protected him in gun battles. Drawing by unknown artist at Ned Kelly's last stand at Glenrowan (1880). Courtesy Glenrowan Tourist Centre, Victoria

Banjo Paterson was inspired to write 'The Man from Snowy River' after hearing a story about an exceptionally good horseman, the only one in a group of mountain men chasing an escaped horse who was able to keep going and round up the rogue colt. Photo by John Olsen, courtesy William Moore Agencies

1804
FLINDERS PUTS AUSTRALIA ON THE MAP

'Australia—that's it!' Flinders exclaimed, looking up from the chart he was drawing of the great southern continent. 'Not Terra Australis and certainly not New Holland—let's forget the Dutch,' he said, talking to himself. 'And I certainly don't want it to become Terre Napoléon if the wretched French win this war,' he mused, twirling his quill. 'That French cartographer I met exploring Terra Australis recently, Louis de Freycinet, will no doubt mark his chart Terre Napoléon when he gets back to Paris.

'But Australia certainly sounds better than New South Wales—and anyway, the place looks nothing like south Wales. I don't know what Cook was thinking about,' he said, striding to the window to look out at the cattle grazing in the lush green fields on the French island of Mauritius. 'Australis means south, and the island is in the southern hemisphere and has been known for ages as the Great South Land,' he said, more sure at every moment that he had flashed on the right name.

'Mind you, if only my dear, long-suffering wife Ann were here instead of stuck in England, she would help me,' he muttered. 'But of course the mean-spirited Admiralty wouldn't let me bring her when I sailed for Australia—they even ordered her off my ship. Well, at least now she isn't trapped in this damned French prison.'

Pacing up and down in the house he had been assigned since his arrest, Flinders had another thought: 'But I must be careful of putting "Australia" on the chart, lest I alert that treacherous French Governor Charles de Caen, who still claims I am a spy. Then he might confiscate the map and change it to Terre Napoléon.'

Then, looking out the window again, from where he could see a native climbing high into a tree to pick fruit, he said to himself: 'That's it: I'll aim for the top. I will get this chart off the island in a sealed diplomatic package and send it straight to Sir Joseph Banks and the Admiralty so they can put Australia on our charts before the French publish their map as Terre Napoléon. I shall be the first navigator to publish a map of the whole continent, and I want it called Australia.'

Dipping his quill into the ink, Flinders lowered it onto the chart he had made after sailing around the continent and boldly wrote, in the middle, one word: 'Australia'.

Matthew Flinders was still imprisoned for eight years on trumped up espionage charges when he called into the French port of Mauritius for assistance on his return voyage to England. Painting by Antoine Toussaint de Chazal (1807).

IT WAS A GREAT MOMENT because the ill-fated British navigator had just given the last continent to be settled the name that would stick. It had been a long time coming. Europe's scholars had supposed there must be a great south land for centuries, mainly because they believed it was needed to balance the land masses in the north. But it was Flinders who defined its shape by circumnavigating it.

At first referred to vaguely as Terra Incognita (Unknown Land), then Terra Australis (Southern Land), the continent was called New Holland by Dutch navigators who charted some of the west coast on their voyages to the Spice Islands in the seventeenth century. Captain Cook, who discovered the east coast in 1770, thought it looked like Wales, so called it New South Wales. The British did not want to offend the Dutch at the time, so they claimed only the eastern half for the Crown and left 'New Holland' written on the western half of their maps. The ill-fated French navigator Nicolas Baudin and his cartographer Louis de Freycinet, whom Flinders had recently met in Encounter Bay, had also mapped part of the continent, bestowing French place names on the parts they explored. They told Flinders they were going to use the name Terre Napoléon.

Clearly this confusion could not continue. Flinders did send his 1804 map to Sir Joseph Banks in England on a passing ship, but with the British busy fighting the French, the name did not catch on until Flinders' book, using the name Australia, appeared in 1814, ten years after his Eureka moment. Governor Lachlan Macquarie later approved the name, and the New South Wales Legislative Council adopted it in 1824.

Historical background

Matthew Flinders finished his chart during his imprisonment on Mauritius, where he was held on a trumped-up charge after being forced to call at the island on his way home because his ship was leaking. As the British were again fighting the French in the Napoleonic Wars, De Caen seized Flinders even though he was clearly a navigator on a scientific voyage of discovery.

Flinders had sailed first north and west on a challenging voyage around Australia in 1802–1803, charting and naming places undiscovered by Cook or any others. Before that, he and George Bass had discovered the strait separating the mainland from Van Diemen's Land (Tasmania) and named it Bass's Strait; the pair also sailed around Tasmania, proving it was an island.

After returning to Sydney in 1803, Flinders had to abandon his rotting ship. Unable to find another one suited to exploration, he eventually set sail for England on the schooner *Cumberland*, but its dangerous leak forced him to visit Mauritius for repairs. Even though Britain and France were at war again, Flinders hoped his passport and the scientific nature of his mission would allow him to continue on his way. Instead he was arrested—but with all his research papers, and now with plenty of time to create his breakthrough 1804 map.

'Australia' had been used in references to the general region, but Flinders was the first to apply the name specifically to the continent. In 1804 he wrote to his brother: 'I call the whole island Australia, or Terra Australis.' Later that year he wrote to Banks and mentioned 'my general chart of Australia'. That 92 cm x 72 cm map, made in 1804, was the first on which Australia was used to name the land mass whose outline is so familiar today.

In March 1806, after twenty-seven months of detention, Flinders had his release approved by Napoleon, but De Caen, who by then hated the proud and dignified prisoner whom he could not humble, refused to let him leave, claiming Flinders' knowledge of Mauritius's defences would encourage Britain to try to capture it. In June 1809 the Royal Navy began a blockade of the island, and a year later Flinders was finally freed.

Back in England, he continued to promote Australia as a name, especially after he learned that the French had—as he'd feared—published the first map of the continent in 1811 and named part of it Terre Napoléon. It had been a race between Flinders and the French duo of Baudin and De Freycinet to 'brand' the continent. Baudin had since died of tuberculosis, but De Freycinet had sailed back to Paris with all the paperwork while his government imprisoned his main

'I shall be the first navigator to publish a map of the whole continent, and I want it called Australia.'

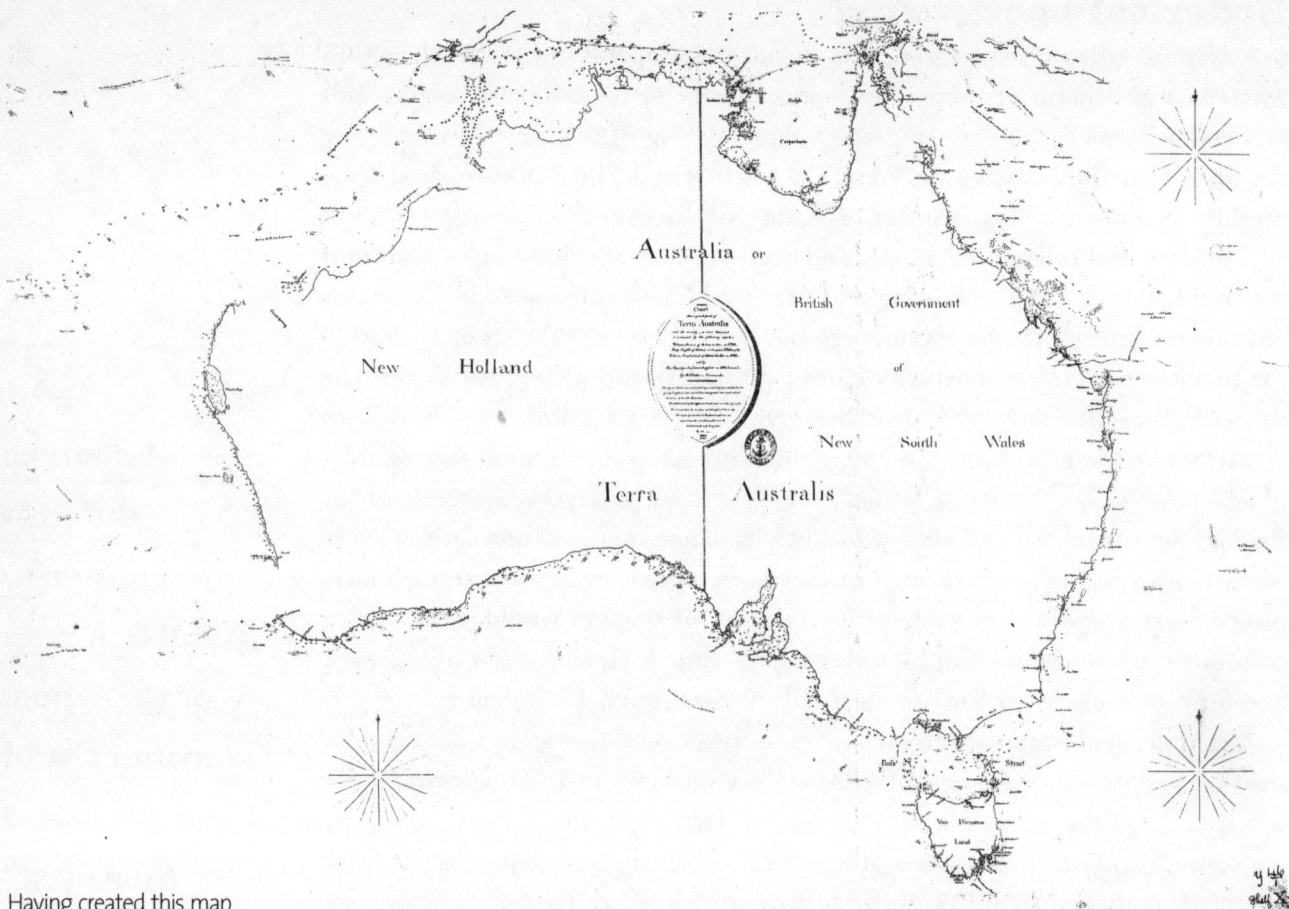

Having created this map in 1804 after charting the coastline, Matthew Flinders became the first to call the continent 'Australia' (when he wrote this name at the top of the map) instead of New Holland, New South Wales or Terra Australis. His superiors in England thought the new name was too radical, so initially refused his recommendation.

rival. Had the French defeated Britain in the Napoleonic Wars they might have seized her colonies—in which case New Holland would almost certainly have been called Terre Napoléon.

Back in London, Flinders raced to get his own book out—but Sir Joseph Banks did not take to the name Australia, preferring New Holland or Terra Australis. As a result, the book of Flinders' adventures had to be published under the title *A Voyage to Terra Australis*. Flinders, by now desperately ill, did see copies of the maps (of 'Australia') that were to be published with the book, but the final page proofs were only brought to him on the eve of his death on 19 July 1814.

The book however, was widely read and the name Australia soon became official.

Postscript

The dedicated navigator's health had been ruined by his exhausting voyages and his long imprisonment. Flinders had just enough time to write the book on his crowning achievement as a navigator before dying at the age of forty. Sadly, despite his self-sacrificing service to the Admiralty, the British Government refused his widow Ann a pension, and she had to raise their daughter without an income. Some funds were finally raised for them by appreciative people in Australia, but the help came too late for Mrs Flinders, who died in 1852. The benefactors agreed to transfer the endowment to her daughter, Anne, who by then had married, so the delayed pension finally went to Mrs Anne Petrie. This at least helped her pay for the education of her son and Flinders' grandson, William Matthew Flinders Petrie (1853–1942), who became a noted Egyptologist. Petrie offered all Flinders' papers and possessions to the first government in Australia to build a statue to his grandfather. Victoria and New South Wales competed for the prize, but New South Wales built its statue first—which is why there is a prominent memorial to Flinders in each of the nation's biggest cities.

That French Connection

Although most people think Matthews Flinders published the first map of Australia, he did not. He may have drawn the first map himself while he was in a French prison on Mauritius in 1804, and also been first to name the continent Australia, but when the British Admiralty received his map they just put it in a drawer until Flinders was released from prison in 1810. Meanwhile rival French navigator Captain Louis de Freycinet, who had also been charting Australia (with Captain Nicolas Baudin), had published the first definitive map of Australia by 1811—following the earlier publication of books telling the epic story of their voyage. De Freycinet did not call the continent 'Australia' of course but instead gave different names to different parts of the continent, including the southern coast which he called 'Terra Napoleon'. Flinders' book, with its map of Australia, was not published until 1814.

What would have made this French *coup* even worse for Flinders (had he lived long enough to find out) was the fact that de Freycinet had smuggled his wife on board disguised as a cabin boy to keep him company on the long voyage, whereas the British Admiralty had expelled Flinders' new bride from his ship just before he sailed off, forcing him to spend many years on his own.

De Freycinet was just one French navigator in a long line of busy French navigators hot on the heels of the British, including the Comte de la Perouse, who had arrived in Botany Bay just five days after the British First Fleet arrived in 1788. But thanks to the 1789 French Revolution and Napoleon's military ambitions the French exploration of Australia soon came to an end.

1805
JOHN MACARTHUR 'STARTS' WOOL INDUSTRY

'So, just back from England, eh? And what have you got there, Macarthur?' Governor King asked, showing the New South Wales Corps officer into his office. 'Government papers confirming your court martial, I presume?'

'On the contrary, your Excellency,' John Macarthur replied with a grin as he took a seat opposite the governor's desk. 'This here official document promotes me from military officer to pastoralist—with the largest land grant in the colony to boot,' Macarthur said, handing over a scroll bound with pink ribbon.

'Land grant? What rubbish!' King spluttered. 'What about the court martial? After all, I expelled you from the colony for rebelling against my government and nearly killing your commanding officer and my friend, Captain William Paterson, in that duel in 1801.'

'He couldn't shoot to save his life, which is why I could have taken it,' Macarthur said coldly.

'But I sent you back to London to a court martial,' King said. 'Where are the papers confirming that trial?'

'Huh! There was no court martial, your Excellency,' Macarthur replied. 'I resigned from the New South Wales Corps when I got to London, didn't I? So how could I be court-martialled?' said Macarthur, enjoying himself. 'Now please be kind enough to read that order.'

'Confound it, man! I knew you could not be trusted, but this is unbelievable,' the frustrated governor said, reaching for his port bottle and pouring out a medicinal glassful for his gout. 'So you are no longer an officer?'

'No, but I am still a gentleman, as we both are—even though both our fathers were drapers back in the West Country,' Macarthur retorted, opening both arms wide and looking down proudly at his fine waistcoat and gold-buckled shoes. 'Now, please,' he said, pointing impatiently to the scroll.

'Who's it from?' King asked, putting down his glass and untying the ribbon.

'The Secretary of State for Colonies.'

'Lord Camden!' King said, as he began reading the scroll. 'What! The Secretary has granted you 5000 acres?' 'Five thousand acres at the Cow Pastures?' He sat back, flabbergasted.

'That's what it says, and when I demonstrate the viability of my plans, they will give me another 5000,' the new landowner crowed. 'Sir Joseph Banks vouched for my credentials, he did.'

'Credentials?' King said. 'Banks wouldn't be taken in by you, surely?'

'Well, that's how I got the land, and I'll soon be stocking it with my merino sheep,' Macarthur said, further baiting the governor.

'What do you mean, your merinos? They are the same twenty-six Spanish merinos that I bought for the government in 1796. You didn't import them, I did!'

'That may be so, your Excellency,' Macarthur replied, 'but I bought them after that, didn't I?'

'Not from us. We refused to sell them to you as an army officer of bad standing,' the governor said.

'That may be so, but I succeeded in buying them anyway—from the farmers who bought them from the government,' Macarthur said.

'But don't forget, Macarthur, it was I who—at your request—wrote to ask the Secretary of State if the government could buy them back from you. And I sent your fleeces to London for inspection.'

'More fool you, King,' Macarthur replied, taking off his white gloves absent-mindedly. 'Because those are the very fleeces that inspired Camden to give me 5000 acres of prime grassland—those and some other fleeces I took back in 1801.'

'You're a shameless opportunist,' King said, throwing down the scroll.

Self-serving colonial power-broker John Macarthur shows the face that tormented, undermined and outwitted four governors: Hunter, King, Bligh and Macquarie.

'One has to be,' Macarthur shot back smugly. 'And I now intend to start a wool industry with that flock, along with even higher-quality merinos I've just bought from the royal flock of King George himself—five rams, in fact, and one beautiful ewe—which I transported with me on the ship.'

'I hardly thought you had either the time or the interest for the hard work such a farm will need.'

'Ah, but I can depend on Elizabeth—my wife is a very hard worker,' Macarthur gloated. 'She's quite capable of managing Camden—especially with free convict labour from your government.'

'Camden?'

'That's what I'm calling my new property, after my benefactor. He also introduced me to buyers in England—and they've already ordered shipments of wool.'

'Damn it, man, it seems you have all the powerful men on side,' the governor said, standing up and handing back the scroll. 'So I suppose it is now my job to encourage such new business for this penal colony.'

'I should hope so,' Macarthur replied. 'If you want to please your masters back home.'

'Well, having imported that first flock I obviously have faith in the future of wool for exports,' the governor said philosophically, as he ushered Macarthur to the door. 'So I suppose I must wish you well—for the sake of the colony.'

IT WAS A GREAT MOMENT because Macarthur—using the sheep King had imported in 1797, along with top-quality merinos he had now brought from England—was about to found Australia's wool industry. King supported the venture, even though Macarthur had criticised him and his administration while in London. It was 1805 and Macarthur—helped greatly by his wife, Elizabeth— soon succeeded in producing good wool for export from their flock, which bred well on the fine grasses at Camden. The Macarthurs exported their first bale two years later, and the quality steadily improved, until buyers in England preferred it to Spanish or German wool and demand increased exponentially. Macarthur may have been an unprincipled entrepreneur, but he was just the type the colony needed to defy authority and raise the flag of free enterprise in the midst of a convict settlement. Within a decade the officer turned grazier—or, more precisely, his hard-working wife, Elizabeth—had set Australia well on the way to becoming the nation that 'rode on the sheep's back'.

Having already established his flourishing Elizabeth Farm, Macarthur used the additional land grant he obtained from Lord Camden to establish a firm foundation for the wool industry in the colony. Painting by Joseph Lycett (1822).

Historical background

King may have bought the first breeding flock on his own personal initiative and so technically founded the colony's wool industry in 1796, but Macarthur—an entrepreneur, not a government official—turned that flock into the foundation of a successful industry by breeding a larger flock and developing wool of the highest quality. The newly developed steam-powered textile mills in England badly needed fine wool. Macarthur supplied wool brokers in London, producing heavier fleeces than any colonial rivals. By 1822 he had won two medals from the London Society of Arts for producing 68,000 kg of wool superior to the celebrated output of Saxony, in today's Germany.

Postscript

The credit should really have gone to Elizabeth, who managed the Camden sheep property alone for many years while Macarthur made repeated trips to England—including the eight years during which the political troublemaker was banished from the colony for his role in deposing Governor Bligh in 1808. Macarthur was too often in trouble and, although the Rum Rebellion against Bligh was his greatest political coup, he tried to undermine the administration of all four governors who followed Phillip—Hunter, King, Bligh and Macquarie. Elizabeth meanwhile got on with improving the flock and fleeces, developing the property—which was eventually 28,000 acres—and building the Camden homestead, which Macarthur did not live to see completed. She also had to make all the decisions towards the end of Macarthur's life, because he went insane; he died in 1834.

'What do you mean, your merinos? They are the same twenty-six Spanish merinos I bought for the government in 1796. You didn't import them, I did!'

1808
RUM REBELLION DEPOSES GOVERNOR BLIGH

'**D**amn the law of England! I am Governor and I make the laws in this colony!' William Bligh shouted through the locked front door of Sydney's Government House at Major George Johnston, the leader of the small army of redcoats Bligh had seen through the window.

'But the law of England is still supreme, Your Excellency,' Johnston shouted back. 'I demand that you let me in—I have a warrant for your arrest on charges of breaking that law.'

'Damn you, didn't you hear me? Go away!' Bligh yelled.

'Your Excellency,' Johnston warned as he rattled the door handle, 'I have the full New South Wales Corps assembled out here with bayonets fixed, ready to take action if you resist arrest.'

'I heard your damn band playing and saw the colours flying as you marched up here,' Bligh said, 'but that pretty show carries no authority.'

'I am Commandant of the New South Wales Corps, and I must tell you that in the circumstances I have also appointed myself Lieutenant Governor,' Johnston said. 'I have already asked you to resign, as ordered by John Macarthur. If you continue to refuse, Sir, I will execute the warrant to arrest you.'

'Damn your warrant. What possible grounds could be specified for my arrest?'

'It says "The present alarming state of this colony in which every man's property, liberty and life is endangered induces us most earnestly to implore you instantly to place Governor Bligh under an arrest, and to assume the command of the colony".'

'Who signed it?' spluttered Bligh.

'Macarthur—Captain John Macarthur.'

'Ah, I thought so. Well, he is no longer a captain, nor a member of the Corps, and he has no legal authority in this colony,' Bligh retorted. 'Macarthur is just enraged because I have stopped the rum trade by which you redcoats almost ruined this colony.'

'This is a popular revolt, Sir!' Johnston said. 'Macarthur has the support of all leading colonists, including the Blaxland brothers, and we are collecting 150 signatures supporting this warrant.'

'I don't care how many signatures you have from mere colonists. I am the Governor and law-maker. Now be gone, I tell you.'

There was a loud crack as Bligh's front door gave way under the pressure of the impatient redcoats' shoulders.

'I'll wait no longer,' Johnston shouted into the ragged hole. Waving his warrant, he stepped through the remains of the door, closely followed by two of his soldiers—but Bligh had vanished.

Finding nobody on the ground floor, the soldiers ran up the stairs, broke through the only door that was locked and burst into Bligh's bedroom.

'Where are you, Sir?' cried Johnston breathlessly.

'Look, the Governor's under the bed,' shouted a soldier, catching sight of Bligh's boots. 'I see him,' called the second soldier, who rushed up to the bed, then hesitated.

'Don't just stand there, men. He may be the Governor, but we have a warrant for his arrest,' Johnston ordered angrily. 'Pull him out by his boots!'

The controversial Governor William Bligh may have established a formidable reputation at sea, surviving a mutiny and subsequent epic longboat voyage, but was still no match for John Macarthur and the New South Wales Corps.

IT WAS A GREAT MOMENT because it was the only overthrow of civilian authority by the military in Australia's history and because, for better or worse, the successful revolt by colonists curbed the dictatorial powers of the Governor, at least temporarily (coup leaders Macarthur and Johnston were soon recalled by the British Government). With a keen sense of occasion the rebels had chosen 26 January 1808, the twentieth anniversay of the colony's founding. Unjustified though the so-called Rum Rebellion was, it represented a turning point. Macarthur and Johnston's coup forced the British Government to stop using ill-trained naval officers as governors and replace them with military officers such as Lachlan Macquarie (1810–1821), who took over from Bligh and dealt far more effectively with the local military.

The mutiny was led by the self-serving former New South Wales Corps captain and inveterate troublemaker John Macarthur, who wanted to assert his power over the colonial administration so he could continue to operate his illegal businesses unchallenged. The richest businessman and largest landowner in the colony, the wilful and devious Macarthur had become its de facto ruler, creating factions to support his enterprises, vilifying his opponents, and manipulating corrupt officials whose debts he bought up. Macarthur was the forerunner of the many self-made and unscrupulous men who have dominated Australian political and economic life.

A subsequent great moment was the dismantling of Johnston's New South Wales Corps, which had used rum as a de facto currency for so long it was openly called the Rum Corps—rum also meant 'dodgy'. The incoming Governor Macquarie replaced it with his own trustworthy 73rd Regiment.

Historical background

Macarthur thought Bligh would be fair game because when he was at Tahiti in 1789 he had already been deposed as captain of HMS *Bounty*. The mutineers loathed his harsh discipline and did not want to leave their Tahitian girlfriends. After casting Bligh and loyal crew members adrift in a longboat, they collected their women and sailed to an uncharted island (Pitcairn), where they spent the rest of their lives. Bligh, meanwhile, safely guided his longboat to Timor and returned to England, where a naval court cleared him of all blame and sent a ship to Tahiti to round up and punish the mutineers.

Although he was the colony's military leader, Major George Johnston—who, ironically, had been commended for putting down the 1804 uprising of Irish nationalists known as the Vinegar Hill Rebellion—overthrew Bligh on behalf of his friend Macarthur. Bligh had made the mistake of arresting Macarthur for letting a convict escape to Tahiti on a ship he part-owned. Macarthur refused to pay a fine for the offence, whereupon Bligh imprisoned him for breaking the law.

Macarthur claimed Judge-Advocate Atkins was unfit to judge him and also owed him money. The other members of the court—six soldiers—agreed with Macarthur. Since most of the leading men in the colony did too, his friend

'Don't just stand there, men. He may be the Governor, but we have a warrant for his arrest. Pull him out by his boots!'

When the leader of the mutiny on the *Bounty*, Fletcher Christian, cast Captain Bligh adrift near Tahiti in 1789 he never dreamt the great navigator could sail his 23-foot open boat crowded with nineteen crew to safety in Timor. He covered 3618 miles (5823 kilometres) in 41 days. Painting by Robert Dodd.

Johnston ordered Macarthur's release from prison. Macarthur then drew up and signed the warrant that ordered Johnston to arrest Bligh for endangering the stability of the colony and placed Johnston in charge. He collected nearly 150 signatures to legitimise his coup d'état—which became known as the Rum Rebellion.

Bligh remained under house arrest at Government House for a year before a suitable ship could be found to dispatch him back to England. Although Bligh tried to muster support from free settlers in both New South Wales and Tasmania, they all—apart from Hawkesbury River settlers who resented being forced to trade with Macarthur on his extortionate terms—refused to help him, so he had no choice but to return to London. When his replacement, Governor Macquarie, arrived in December 1809 he confirmed British Government orders for Bligh's recall, and Bligh finally sailed for England in May 1810.

Postscript

Returning to England after their mutiny, Johnston and Macarthur arrived well before Bligh, but they failed to win the authorities over to their cause. Johnston was cashiered and sent back to Sydney as a civilian settler, a relatively minor penalty. Macarthur was ordered to stay in England until further notice and a warrant was issued for his arrest in the event of his return to Sydney. This kept the troublemaker out of the colony until 1817, allowing Macquarie to establish badly needed order. Meanwhile, Bligh was completely exonerated by the British Government, as he had been over the *Bounty* mutiny, and eventually promoted to Vice Admiral. He died in London in 1817.

A Rum Business

From the moment the New South Wales Corps—the Red Coats—were employed for military duties in the British penal colony they insisted on getting as much rum as they could. They even threatened to delay the sailing of the First Fleet if they were not allowed extra rations of rum on the voyage out and then during their service in the colony. Not surprisingly they were soon called 'the Rum Corps'. Once entrenched in the colony the Corps sent ships to the nearest suppliers and imported shiploads of rum to drink, trade, sell at exorbitant profits and buy favours.

Worth more than money—especially in the absence of any standard currency—rum became a basic commodity with an agreed value. As life in the far-flung penal colony was so miserable for many of these English misfits they drank to drown their sorrows. Only a small volume was required to make the drinker drunk. Employers also paid workers in rum—most famously those workers on the Sydney Hospital known as the Rum Hospital.

The leader of the Rum Corps and the most powerful power-broker Captain John Macarthur also imported a copper still to increase his control over the rum trade. As Governor King complained, 'One half of the colony already belongs to him and it will not be long before he gets the other half.'

Successive governors tried in vain to stop the Rum Corps importing, trading and drinking rum; the Rum Corps gained a stranglehold after Governor Phillip retired, and ran the colony until his replacement, Governor John Hunter, arrived. Hunter failed to curb the rum trade, as did Governor King—even though King turned ships away loaded with rum and introduced beer and wine as alternatives. The Rum Corps then reached the peak of its power when they mounted the Rum Rebellion, deposing Governor Bligh. But once these naval governors were replaced by a military governor, the stronger Lachlan Macquarie—who brought his own military force, the 73rd Regiment, in 1810—the government disbanded the Rum Corps and curtailed the power of demon drink that had ruined the early days of the colony.

1810
LACHLAN MACQUARIE LAYS FOUNDATIONS FOR A GREAT CITY

'**Y**ou'll do as you are ordered, Reverend Marsden,' Governor Macquarie said, as his aide-de-camp pinned a page of *The Sydney Gazette* bearing his latest official proclamation on the noticeboard outside Marsden's church. 'We need three responsible people as trustees of the new road to the Hawkesbury settlement, and you have been appointed.'

'I don't take my orders from the likes of you, Macquarie,' the Reverend Samuel Marsden said, stamping his long-staffed cross into the dirt in front of his little wooden church. 'And you should not have printed my new appointment in the *Gazette*.'

'So who *do* you take orders from, Reverend?'

'From God Almighty,' said Marsden, drawing himself up to his full height. 'Certainly not from a friend of the Emancipists such as you. I am not going to serve alongside ex-convicts like Simeon Lord and Andrew Thompson, who are also living in sin with convict women.'

'But they've served their time, been pardoned and must be forgiven their sins—especially by a man of God,' Macquarie replied. 'And to think you were recommended for this job by William Wilberforce, the champion of slaves, himself. As for women of convict stock, there is not much else to choose from, even for you Exclusives.'

'You and your emancipation policy! Bah!' Marsden spat out. 'Fancy treating convicts like royalty and stopping the floggings. Their souls cannot be redeemed. We Exclusives are the only future this colony has.'

'No wonder they call you the flogging parson,' Macquarie said coldly.

'If you had a military commission I would have you court-martialled for disobedience.'

56

'It does those sinners good. As for you appointing an ex-convict, Francis Greenway, to design and build all your fancy buildings, which the convicts don't deserve and which cost a fortune—you'd think he was Christopher Wren! It's time you stopped favouring the convicts.'

'Yes, Greenway is an Emancipist,' Macquarie said. 'But I would have thought that you, as God's representative, would have more faith in the colony's future. I realised as soon as I arrived that this colony badly needed public buildings, and Greenway is a most gifted architect and builder.'

'But he came here as a convict, a man of sin,' Marsden said, looking to the heavens as if for confirmation. 'Until your soft-headed emancipation whitewashed him.'

'Emancipation frequently renders a convict as good a subject of His Majesty as any other class of person,' Macquarie said.

'I still refuse to act as commissioner on your so-called public road without orders from London,' Marsden said, puffing out his chest. 'You should not be allowing *your* flock freedom to go beyond the boundaries of the original penal colony. Soon they'll be too far away to be controlled, let alone punished for their sins.'

'It is just as well that you hold a civil commission, because if you had a military commission I would have you court-martialled for disobedience.'

'Damn your new buildings and roads. Now take that notice off my board.' Marsden turned on his heel to enter his church.

'I won't be stopped,' Macquarie called after him, 'with either my emancipations or my building!'

'You'll get your come-uppance,' the preacher called back. 'The British Government will not approve, you wait and see. You'll be dealt with by the higher authority I am quoting now—our London masters.'

The reforming Governor Lachlan Macquarie won the hearts of the convicts through his compassionate policy of emancipation, but alienated class-conscious 'Exclusives' who undermined his authority and ruined his reputation.

IT WAS A GREAT MOMENT because against formidable odds, including opposition from one of the colony's most influential men, Governor Macquarie did build his road to the outlying settlements. He found another trustee in place of Marsden, expanded the settlement, and erected new public buildings. He overruled the leading cleric in the fledgling colony to ensure an upgrading of the main road north-west from Sydney to the fast-growing farming region on the Hawkesbury River that was becoming the bread basket for the burgeoning colony. By 1811 five so-called 'Macquarie towns' had been established in the area—Windsor, Richmond, Castlereagh, Pitt Town, and Wilberforce, named for the anti-slavery campaigner.

Historical background

Macquarie took office in 1810, replacing Governor William Bligh after the Rum Rebellion and bringing in his own 73rd Regiment of Foot to control the unruly New South Wales Corps. In the next few years, a new confrontation came to a head, between Emancipists (former convicts who had been pardoned or served out their sentences) and Exclusives (free settlers, colonial officials and members of the military), who sought to shut Emancipists out of the full social and economic life of the colony. Macquarie's face-off with Marsden marked a turning point in this conflict. Against the Exclusives' protests, he not only pushed that roadway through to the Hawkesbury but also boldly extended the settlement's boundaries in other directions, including west to the Blue Mountains. A visionary planner with faith in the future of a reformed penal colony, Macquarie spent his twelve years as Governor laying grand bricks-and-mortar foundations for the future city of Sydney in a massive construction program of public buildings, many of which stand to this day.

Known as 'the flogging parson' the self-seeking 'Exclusive' Reverend Samuel Marsden was more interested in acquiring wealth than saving souls, so opposed Governor Macquarie's policy of offering convicts a second chance.

By the time he left New South Wales, Macquarie had achieved minor miracles. The colony's best governor so far, he was also its most optimistic, confident and successful nation-builder. His impressive array of public works included a post office, a hospital, a military barracks and schools. He encouraged the establishment of the Bank of New South Wales in the face of London's opposition, and fostered exploratory journeys—such as the 1813 crossing of the Blue Mountains—that steadily expanded the area of settlement. Macquarie stated that under his rule 'the colony has . . . greatly improved in agriculture, trade, increase of flocks and herds, and wealth of every kind; that the people build better dwelling houses, and live more comfortably; that they are in a very considerable degree reformed in their moral and religious habits; that they are now less prone to drunkenness, and more industrious; and that crimes have decreased'.

Postscript

Marsden was right about the judgement of the British Government. Worried by rumours of overspending spread by Exclusives such as the former New South Wales Corps captain John Macarthur, London sent Commissioner John Bigge to assess Macquarie's administration. Bigge, who had come under the influence of Macarthur, claimed Macquarie had wasted public funds on an extravagant and unnecessary building program. He said he was too tolerant towards the convicts and did not punish them enough, had pardoned and emancipated too many, and was misguided in trusting Emancipists in positions of public authority. He concluded that Macquarie was not equipped to govern without the help of an advisory body. Macquarie finally resigned and returned to his native Scotland. Denied recognition for his achievements and allocated a minimal pension, he died in London in 1824, a disappointed and embittered man.

It was difficult for Governor Macquarie to expand the boundaries of the penal colony because pioneers brave enough to start farming beyond the settled districts were often attacked by Aborigines.

1813
BLAXLAND, LAWSON AND WENTWORTH CROSS BLUE MOUNTAINS

'The roughness of this country I found beyond description. I cannot give you a more expressive idea than travelling over the tops of houses in a town.'

'There it is!' expedition leader Gregory Blaxland yelled from his saddle.

'What mirage is it this time?' complained the youngster of the exploring party, William Charles Wentworth, leading his stumbling horse through thick bush up to the rocky outcrop where Blaxland stood in his stirrups. 'I can't see anything for these wretched trees.'

'Trees! If we don't get out of the trees soon I'll go mad,' an exasperated Lieutenant William Lawson complained from further down the ridge as he led his horse behind Wentworth. 'At least in the Army we march along roads, so I hope you are not hallucinating, Greg.'

'No, I'm not—and would I lie to a fellow grazier? Clear plains for our hungry sheep and cattle as far as the eye can see . . . I told you we'd get through, lads, if we followed the tops of the ridges,' Blaxland said proudly. 'But come and see for yourself. Get back on your horse and ride up here. Look—wide, open valleys big enough to take all the livestock in the colony.'

'You're right,' Wentworth said, after riding up beside Blaxland and catching his breath. 'It's enough grassland to support all the stock in the colony for the next thirty years.'

'At least—and there will be more open land beyond, lads,' Blaxland said. 'We have done our duty. Now the colony can expand westward forever.'

'We've certainly earned our 1000-acre prize, eh, Greg,' Wentworth said, imagining his future herds and flocks filling the far grasslands.

'What a rich and bountiful land we British have settled,' Blaxland mused aloud, overcome by the enormity of the moment.

'Can you see China?' Lawson joked, pulling up on his horse. 'Some convicts used to say they could escape to China if they could only cross the Blue Mountains.'

'Well, they must have been Irish convicts,' was Blaxland's wry response. 'Anyway, we've long since dispelled that myth.'

'But look! It stretches as far as the eye can see,' Wentworth said excitedly, shielding his eyes from the sun. 'And you're right, Greg, there may be yet more grassland beyond.'

'Well, lads, don't get too carried way . . . we're so short of supplies and water I reckon we should head back now,' said Lawson, who was used to organising military expeditions.

'Of course, Lieutenant Lawson, of course,' Blaxland replied.

'But one more look before we go, lads,' young Wentworth pleaded. 'This view is as sweet as the Israelites' must have been when they gazed on the Promised Land. This is the Land of Canaan for our hemmed-in lot.'

'Now, gentlemen, let us return to Sydney and our prize,' Blaxland said briskly. 'We have breached the barrier that's kept colonists chained to the coast since the First Fleet arrived in 1788. If only we had some rum—we could toast this great moment!'

William Charles Wentworth became the most successful of the three explorers, expanding his reward of 1000 acres with vast landholdings, empowering him to become a major political force in New South Wales.

IT WAS A GREAT MOMENT because the explorers had broken out of Sydney's topographical prison. They had cut a path across the Blue Mountains, which had formed an impassable wall since the colony's founding. It was late May 1813, and after nineteen days of exhausting bush-bashing, Gregory Blaxland, William Lawson and William Charles Wentworth had succeeded where so many had failed. They just reached a vantage point—now Mount Blaxland—from which they could clearly see the grasslands beyond. It was the first real confirmation that James Mario Matra and Sir Joseph Banks back in the 1780s had been right: the land discovered by Cook and settled by Phillip would indeed be a valuable asset to Britain and her people.

Historical background

From the time Sydney was settled, the colonists had struggled to find suitable grazing land. They knew little about the land to the west along the Parramatta

The experienced Gregory Blaxland, who had mounted earlier expeditions, successfully led Lawson and Wentworth through the rugged terrain until they caught sight of the grassy plains to the west.

River—some convicts even believed they could escape to China by crossing the mountains, perhaps because convict transports sailed on to China to collect tea after dropping their human cargoes. The settlers soon realised they were hemmed in by the Blue Mountains, part of the Great Dividing Range, whose sandstone heights and steep, sheer cliffs were covered by thick forest. Though they were never more than 914 metres above sea level, the hills that seemed from afar to be blue seemed impossible to scale. Nevertheless, the dream of open pastureland kept alive plans to cross them.

Not long after Governor Macquarie took over as governor in 1810, he could see the shortage of grazing land was severe. He offered a reward to anyone who could cross the mountains and find the needed grassy plains. As a Scotsman familiar with the Highlands, the visionary Macquarie was confident there would one day be a settlement beyond the Blue Mountains.

He knew crossing the barrier would be hard because so many had tried without success. William Dawes and Lieutenant George Johnston made the first attempt in 1789, but 'were obliged to relinquish their object' because 'they found the country so rugged and the difficulty of walking so excessive that in three days they were able to penetrate only fifteen miles'. Johnston tried again with Captain William Paterson of the New South Wales Corps in 1793, but their boats were damaged as they followed the rivers. Three years later Henry Hacking was forced to turn back on reaching 'an impassable barrier which seemed fixed to the westward, with little hope of extending cultivation beyond the present settlement'. Explorer George Bass in the same year reported 'the impossibility of going beyond those extraordinary ramparts'. Ensign Barallier of the NSW Corps penetrated further west in 1802 but was turned back by hostile Aborigines and steep cliffs and told Governor King, 'this formidable barrier is impassable for man'. The botanist George Cayley also failed: in 1804, he reported to his patron, Sir Joseph Banks, that 'the roughness of this country I found beyond description. I cannot give you a more expressive idea than travelling over the tops of houses in a town.'

It was Gregory Blaxland, a free settler and grazier, who came up with the strategy of following the ridges with their commanding views instead of steep-sided river valleys in which explorers were blocked by cliff faces or got lost.

Blaxland made some preliminary trips starting in 1810. After exploring the Warragamba River by boat—once with Macquarie himself—he announced it was time 'to climb up on to the plateau to the north of the Warragamba and press westward keeping to the ridges'. On 11 May 1813, he set out in a well-organised expedition with two men who also stood to gain from finding new land—Lieutenant William Lawson, a soldier turned grazier, and William Charles Wentworth, a twenty-year-old landowner.

Taking four servants, four horses loaded with provisions and five dogs, they set out from Sydney, crossed the Nepean River and began to climb up the ridges and onto the plateau, which they then followed westward. They 'kept the streams of water which appeared to empty themselves into the western river [Warragamba] on their left hand . . . the streams of water which emptied themselves into the River Grose or any other river on their right'. It was very tough going. They had to cut their way through thick bush as they followed the ridges, taking care not to fall down either side and often leading their horses because they could not ride them. They went out of their way down to creeks to replenish their water whenever they could.

Early explorers researched the crossing of the Blue Mountains by travelling up the Warragamba River, from which they could see the rugged terrain they had to cross towering above them. Drawing by Marchais (1820).

On May 31, they reached a peak they named Mount Blaxland from which they could see open grasslands. Blaxland said they 'saw land all around them sufficient to feed the stock of the colony in their opinion for the next thirty years'. The summit deserved to be called Blaxland, because although Wentworth went on to become a leading figure in the colony, it was Blaxland who led them through. Having achieved their goal the men returned to Sydney, reaching home on June 6.

For this achievement, Governor Macquarie eventually gave each of the explorers 1000 acres (405 hectares). Macquarie sent Surveyor George Evans to confirm the crossing, which he did, reaching Mount Blaxland by the clearly blazed trail in six days before moving further west to the future site of Bathurst. Based on Evans's favourable report, Macquarie boldly commissioned the construction of a road over the previously impassable mountains, ordering William Cox to build it with convict labour to a place where he could establish a settlement to be named Bathurst after the Secretary of State for the Colonies. This permanent road was built within two years, a remarkably short time. In 1818 Macquarie proudly erected a stone obelisk in Macquarie Place, Sydney, from which settlers could measure the distance to all localites along his roads.

Former Lieutenant William Lawson introduced badly needed military discipline to guide his fellow explorers Wentworth and Blaxland as they crossed the Blue Mountains but lost his own way later in life and committed suicide.

Postscript

Despite their success, the explorers had not actually crossed the Blue Mountains. They had crossed the sandstone plateau—the hardest part—but not the whole of the Great Dividing Range. They did not realise that the barrier between the coastal and inland rivers in fact lay further west.

The Sydney Gazette devoted only a single paragraph to their crossing, and they had to wait nearly a year to gain official recognition. Nevertheless, on 12 February 1814 Governor Macquarie issued a general order: 'The Governor is happy to embrace this Opportunity of Conveying his Acknowledgements to Gregory Blaxland and William Charles Wentworth Esquires and Lieutenant Lawson of the Royal Veteran Company for their enterprising and arduous Exertions on the Tour of Discovery when they effected a Passage over the Blue Mountains.' He also honoured his promise of a prize, saying: 'The Governor,

desirous of conferring on the Gentlemen substantial marks of his Sense of their Meritorious Exertions on this Occasion, means to present each of them with a Grant of 1,000 Acres of Land in this newly discovered Country.'

Of the three explorers, W.C. Wentworth best used this fame as a stepping stone to success. Building on his grant, he bought up as much land as he could, becoming a grazier with vast holdings. He then became a lawyer, founder of the Patriotic Association and founding owner of the highly opinionated newspaper *The Australian*, which campaigned for press liberty, freedom of speech and political reforms that included democratic institutions and a Constitution. His efforts helped bring about a more representative government for New South Wales in 1842, and fourteen years later, self-rule for the colony. Wentworth's fellow explorers were not so fortunate. Although Lawson fared well enough, he never matched Wentworth's achievements. Blaxland, after various attempts to establish vineyards, committed suicide in 1853.

It may have taken many years for the first explorers to cross the Blue Mountains, but the impatient Governor Macquarie ordered the first road built across this rugged barrier within two years. Painting by Augustus Earle.

1834
BUCKLEY 'MURRANGURK': WILD WHITE MAN RETURNS FROM DEAD

'What the hell is that?' Jack Jones said, looking up from the hole he was digging in a clearing in the bush at Indented Head. 'Where'd you put the gun, Willie? Quick!'

'My God. It's a blackfella,' Willie Smith said, dropping his spade. 'He's gigantic! Gun's over by the tent,' he said, rushing off. 'I'll get it.'

'Hurry, Willie,' Jones warned, holding his shovel in front of him like a shield as the warrior approached. 'The blackfella's got a spear and nasty looking club. Make haste, man!'

'Got it,' Smith panted, rejoining Jones at the post holes. 'Just in time, eh?' he said, raising the muzzle and cocking the hammer. 'Big beggar, ain't he?'

'So far as we can see, anyway,' Jones said. He tightened his grip on the spade as the intruder looked around the clearing. 'He seems peaceful. We should be able to handle him. Maybe he only wants an axe.'

'Yeah, like the ones that were pinched from Mr Batman's toolbox the other night while we were sleeping in the tent,' Smith said, levelling the gun at the approaching giant's chest.

'But have a look at the beggar. Funny looking blackfella, isn't he? His skin!' Jones hissed as the intruder drew nearer. 'His skin ain't black like the other savages! It looks white.'

'Mebbe he's painted white, like they do for their fireside corroborees,' Smith whispered.

'No. That's white like ours.'

'Stop! Stop right there!' Smith yelled, thrusting his gun forward. 'Don't come any closer, blackfella, or I'll shoot. Stand where you are!'

The intruder stopped in his tracks a few metres from John Batman's two workmen and stood perfectly still, looking from one face to the other. Almost two metres tall, with a long, white, waist-length beard, he towered over them. Apart from a worn old kangaroo skin, he was barefoot and naked.

'Drop your spear and your club,' Smith ordered. 'Come on, put it down.'

'He doesn't understand,' Jones said. 'I'll show him.' He laid his shovel on the ground, pointing to the intruder to do the same.

'Murrangurk,' the man said in a low, gravelly voice as his large form bent forward to place his spear and club on the ground. 'Murrangurk, Murrangurk,' he repeated, tapping his barrel chest.

'What the hell's that supposed to mean?' Jones asked, stepping backwards in fear.

'Mebbe Murrangurk's 'is tribal group,' Smith ventured nervously, his gun still aimed at the intruder's chest. 'Or maybe it's his name.'

'But how come his skin is so white?' Jones asked, patting his own bare arms.

'Ah, ah, Murrangurk,' the intruder said excitedly, pulling the kangaroo skin off his left shoulder and pointing to his upper arm. 'Murrangurk.'

'What is it?' Smith asked, gun still at the ready.

'Might be a trap,' Jones warned.

'No. I'll take a look, me gun's loaded,' Smith said, stepping forward gingerly. 'My God! It's writing. Two letters!'

'What's it say, Smithy? You can read, can't you?'

Smith peered at the visitor's arm. 'It says W.B., it does—W.B. It's a bloody tattoo.'

'Murrangurk, Murrangurk,' their visitor said over and over excitedly, as if pleased that the two men had recognised his tattoo.

'How the hell did he get that?' Jones asked. 'Blacks scar their bodies, but only white men do tattoos.'

'That's it, Jack,' Smith said. 'He's not a blackfella at all—just a bloody ship-wrecked sailor who's been living with the savages for so long he can't even talk the King's English!'

'You may be right. Unless he's an escaped convict from that old 1803 settlement over there,' Jones said, pointing across the bay. 'You know, that one abandoned by Lieutenant Governor Collins.'

'Almost entirely naked, enduring nearly every kind of privation, sleeping on the ground . . . year after year, and deprived of all the decencies and comforts of life, still I lived on.'

'Yeah. Come to think of it, I did hear Mr Batman say there was a few convicts escaped back then. Wouldn't it be marvellous if he was one of them, eh?' Smith said.

'Well, let's offer the poor bastard a cup of tea and some ship's biscuits,' Jones said. He walked towards the tent in the middle of the clearing, and the visitor, still mumbling 'Murrangurk, Murrangurk', followed him.

IT WAS A GREAT MOMENT because the giant 'blackfellow' was none other than escaped convict William Buckley, who had bolted into the bush just before Lieutenant Governor Captain David Collins abandoned the settlement at what is today Sorrento, near Melbourne, in 1804. It was now 12 July 1835. Buckley had lived during the intervening years with the local tribes of Port Phillip, mainly the Watharung people.

Historical background

Buckley had been transported to the new penal colony planned for Port Phillip (and soon established at Sorrento). After arriving in 1803, he bided his time until he could escape: he hoped to make it north to Sydney. Armed with a gun, he bolted into the bush with three other convicts named Gibson, Marmon and Pye, but one of these was shot by an alert sentry and, after a few days on the run, the other two decided to return to the settlement, taking the gun with them. They were never heard of again. The following year the settlement, still under the command of Collins, was moved to Sullivan Bay, on the Derwent River in Tasmania.

Buckley found a creek near Mount Defiance and built himself a hut there. Three Aboriginal hunters brought him some fish and offered to take him into their tribe, but Buckley refused. Then he changed his mind and went searching for them in the Otway Forest area. Failing to find them, the lonely convict tried to return to Sorrento to give himself up but broke down from exhaustion and malnutrition near the Barwon River. He lay down on a mound of earth, where he picked up a broken spear to use as a crutch before collapsing completely. Two Aboriginal women who had seen him staggering along followed him, then called some warriors, who carried the sick convict back to their camp. They nursed him back to health and called him Murrangurk—which he later learned was the name of a tall, strong warrior who had just been buried under the mound where Buckley

Escaped convict William Buckley, who joined the Aborigines, certainly stood out whenever they performed a corroboree, but it was only the tattoo on his arm that confirmed his identity when he returned to the settlement after thirty years. Painted by Tommy McRae (1870).

had rested. The Aborigines thought the white Buckley must have been Murrangurk come back to life, as they associated the colour white with the spirit world.

The tribe revered Buckley-Murrangurk, waiting on him hand and foot and providing him over the years with wives with whom he had children. They taught him their language and how to use their weapons for hunting, and enlisted Buckley's help in tribal battles, which mostly arose from squabbles over women. Buckley's later account suggests he acquitted himself very well as Murrangurk.

He might have lived the rest of his life among the Aborigines if John Batman, who had been living in Tasmania, had not decided to settle Port Phillip in 1834 with his associate William Fawkner. Batman and Fawkner sent an advance party, including would-be settlers such as Jack Jones and William Smith, to prepare a site on the Bellarine Peninsula near Indented Head, on the western side of Port Phillip. It was there that Murrangurk was reunited with his fellow Britons.

After some time back in the white settlement, Buckley relearned English and was able to tell his full story. Born in 1780 in Cheshire, he was apprenticed to a bricklayer before joining the army. He then struck an officer and may also have stolen goods, and was transported for either or both offences as part of the abortive expedition to Port Phillip led by Lieutenant Governor David Collins. In his official report, Buckley said:

69

I had almost given up all hope of ceasing my savage life, and as man accustoms himself to the most extraordinary changes of climate and circumstances, so I had become a wild inhabitant of the wilderness, almost in reality. It is very wonderful, but not less strange than true. Almost entirely naked, enduring nearly every kind of privation, sleeping on the ground month after month, year after year, and deprived of all the decencies and comforts of life, still I lived on, only occasionally suffering from temporary indisposition.

Postscript

It took many years, but Buckley managed to readjust to life as a white man. But although he washed, shaved, put on European clothes and began to speak halting English again, he never really seemed to commit to the colony or its values. He certainly opposed any attempts to marginalise or punish Aboriginal people outside the settlement.

At first he made occasional visits to his tribe, where he was always very welcome. Joseph Gellibrand, who accompanied him once, reported: 'When we arrived at the natives' camp I witnessed one of the most pleasing and affecting sights. Buckley had dismounted and there were three men, five women and about twelve children all clinging to him and surrounding him with tears of joy and delight running down their cheeks, which proved the affection which these people entertained for Buckley.'

Buckley certainly fared much better than Bennelong, who was ostracised by his Eora tribe after deserting them in the 1790s to live with the whites in Sydney. The ex-convict was pardoned by Governor George Arthur of Tasmania and worked for the settlement in Port Phillip Bay as an ambassador, explaining the settlers' needs to the tribespeople. Eventually he lost interest in his Aboriginal ways and in 1837 moved to Tasmania, where he found well-paid work with the government, first as a storekeeper, then finally as gatekeeper of a female prison.

In 1840, he married Julia Eagers, a widow with one child. Having survived thirty-one years in the bush, Buckley was killed at the age of eighty when the carriage in which he was travelling collided with another carriage in Hobart.

The cave where Buckley sheltered during his time with the Aborigines can still be seen in the cliffs below Point Lonsdale, Victoria.

1851

HARGRAVES DISCOVERS GOLD AND TRANSFORMS COLONIES

'Are you sure you saw gold?' Edward Hargraves asked, in his newly acquired American accent. He stared at the rocky creek bed in the bush not far from Bathurst. 'These certainly look like the same kind of rocks I saw in California where the Forty-Niners found gold.'

'Yes, Eddie. We wouldn't lie to you,' Mrs Lister said, with her hands resting on the soiled apron covering her hips. 'You having been apprenticed to me 'usband at only fourteen and all.' She shook her head. 'Merchant seamen don't lie, Eddie. You should 'ave learnt that during your time with 'im. Anyhow, you tell 'im, Johnny—go on, son, show 'im.'

'Right then, Mum,' John Lister said, stepping forward to the edge of Lewis Ponds Creek. 'I come down to get some water for me dog and pulled back some rocks so I could dip me hat in—and then I seen it.'

'Saw what?' Hargraves asked, looking intently into Johnny's face and thinking of the New South Wales Government's offer: £500 for the first person to find a commercial gold deposit. 'You know I've just come back from America, don't you, son, where the only gold found by most of the Forty-Niners was fool's gold?'

'Nope, this weren't fool's gold. I know that stuff—this were gold, all right,' Johnny said, pointing to the rocks he had removed from the creek.

'Here, hand me that pan,' Hargraves demanded. He rolled up his sleeves and waded into the water. 'You grab that other pan, and we'll soon see how right you are. And if it's promising, I'll show you how to build a Californian cradle.'

The men spent some time patiently panning and washing out gravel from the creek bed. Then Lister called out: 'Gold! I've found it!'

Overleaf: Once commercially viable gold was discovered at the tranquil junction of Lewis Ponds and Summerhill Creek near Bathurst, it started a hectic gold rush that transformed the former penal colonies.

71

Although young John Lister discovered the first gold, once he showed Edward Hargraves it was self-promoting Hargraves who announced the discovery, claimed credit, received the rewards and sparked the gold rush.

'Show me,' the doubting Hargraves demanded, rushing towards the younger man.

'I told you,' Lister said, showing the glittering golden sprinkle in his hands. 'What do you reckon that is, then?'

'It certainly looks like the real thing,' Hargraves exclaimed. 'Let me take a closer look.' He scrambled forward. 'Yeah, I reckon there'd be at least £10 worth of gold dust there, Johnny. Well done! You keep looking, son, and I'll go and talk to the authorities.'

It was 12 February 1851, and Hargraves was right. The gold John Lister found was actually worth £13, so they had a substantial find. Lister found more, teaming up with the young settlers Henry James and William Tom and digging closer to the town of Orange, using the techniques Hargraves had shown them. A loyal friend of Hargraves, Lister pleaded for secrecy, but now Hargraves decided it was time to spill the beans. He called the area Ophir, after King Solomon's fabulous Old Testament mines. By then others, too, had found gold in payable quantities nearby.

Having confirmed that this was indeed gold country, he hurried to Bathurst and announced the news in a popular pub, Arthur's Inn. As gold fever swept the town, Hargraves also wasted no time in claiming as much personal credit as he could. He had a letter published in *The Sydney Morning Herald* confirming the gold strike, and contacted the Governor, Sir Charles FitzRoy, and the Colonial Secretary, Edward Deas Thomson, whose geologist certified that Hargraves (and others) really had discovered gold. The government, true to its word, then paid Hargraves a reward, which the consummate self-promoter parlayed from £500 to an astounding £10,000. He also secured a job as a commissioner of Crown lands for the gold districts and a justice of the peace—and eventually a princely pension of £250 a year.

IT WAS A GREAT MOMENT because the dicovery of gold transformed the struggling, sparsely populated former penal colony—and later its neighbours—into flourishing economies. Hargraves' find started a massive gold rush, bringing settlers flocking from around the world—exactly the catalyst the colonies needed to grow beyond a dumping ground for convicts. Other prospectors soon found more gold not only at Ophir, but in other New South Wales fields such as Gulgong, Hill End and Wellington. Prospectors also found gold deposits in the Victorian colony at Ballarat, Bendigo, Castlemaine, Beechworth and numerous other sites.

Historical background

Born in Britain, Hargraves was a devil-may-care opportunist who had tried his hand as a sailor, publican and unsuccessful gold prospector in California. With his move to New South Wales in January 1851, however, his luck changed. The colonies' luck changed too: in the ensuing gold rush, thousands of Europeans set sail—voluntarily—for the colonies. Just as importantly, the badly needed workers who had absconded for the Californian goldfields came home. If Melbourne and Sydney still suffered for a time from labour shortages, they benefited in other ways. The gold seekers who rushed to the three Australian colonies increased their total population nearly threefold. Victoria's grew most: from 77,000 in 1850 to 540,000 in 1860. At least 130,000 lived in Melbourne, making it the continent's largest city. In 1852 alone, more than 1800 migrants arrived there every week.

The social and political culture changed dramatically as ex-convicts became a fast-shrinking minority. Many of the new arrivals were educated, and most brought professional and industrial skills with them. The increased population also helped boost the wool, meat and wheat industries by providing a larger domestic market and producing capital for investment, particularly in railways, which in turn spawned iron and steel production and other industries.

'Nope, this weren't fool's gold. I know that stuff—this were gold, all right.'

Postscript

Hargraves and his friend Lister were not the first to find gold in Australia. Numerous earlier discoveries had been hushed up by the authorities, who thought the colonies were not ready for a gold rush—and that the Crown owned the gold anyway. Hargraves himself never found substantial amounts: though he claimed the fame and the government rewards, the biggest nuggets were turned up by others—like the seventy-two-kilogram Welcome Stranger, found by two Cornishmen, Richard Oates and John Deason, at Moliagul, north-west of

Melbourne. In June 1893, in Western Australia, Paddy Hannan and his mates Thomas Flanagan and Dan O'Shea found much more gold than Hargraves and his associates ever did; the Crown rewarded them with annuities and land grants.

What Hargraves did succeed at was promoting his meagre finds and sparking the gold rush that transformed the colonies into flourishing societies with rich rewards for clever entrepreneurs. Hargraves promoted the rush and his role in it on speaking tours in England. The Victorian Government awarded him £2381, but further payments were withheld after protests by James Tom. An 1853 inquiry upheld Hargraves' claim that he was the first to discover a viable goldfield, but that triumph was brief: just before he died in Sydney in 1891, a second inquiry ruled that the honour belonged to John Lister and James Tom.

1854
PETER LALOR LEADS EUREKA REBELLION DEMANDING DEMOCRACY

'Now, men, as your newly elected commander-in-chief, I order you to take the oath under the Southern Cross,' Peter Lalor said to the Ballarat gold miners who had gathered about him as he hoisted the hastily sewn flag on a tall pole. He propped his rifle against a pile of the timber that was being used to build the Eureka Stockade.

'What kind of oath, Pete?' his comrade George Black asked. 'You're not expecting us to fight like blood brothers to the death are you, mate, like those poor bloody Vinegar Hill Paddies back in 1804?'

'Yeah, what was their battle cry?' Frederick Vern asked. '"Death or liberty", wasn't it?' He looked around nervously.

'And that bloody Governor King hanged nine of the poor bastards,' Black said, 'almost as many as what was killed in the battle. Let's hope Governor Hotham don't do that to us, eh?'

'He won't,' Lalor said. 'They were convicts, and we free miners should have more rights. The oath is just what our army of the revolution agreed at the Reform League meeting this arvo, Blackie.' The tall, handsome leader pulled himself up to his commanding height: 'Listen, everyone, it's my duty now to swear you all in. We must take the oath together—the Oath of the Southern Cross.'

He looked around at the assembled men. 'Hear me with attention. The man who, after this solemn oath, does not stand by our standard is a coward in heart.' Looking at every man in turn, he added: 'I order all persons who do not intend to take the oath to leave the meeting at once.'

'We swear by the Southern Cross to stand truly by each other and fight to defend our rights and liberties. Amen.'

When no one broke ranks, Lalor continued: 'Right! Let all divisions who are under arms fall in around the flagstaff.'

Kneeling on one knee, Lalor pointed to the blue flag with its broad cross of white stars. 'Repeat after me: "We swear by the Southern Cross to stand truly by each other and fight to defend our rights and liberties. Amen."'

Then, leaping into action, the miners hurried to complete the stockade. Some overturned carts to close gaps in the crude barrier of timber slabs and enclose a large area of open ground. Others collected what supplies and arms they could find or hastily forged pikes. They didn't have long: three days later, on 3 December 1854 government troops attacked. It was a bloodbath for the miners, but it was also a baptism in blood for democratic rights, and it changed colonial politics forever. It would go down in history as the battle at Eureka Stockade.

Peter Lalor, the leader of the violent 1854 Eureka Rebellion, who lost the battle against government troops and his left arm in the conflict, nevertheless succeeded in introducing badly needed democratic reforms in Victoria.

IT WAS A GREAT MOMENT because free citizens of colonial Australia had banded together for the first time to fight for democratic rights against an autocratic government, and because in the long term they succeeded. Not only did they win more individual rights for prospectors on the goldfields, but their action inspired democratic reforms in Victoria and the other colonies. Their campaign added weight to earlier agitation for reform. Within two years of the rebellion, all colonies save Western Australia had achieved self-government and were on the way to true democracy.

Historical background

The seeds of this rebellion were sown in 1851, when thousands of free-spirited prospectors—soon to be known generally as diggers—flooded into the penal colonies after Hargraves and Lister discovered gold. Many were political radicals, chiefly English Chartists, who demanded universal (male) suffrage, regular elections, secret ballots and payment for members of parliament. Although most were short of funds, these ambitious seekers of an Australian El Dorado expected better treatment than the convicts had received, and they began agitating for political rights, including greater representation in government. The miners had a case: they certainly got nothing for their licence fees but harassment. Like the American rebel colonists of 1776, they did not want to pay 'taxation without representation'. These free spirits also wanted the right to vote and to buy the land they worked.

The incoming Lieutenant Governor of Victoria, Sir Charles Hotham, provoked the new arrivals when, on a visit to the goldfields in 1854, he insisted all miners pay licence fees, increased those fees, and stepped up police licence inspections to boost public revenue. The miners were incensed. On 11 November 1854, at Bakery Hill, a meeting of 11,000 diggers formed the Ballarat Reform League to agitate for administrative reform on the goldfields and abolition of the licence. Their leaders included Lalor, Vern, Black and Raffaello Carboni. Although Hotham agreed to include a representative of the miners in the Legislative Council, he then sent more soldiers to the diggings and provoked the miners further. At a protest meeting on November 29 the German-born Vern successfully proposed that the miners burn their licences and, in defiance, hoist their own home-made flag: the Southern Cross.

The diggers elected the Irish miner Peter Lalor as their leader, and at his behest about 500 men swore allegiance to the Southern Cross flag. When the

The ill-equipped and poorly disciplined gold miners hiding behind their flimsy stockade at Ballarat had little hope of defending their timber fortress against the hundreds of troops sent by the government to crush the revolt.

With most gold miners making so little money from the diggings they could not afford to pay the expensive licence fees imposed by greedy government officials and rose up in arms against the draconian tax. Cartoon from Melbourne *Punch*.

goldfields police again began rounding up miners who had no licence, many refused to go into custody, while others yelled, fought with the police and threw stones. The Riot Act was read, more troops were ordered in from Melbourne, and the miners took their stand at the Eureka Stockade.

After three days, with government troops still making no move, many diggers left the stockade. It was Saturday afternoon and, assuming that there would be no attack on the Sabbath, they planned to stay away until Monday. Police spies were quick to tell the authorities of the depleted numbers. At 3 a.m. on Sunday, December 3, regular infantry, cavalry, mounted and foot police attacked the stockade in the dark, catching many of the rebels asleep. They overpowered the fort's defenders in twenty minutes, killing fourteen miners and wounding twenty, including Peter Lalor, who was shot in the left shoulder. Eight of the wounded miners later died; another 100 were taken prisoner. Some of the troops ran amok and killed two bystanders before destroying the miners' tents and property. Despite being caught unawares, the rebel miners killed the commanding officer, Captain Henry Wise, and four privates. Other accounts claim that as many as thirty miners died.

Although it was swiftly crushed, the Eureka rebellion became a turning point. The miners had lost the battle but won their war. When diggers were put on trial in Melbourne, the public was overwhelmingly on their side. A meeting condemned the assaults on the stockade, forcing the Colonial Secretary, John Foster, to resign, and thirteen miners charged with high treason were acquitted. A royal commission was appointed: it recommended change, and the miner's licence fee was soon replaced by a £1-a-year Miner's Right, which brought with it the right to vote. These reforms facilitated the introduction of suffrage for all white males when Victoria became self-governing in 1856. Because of the public support it inspired for these reforms, Eureka came to be seen as the birthplace of democracy in Australia.

Newly arrived Governor, Sir Charles Hotham sparked the Eureka rebellion after visiting the diggings, increasing police presence on the gold fields and calling for more licence inspections and increasing punishment for miners found without licences.

Postscript

Although his troops defeated the rebels, Sir Charles Hotham collapsed and died suddenly the following year, worn out by the challenges of eighteen months governing the turbulent colony. Despite being hunted by police after the rebellion (WANTED posters offered a reward of £400 for his and George Black's capture), the following year Peter Lalor tempered his fiery radicalism and was appointed to the Victorian Legislative Council. He was later elected to the new Legislative

Charting a New Course

The trade unions formed by the stonemasons grew out of the increasingly popular Chartist movement, which had been formed by radical members of the working class in England who had protested for better working conditions from the 1830s onwards. The objectives of the Chartists were democratic rights for all men and they took their name from *The People's Charter* published in 1838. They fought for six reforms: universal manhood suffrage; the abolition of property qualifications for members of parliament; parliamentary electorates of equal size; a secret ballot; payment for members of parliament; and annual general elections. Although the British parliament rejected their demands when the Chartists petitioned for reforms in both 1839 and 1842, the never-say-die members formed trade unions, which eventually achieved most of their six targets.

Fuelled by assertive immigrants, the trade unions in the colonies pioneered reforms and achieved much better conditions far earlier than their English counterparts, such as the eight-hour day won in Melbourne by the former English Chartist James Stephens in 1856. In turn, the trade unions formed the Labor Party, which won government on behalf of the working classes in Australia by 1904—something the Chartists could never have dreamt of back in the 1830s.

Assembly, and served as Postmaster-General, Commissioner of Trade and Customs, and finally Speaker, until poor health forced him to resign in September 1887. He married Alicia Dunn, the schoolmistress who sheltered him after his escape from the stockade and nursed him back to health after a doctor amputated his left arm. His grandson, Captain Joseph Peter Lalor, was to show similar courage in 1915 at Gallipoli, where he reportedly carried the sword used by Peter Lalor at Eureka.

1856
TRADE UNION LEADER JAMES STEPHENS WINS EIGHT-HOUR DAY

'**D**own tools, men,' James Stephens barked in his thick Welsh accent at his fellow stonemasons laying the foundations of Melbourne's new university. 'Today is the day.'

'What day?' Jim Galloway asked. 'We gotta finish shaping these bloody bluestones for the foundations. We can't knock off now.'

'I surely can't stop,' Tommy Vine added. 'I don't want me pay docked. I need all the dough I can find with a pregnant wife and kids to feed—lost too much time and money scratching around on the bloody goldfields. We should get these stones shaped if we work till dark.'

'That's the whole bloody point,' Stephens said, strapping up his tool bag. 'We're not working from dawn till dark any more. Those days are over.'

'Well, that's the deal we signed with the builder,' Galloway said, standing up stiffly and starting to sharpen his chisels.

'You've got short memories,' Stephens exclaimed, stepping forward and grabbing Galloway's chisel. 'Have you forgotten what we agreed at our meeting last month?'

'We elected you leader of the stonemasons, but what was the plan?' Galloway said.

'You're a Chartist, Jimmy. You voted for all the stonemasons working on this back-breaking site to march on Parliament, collecting other workers on the way, and demand an eight-hour work day, right?' Stephens said.

'Oh yes, I was there with you and Tommy Vine—we'd had a few beers. Is it today we march?' Galloway asked.

'You know it is—April 21. Come on, men, help me unfurl the banner we're carrying at the head of the procession.'

'What, the Operative Stonemason's Society?' Vine asked. 'We leading all the other building trades down to Parliament House?'

'What if the police attack us the way they went for poor old Peter Lalor and the Chartists up at the Eureka Stockade a couple of years ago?' Galloway asked.

'The police would never dare fire into our peaceful procession—we're not even armed,' Stephens barked back, holding out one end of the big banner to Galloway. 'Anyway, the reporters and artists from that new rag *The Age* will be watching the troops this time.'

'Lets hope they don't call you "a stupid mischievous blockhead—the worst enemy of the colony" like *The Herald* did,' Galloway teased.

'But d'you reckon the government will allow us to work an eight-hour day, just by us marching to Parliament?' Vine asked. 'They might just sack us instead. Then how will I feed me family?'

'We have strength in numbers—there's hundreds of us,' Stephens said, striding out ahead with Galloway and the banner. 'And we'll stay on strike until we get the eight-hour day. That's the only way to make conservative politicians listen.'

'James is right,' Galloway agreed. 'Come on, Tommy, where's yer backbone? Do you want the lads to think yer a scab?'

'All right—damn the bosses,' Vine said. 'We'll need a big crowd if we're to get our eight-hour workin' day.'

IT WAS A GREAT MOMENT because the march of the stonemasons and allied workers succeeded. They and others employed on public works won their eight-hour day—and without a reduction in pay. It was a world first. James Stephens, fellow Chartist Jim Galloway, Thomas Vine and their fellow masons had done well. It was 21 April 1856, in a Melbourne flush with money, migrants and fresh ideas from the goldfields, and where people were still talking about the democratic gains achieved by the gold miners at Eureka two years before.

James Stephens, who led the march in 1856 that won the eight-hour day for Victorian stonemasons and other tradesmen, later fell off a scaffold and was unable to work, ending his life in poverty in the absence of any worker's compensation. Contemporary wood engraving done for *The Illustrated Australian News and Musical Times*.

A month later, when the new regulation came into force in Victoria, the stonemasons celebrated by taking a day off and marching through Melbourne again with 700 workers from nineteen associated trades. By 1860 the eight-hour day applied to all industries. Victoria later declared May 21 a public holiday to celebrate this working-class breakthrough; in 1903, an Eight Hour Day monument was built outside the Melbourne Trades Hall.

The new law confirmed the value of the newly developed trade unions and showed how much workers could achieve when they joined forces. It created a successful foundation for the growth of a national trade union movement, which developed exponentially in Australia from that time, well ahead of the rest of the Western world.

Historical background

James Stephens, a Welsh-born Chartist and a member of the Melbourne Lodge of Operative Masons, had organised similar protests in London, where he had worked on the new parliamentary buildings. The masons were able to win their eight-hour day in Melbourne because so many free migrants like Stephens had flooded into Victoria with the gold rushes that they transformed the political culture.

These new arrivals from Europe and the United States included educated, militant reformers with strong democratic views. They would not accept the status quo of twelve- to sixteen-hour workdays—and they knew that skilled workers had bargaining power because they were so badly needed. Some also knew of the Scottish industrial activist Robert Owen (1771–1858), who had advocated the eight-hour day from 1817. The time was right, as Stephens recorded after the march: 'It was a burning hot day and I thought the occasion a good one, so I called the men to follow me. I marched them down to a new building then being built in Madeleine Street, thence to Temple Court and on to Parliament House, the men at all these works immediately dropping their tools and joining the procession.'

The Victorians had been inspired by similar agitation in Sydney. Stonemasons working on two churches and a brewery had taken industrial action the year before and negotiated eight-hour days, though they had been forced to take a pay cut. The more militant Melbourne masons refused to give up a penny of their pay. Their triumph was to secure more leisure time while keeping the same wage.

'We have strength in numbers . . . And we'll stay on strike until we get the eight-hour day.'

Trade unions fought for the eight-hour day in 1856 because most tradesmen and their families could not afford basic accommodation, while members of the entrepreneurial upper classes wined and dined at society balls. Drawn by Cousins for *Humbug*.

Postscript

James Stephens might have improved the lot of the workers, but he died in poverty. After achieving the eight-hour day he fell off a scaffold, which left him 'maimed, half-blind and unable to work for his living'. But the Trades Hall Council, where he had served as a treasurer, passed the hat around and raised £500 to help him survive.

Despite the example of the stonemasons, it was years before the eight-hour day became standard. Other New South Wales workers did not win this right until 1916, and unions were still campaigning in the 1920s to make it common practice throughout Australia.

The eight-hour day was not formally approved by the Commonwealth Arbitration Court until 1948—nearly a century after the stonemasons first secured it. But the Australians were so far ahead of their British counterparts that when the Fabian socialists Beatrice and Sidney Webb toured Australia in the late 1890s, they described the place as 'a working man's paradise'.

1860
BURKE AND WILLS CROSS CONTINENT FOR FIRST TIME

'Well, Mr Wills, it tastes salty to me! What do you say?' Robert O'Hara Burke said, spitting out a mouthful of seawater he had just scooped up from the base of a mangrove tree while standing knee deep in swamp water.

'Most certainly, Mr Burke,' William Wills replied with an excited nod, swilling a mouthful of salt water. 'From prior experiments and if my taste buds are still reliable, I confirm it contains sodium chloride.'

'Damn it, man, do you surveyors always have to be so scientific? Can't you just say it's salty?' Burke said tiredly, grabbing the trunk of the mangrove for support. 'If it is, then we don't have to force our way any further through these vile swamps just to see to the blasted Gulf of Carpentaria.'

'Yes, Mr Burke,' the equally exhausted Wills replied, leaning forward to peer into his companion's tortured face. 'It is indeed salt water.'

'Capital, Mr Wills,' Burke said, leaning forward to shake his hand. 'Do you realise what that means? We have actually reached the Gulf—we've crossed this wretched continent at last!'

'Well done, Mr Burke, well done,' Wills replied, collapsing to sit in the swampy water. 'You have succeeded in leading the first expedition across Australia from south to north. The Victorian Exploration Expedition has achieved its goal.' He splashed handfuls of salty water over his head.

'Thank you, but I could not have done it without my loyal deputy,' Burke said.

'And we could not have done it without the generous support of the Royal Society of Victoria, either,' Wills added. 'They will be most grateful when we tell them the good news.'

The country police officer—Robert O'Hara Burke—picked to lead the 1860 expedition across the continent, had never been to the outback, could not navigate by day or by the Southern Cross at night, and made a series of fatal mistakes that undermined the expedition.

'It will be fair to say we reached the sea,' said Burke, 'but we will have to tell them we could not obtain a view of the open ocean, although we made every endeavour to do so.'

'We haven't the supplies, strength or time to cut our way through these mangroves, and it would be dangerous to try,' Wills warned. 'My navigation also confirms that we have reached the latitude of the Gulf, and this salt water can only be from the sea.'

'It's certainly not an inland sea, is it?' Burke laughed. 'This is the Gulf! We can return to Cooper's Creek.'

'The sooner the better, Mr Burke. After all, we told the party there we'd only be away three months and it's taken us two months just to get here. We cannot waste a minute—our food supplies are too low.'

'Don't worry. We can travel faster on the way back. But now we must get back to King and Gray at Camp 119 and tell them our good news.'

'Yes, indeed,' Wills agreed, struggling to his aching feet. 'But I won't forget this moment!'

'We've made history, Mr Wills!' Burke exclaimed. 'Back to Cooper's Creek it is, then. Oh, wait till we tell Brahe we were the first to cross the continent!' And for the first time in two months, he and Wills headed south.

IT WAS A GREAT MOMENT because at last the vast southern continent had been traversed from south to north. Burke and Wills had also discovered vast tracts of well-watered grazing land, which would enable pastoralists to spread further inland. Australia's arid interior was still largely a mystery, but Burke and Wills' explorations, added to those of Edward Kennedy, Ludwig Leichhardt, Charles Sturt and John McDouall Stuart, had begun to lay firm tracks across the great blank space on the map.

Historical background

At the request of the Royal Society of Victoria, Burke and Wills set out from Melbourne on 20 August 1860 with a large and well-equipped (some would

1860

say over-equipped) party. The Society, which sank more than £3000 into the expedition, hoped Victorians would cross the continent ahead of their main rivals, a South Australian party led by John McDouall Stuart. They also hoped Burke and Wills would discover and claim useable land and plentiful supplies of water, enabling the expansion of the pastoral industry. The Irish-born Robert O'Hara Burke had served in the Austrian army before migrating to Australia and becoming a police superintendent in the goldfields town of Castlemaine. William Wills, his twenty-six-year-old deputy, was a medical doctor turned assistant at the Melbourne Observatory, where he specialised in astronomy and surveying. Burke, thirty-nine when he set out, selected nineteen people for the expedition from 700 applicants. They were farewelled by 'nearly the whole population, who suspended ordinary business and turned out to witness the imposing spectacle', according to Wills's father. In his parting speech, Burke said: 'No expedition has ever started under such favourable circumstances as this, and we will do our best to justify this support.'

An advance party reached Cooper's Creek on November 11 and set up a depot to hold the supplies that were being brought up. Putting William Brahe in charge, Burke told him to wait for three months after the supplies arrived; then he set off for the Gulf of Carpentaria, 1500 kilometres to the north, with Wills, Charles Gray and John King, six camels, one horse and three months' provisions. On 11 February 1861, after a two-month trek, they reached the Gulf. Having taken far longer than anticipated, they had to hurry back. Aborigines brought them fish from time to time, but they were still forced to eat a horse and all four got dysentery. Gray died on April 17.

Four days later, they struggled into Cooper's Creek depot, just hours after Brahe had left, believing they had perished. They had walked 3000 kilometres in four months and four days, traversing deserts and rocky plains through extreme heat, sapping humidity and torrential downpours. They had no food, their clothes were in rags, their boots were worn through, and they could hardly walk. 'Our disappointment at finding the depot deserted may easily be imagined,' Wills wrote, 'returning in an exhausted state, after four months of the severest travelling and privation and with our legs almost paralysed.' But at least they could eat:

William John Wills was the scientific brains of the 1860 expedition; he navigated the party to the Gulf and back and kept the only reliable journal. He could have led the party to safety but was no match for the bad-tempered Burke.

Both Wills, shown dying near Coopers Creek in John King's arms, and Burke, standing, died in June 1861. King managed to join a local Aboriginal tribe, which looked after him until a rescue party arrived.

Brahe had left some provisions in a box buried near a tree marked 'DIG 3 FT. N.W. APR 21 1861'.

These were limited, however, because the expected extra supplies had never arrived from the south. Running out of food, Burke, Wills and King tried to walk the 240 kilometres to the closest settlement but had to turn back, too weak to continue. Instead, they decided to wait near Cooper's Creek for rescue. While they were away from the depot, Brahe had returned to see if they had come back from the Gulf, but could find no sign of them. They had buried a message in the food box but failed to blaze a mark on the 'dig tree' saying it was there. Assuming they were dead, Brahe left.

Burke and Wills died of malnutrition on June 28 and 29, but King, who joined the local Yantruwanta Aboriginal tribe, survived to be rescued three months later by a search party and tell the tale to a royal commission set up to investigate the tragedy.

The remains of Burke and Wills were taken back to Melbourne for a state funeral that drew 40,000 spectators. A life-size statue was later built in honour of the two heroes of this tragedy of errors.

Postscript

Burke's success in crossing the continent was somewhat surprising, since he had no training or experience in exploration. He did not keep a journal, rarely put his orders in writing, and he quarrelled with other members of the party. He also had difficulty navigating. A Victorian paper claimed: 'He could not tell north from south in broad daylight, and the Southern Cross as a guide was a never-ending puzzle to him.' Nor did it occur to him to seek help from the natives. Although they had bad luck and were let down by others, Burke and Wills might have survived if, like King, they had befriended the Aborigines.

Eighteen months after Burke and Wills died, the highly experienced—but South Australian—John McDouall Stuart returned safely after making his own trek across the continent. His victory parade in Adelaide was held on the day of Burke and Wills's state funeral.

'Our disappointment at finding the depot deserted may easily be imagined . . . after four months of the severest travelling and privation.'

1880
THE LAST STAND OF AUSTRALIA'S MOST FAMOUS BUSHRANGER

'We're surrounded, boys,' Ned Kelly said, turning back from a hastily boarded-up window. 'There are blasted troopers all around the bloody Glenrowan pub. We'll have a fight and a half, to be sure.'

Reaching for his suit of armour, he barked: 'Grab your armour, lads and put it on quick smart.'

'Don't worry, Ned,' Joe Byrne called out from another boarded window. Propping his rifle so the muzzle still poked out from a hole in the wood, he started putting on his iron plates. 'We may be done for, but I always said I'd be happy with a short life as long as it was a merry one.'

'A merry one! It's certainly been that, Joe,' said Dan Kelly, fully armoured now. 'No other gang ever pulled off as many robberies nor amassed such a pile of loot as us, eh, mate?'

'Nay,' said Ned, now speaking through his helmet, 'nor had £8000 on their heads or inspired a whole army of troopers to do battle. So Joe, you can hold your head high when you get to heaven . . . you've shown over and over that you've got the pluck of the Irish.'

'Aye, Ned,' Steve Hart added from across the darkened room. 'None of us mind dyin' as long we can take a few of these English bastards with us and everyone knows we died game.'

'We'll all die game, Stevo, like brothers in arms . . . which is what you and Joe have always been for us Kelly brothers,' Dan Kelly said. 'We all lived like brothers, and we'll die like brothers, too—that's the Kelly gang.'

'Thanks, Dan,' Hart said. 'And we've kept the blasted English police on the run for years.'

'And here they come, boys!' Ned cried above the din. He took aim and fired out the window as bullets slammed into the boards, spraying the room with splinters. 'Let the bastards have it and make every bullet count! We'll show these blasted English what Irishmen are made of.'

All night Ned Kelly and his gang of bushrangers exchanged fire with the police surrounding the hotel. It was the biggest bushranger battle in Australia's history. But hopelessly outnumbered and fast running out of ammunition, the Kelly gang was beaten. Dan Kelly, Joe Byrne and Steve Hart died at Glenrowan, and Ned was captured so badly wounded he could no longer walk.

IT WAS A GREAT MOMENT because the police had destroyed the country's most notorious bushranger gang, ending an era. It was 1880, and the long battle between the law and the outlaws was finally over. Now ordinary people could travel bush roads again without fear. It was also the end of a romantic period of bushranging, especially by the Irish. It was also a new beginning: the demise of his gang only fuelled the legend of Ned Kelly, which has since acquired the status of a national myth.

The notorious bushranger Ned Kelly, who carried out a series of successful bank robberies and outwitted the Victorian police force for years, became a romantic hero in the eyes of the poor, oppressed and Irish until he was gunned down and captured in a police shoot-out at Glenrowan in 1880.

Historical background

Born in Wallan, Victoria, in 1854, Ned Kelly was the son of an Irish convict transported for stealing two pigs. He grew up in a clan who resented the heavy-handed behaviour of the largely English police. Jailed at the age of sixteen for stealing a mare, he vowed revenge. When police broke down the door of the family home while trying to arrest Ned's younger brother, Dan, for alleged cattle duffing in 1878, the boys' mother, Ellen, stood up to them—and was jailed too. An enraged Ned promptly formed his gang, with Dan, Joe Byrne, an experienced cattle thief from near Beechworth, and Steve Hart, a thief from near Wangaratta. When four police approached their bush hideout a few months later, the gang killed three of them in a shoot-out. The Victorian Government declared the

Kelly gang outlaws, offered a £1000 reward for their capture, and formalised this with the *Felons Apprehension Act*.

Infamous overnight, the gang began manufacturing armour, some of it fashioned from ploughshares. These iron suits could stop a Martini-Henry rifle's .450 bullet at ten yards.

The Kellys robbed the National Bank at Euroa, then travelled into New South Wales and occupied the town of Jerilderie. They set up a headquarters in the Bank of New South Wales, where they imprisoned local police and townsfolk. Having thrown a party for their 'guests', complete with alcohol and games, they robbed the bank, taking more than £2000. They also dressed up in the captured policemen's uniforms and paraded around the town.

Between robberies, Ned Kelly promoted the cause of the poor Irish settlers, many of whom he helped with cash handouts. He also called for the redistribution of land to those who tilled the soil and urged the creation of a republic.

'Such is life.'

Although the government raised the reward for the capture of the gang to £8000 (£2000 for each member) and the police stepped up their efforts, the Kelly gang had a well-tuned bush telegraph of sympathisers who kept them abreast of police movements. When they heard a former friend, Aaron Sherritt, was reporting their movements to the police, they shot him dead in his home, despite the presence of four police officers meant to be protecting him.

Police redoubled their efforts to catch the gang, who dared the authorities to send a trainload of troopers from Melbourne. Occupying the Glenrowan Hotel on 27 June 1880, they held local townsfolk as hostages and waited for the police. To stop the special train carrying hundreds of officers, Kelly's men pulled up a section of the track on a sharp bend so the train would crash into a gully. The plan might well have succeeded had Kelly not allowed a schoolteacher to leave the hotel on compassionate grounds. He ran down the track with a lantern and stopped the train just in time. The police then surrounded the hotel and ordered in a field gun and searchlights.

The gang all put their armour on and prepared to give the police hell, but after a valiant fight Dan Kelly, Joe Byrne and Steve Hart were shot and police set the building on fire. Ned Kelly escaped outside, circled the troopers and, laughing as he went, began shooting at them from behind. Police finally felled him by aiming for his exposed feet and arms.

Taken to Melbourne, Kelly was patched up in hospital, put on trial, convicted by Justice Redmond Barry and, on 11 November 1880, hanged at the Old

Melbourne Gaol. The final words of this brave but reckless bushranger were reputed to have been, 'Such is life.'

Postscript

Although the capture of the Kelly gang was seen as a triumph for the police and government of Victoria, many people remained sympathetic to the outlaws. It was widely believed that the English-controlled authorities had picked for too long on the Irish and the Kelly family in particular, marginalising them to the point where they had little alternative but violence. Kelly was especially popular among the poorer people with whom he shared his spoils. More than just a criminal, he also wrote letters calling for legal reforms. Rightly or wrongly, he remains a symbol of courageous and creative defiance of unjust authority to this day.

When Ned Kelly was sentenced he cursed Judge Barry, warning that he would soon follow Kelly to the grave. Barry died suddenly not long afterwards.

1889

SIR HENRY PARKES INSPIRES COLONIES TO FORM A NATION

'This is the moment I have been waiting for,' Sir Henry Parkes said, turning from the window of his train carriage after seeing the huge crowd gathered to greet him at Tenterfield station. 'The time has come to ignite the fire that will forge these colonies into a nation!'

'Are you sure, Henry?' asked his wife, Clarinda. 'Why would the people here care about federating?' She leaned forward and straightened his tie.

'For a start, they're so far from Sydney they are always complaining the New South Wales Government doesn't care about them,' Parkes said, reaching for a suitcase on the rack above. 'And because they are so near Brisbane, a lot of their supplies come from Queensland, so they have to pay trade tariffs every time their goods cross the border,' he added as the train pulled up. 'I think they are looking for something better.'

'How infuriating,' Clarinda said, picking up her hat box.

'Which makes Tenterfield the perfect place of political unrest for me to launch my long-overdue call for Federation,' Parkes said. He opened the carriage door and stood aside for Clarinda. 'They also share that Queensland paranoia we just heard about in Brisbane, dear—expecting yellow hordes from China to land at any moment.' Parkes cautiously lowered his considerable bulk onto the platform after her. The crowd cheered wildly.

'Isn't that a bit far-fetched?' Clarinda asked.

'Not according to the defence report I've just got hold of,' Parkes said.

'That one you were reading on the train? What's it called?' his wife asked politely.

Always keen to win votes from both Labor and Capital, Sir Henry Parkes found it difficult to ride both horses in the lead-up to the New South Wales election because sections of the Labor movement opposed his dream of Federation, which they saw as 'a capitalist plot'. Cartoon by Hop for *The Bulletin*.

'It's a Report on the State of Defences of the Australian Colonies,' Parkes whispered. 'And, my dear, it is simply frightening.'

'Henry, you do carry on,' Clarinda said, walking with him down the platform as the cheers grew even louder. 'You are as bad as the journalists you always complain about—nobody would ever guess you once edited your own newspaper.'

As federating the colonies did not engage popular opinion, Sir Henry Parkes had to behave like a nursemaid, administering badly needed medicine to change public attitudes. Cartoon by Hop for *The Bulletin*.

Hop.

'Actually, I've asked for a *Sydney Morning Herald* journalist to attend this meeting today so I can reach the voters of Sydney with my speech,' Parkes said. 'At any rate, that report is alarming enough to galvanise the uneducated voter. It will serve well to prod these lethargic colonies into uniting.

'So here today in Tenterfield, Dearie, I will call for the creation of a great national government for all Australians,' he said, puffing out his chest as if stirred by his own lofty words.

'Well good luck, dear husband,' Clarinda said, looking up at him proudly. 'If anyone can stir up a hornet's nest, you can.'

'There's no stopping me now,' Parkes said as they neared the welcoming committee. 'These country bumpkins don't know what they are in for!'

After meeting the mayor and the town officials, Parkes and his wife were taken by carriage to the School of Arts in the main street of Tenterfield. And the fiery speech he delivered there achieved its aim, spurring the colonies to unified action on the biggest question they'd yet faced.

IT WAS A GREAT MOMENT because that sabre-rattling oration by Sir Henry Parkes on 24 October 1889 did spur the colonies to federate. Just over a decade later, the political haggling and horse-trading done, the Commonwealth of Australia was proclaimed at Centennial Park, Sydney, on 1 January 1901.

It was an enormous achievement because at the time Parkes spoke, the six colonies were all independent and self-governing. They competed with each other on many levels—especially trade, through tariffs at their borders—and were fiercely jealous of their autonomy. Only an extraordinary speech, and the threat of a common enemy, could overcome these divisions—and that is what Parkes delivered. In *The Sydney Morning Herald*'s account, Parkes 'told the meeting that General Edwards [author of the Report on the State of Defences] had advised that the forces of the various colonies should be federated for operation in unison in the event of war, so as to act as one great federal army. If an attack were made upon any of the colonies, it might be necessary for us to bring all our power to bear on one spot of the coast.'

Parkes, the *Herald* explained, therefore called for a central government, saying that 'if they were to carry out the recommendations of General Edwards, it would be absolutely necessary for them to have one central authority, which could bring all the forces of the different colonies into one army'. This authority would be a 'great national government for all Australia'.

Parkes called upon the colonies to federate as soon as possible because 'the federal system [was] so strongly recommended, and . . . must appeal to the sense of every intelligent man'. If Federation was decided on, 'The great question which they had to consider was, whether the time had not now arisen for the creation on this Australian continent of an Australian Government . . . This meant a distinct executive and a distinct parliamentary power, a government for the whole of Australia and it meant a Parliament of two Houses, a house of commons and a senate, which would legislate on all great subjects.' Parkes said it was foolish to wait any longer, since 'Australia had now a population of three and a half millions, and the American people numbered only between three and four millions when they formed the great commonwealth of the United States. The numbers were about the same, and surely what the Americans had done by war, the Australians could bring about in peace.' This conclusion drew cheers from his audience.

The 'Father of Federation' Sir Henry Parkes, whose imposing appearance had dominated the federal campaign for many years, died just three years before the people voted to form the nation he had dreamed of.

Historical background

The son of a labourer, Parkes was born in Warwickshire, England, in 1815 and began his working life as a bone and ivory turner before attending adult education classes and joining the Chartist movement. He married Clarinda, a local butcher's daughter, and emigrated to Australia in 1839, arriving 'with only three shillings' but getting a job immediately as a farm labourer. He started a number of businesses, all of which failed.

Inspired by the campaign to stop the transportation of convicts, in 1850 Parkes founded a reformist newspaper, *Empire*, to fight for this and other causes. Nearly always short of funds and once bankrupt, he also worked as a journalist and wrote poetry to help support his growing family. Winning a seat as a radical

reformist in the New South Wales Legislative Council and later the Legislative Assembly, Parkes began a long and distinguished career in politics, promoting universal suffrage and 'free, secular and compulsory education for all' and becoming state Premier five times.

Other political figures had recommended Federation over the years, but Parkes's speech did more than any other to win over the mass of people to the cause. His stroke of genius was to invoke the threat of attack, persuading the colonists that disunity could put their very survival at risk.

Earl Grey, the British Secretary of State for Colonies, had started the Federation ball rolling back in 1847, when he recommended the creation of a General Assembly for the colonies to sort out common problems. In 1853 W.C. Wentworth proposed a federal union, and a special committee was set up to examine 'the Federal Union of the Australian Colonies'. In 1881 Parkes himself called for a Federal Council, which first met in Hobart five years later.

But these steps had not produced any decisive change. Then Parkes publicised Edwards' alarming report and also pointed out the benefits for all Australians of a federally established uniform rail gauge, which would save the time and expense of changing trains at colonial borders. (The country's rail gauges have yet to be fully standardised.)

Having issued his clarion call, Parkes organised a Federal Conference in Melbourne in 1890, at which the colonies agreed to proceed. The framework for a national government was hammered out in a further series of conferences over the next eight years. The proposed new Constitution was then put to the vote. Although Federation was challenged by Melbourne-based radical labour groups, pro-Federation politicians finally won the support of the majority. At a referendum in 1899, 377,988 people voted for federation and 141,386 opposed it. Although Western Australia at first refused to join the Federation, the gold miners who had moved there from the east forced the government to hold a referendum at the last minute, and that colony too joined the Commonwealth.

For his role in this historic turning point, Parkes was known ever after as the Father of Federation.

Postscript

Parkes did not, however, live to see his dream realised. He died in 1896, three years before the final referendum crowned his fiery speech at Tenterfield with

'The great question which they had to consider was, whether the time had not now arisen for the creation on this Australian continent of an Australian Government.'

success. Despite his influence as a politician, he was often in financial trouble. Overweight and overworked, he was perhaps lucky to reach the age of eighty-one. On the day the Commonwealth of Australia was proclaimed, a larger-than-life bust of the great man was carried in procession through Sydney to Centennial Park, where a ceremony hailed the great moment he had done so much to bring about. His image was later placed on Australia's $5 note, and the Canberra suburb in which the Federal Parliament was built was named Parkes.

1890
MAN FROM SNOWY RIVER SPRINGS TO LIFE

'**N**ow, Mr Riley, I'll pour another whisky if you'll tell me what happened on that great ride,' Banjo Paterson said, throwing another log on the fire to brighten the dark shepherd's hut and cut the chill of the mountain night.

'It's bloody Jack, I tell ya—none of your fancy "Mr Riley", young fella,' Riley rasped, enlivened by the drink Paterson had carried in his saddle-bag up to Tom Groggin Station, high in the mountains above Corryong. 'And it wasn't far from 'ere, that terrible descent we 'ad to ride down.'

'In the Snowy Mountains, was it?' the bush poet and journalist asked eagerly, scribbling in his notebook by the light of the fire and one flickering candle. 'And the colt you were chasing was sired by the old stallion Regret?'

'We 'ad to chase 'im—he was worth a thousand pound, that bloody colt, so all the crack riders had gathered,' old Riley said, gazing dreamily into the roaring fire.

'So who were the best horsemen riding with you?' Paterson asked, straining to read his notes in the dark.

'There was Harrison, who made his pile when Pardon won the Cup,' old Riley recalled. 'White haired, he was, but I tell you, few could ride beside him when his blood was up—he'd go anywhere horse and man could.'

Paterson managed to catch up with the old stockman's story and asked, 'Who else?'

'Well, Clancy of the Overflow came down to lend a hand,' Riley said, pausing to take another swallow. 'No better horseman ever held the reins, in my view.'

'And which horse were you riding?' asked Paterson, a keen horseman himself.

'Oh, he was pretty small and weedy, a bit undersized,' Riley said, turning from the fire to face the writer. 'He had a touch of Timor pony, so he was tough, but I reckon he was mostly thoroughbred. The old man told me he'd never do for a long gallop, and he tried to keep me back. But Clancy stood up for me. He knew me and me horse both hailed from the Snowy River, and said we'd be there at the end,' Riley said, warming his hands by the fire. 'And so we were.'

'So you went along with them,' Paterson said, scribbling away.

'Just as well, too. Soon after we first seen the wild horses they bolted into the scrub—mountain ash and kurrajong, mostly. Clancy tried to turn 'em and nearly did, but they ran right under 'is whip. We followed 'em to the summit, and then the old man said forget it. But I let my pony have his head, and he chased them down the mountain like a torrent down its bed,' Riley went on, stirring with his poker the old memories along with the fire.

'That must have been dicey.'

'Well, the ground was full of wombat holes, so you can imagine—any slip was death. But my pony kept his feet. He cleared the fallen timber in his stride, till we landed at the bottom of the mountain safe and sound—just like I knew we would.'

'Had you kept up with the wild horses?' Paterson asked.

'Course I did. I ran them up the hillsides single-handed. Wore them out, just about, then turned their heads for home,' the old man said, finishing his whisky with a gulp. 'Yep—all by meself I brought 'em back.'

The poet turned to a fresh page. 'And your pony, how was he?'

'He could scarcely raise a trot, poor bastard, 'e was bleeding all along 'is flank.' Riley sank back into his homemade easy chair, exhausted but determined to finish his story. 'But he never lost 'is pluck for a minute. No, never chucked it in.'

'What a pony he must have been—and what a magnificent ride!' Paterson said, looking up from his notebook after writing down the last few sentences.

But old Jack Riley was already snoring. 'The poet blew out the candle and got into his bunk opposite the fire. 'It might have been the grog talking,' he thought, 'but what a story!'

A dedicated bush poet who spent much of his early life travelling the outback to collect stories for his ballads, such as 'The Man from Snowy River', Banjo Paterson did more to shape bush culture than any other single writer.

Old Jack Riley who claimed to be 'The Man from Snowy River' lived in an old bark hut high in the mountains above Corryong where 'crack riders' were often known 'to gather for the fray'.

IT WAS A GREAT MOMENT because Paterson now had, from the horseman's mouth, the story that would become Australia's greatest ballad—'The Man from Snowy River'. His rhyme version of Riley's account was published in *The Bulletin* magazine in 1890. It struck a chord immediately, and remains popular to this day.

Historical background

Andrew Barton Paterson was born in February 1864 at Narrambla, near Orange in central western New South Wales. Sent to school in Sydney at the age of ten, he spent most of his life pining for the bush. Like 'The Man from Snowy River' itself, much of what we know about the poem's origins is based on hearsay.

However Paterson, who became a lawyer but also wrote verse under the pseudonym 'The Banjo', did travel widely to interview bushmen for material for his rural ballads. In the foreword to the 1895 collection named for 'The Man from Snowy River', he wrote: 'I have gathered these stories afar, in the wind and the rain, in the land where the cattle camps are, on the edge of the plain . . .'

In the mountains high above Corryong in Victoria, the locals claim to this day that Paterson rode up to Tom Groggin Station to interview Riley. All the townsfolk at the time told him Riley was the best mountain horseman around, and could give him the details of a brumby round-up that had become a rural legend, if not a tall tale.

Although Paterson did not think his 'ruined rhymes' were likely to last long, 'The Man from Snowy River' has had a great and lasting impact in Australia. It is still recited around campfires and declaimed in pubs, at home and overseas. It has inspired three movies called *The Man from Snowy River*, one made in 1920 and two in the 1980s; television programs; paintings by artists such as Pro Hart and Robert Lovett; country-and-western songs, horse treks, arena shows, and an annual competition for the modern Man from Snowy River, started in Corryong in 1995 by this author to mark the centenary of the ballad. The films also helped make Akubra hats and Drizabone coats symbols of rugged Aussie manhood. In 1993 Paterson's portrait was placed on a new $10 note: behind his face appear, in microscopic type, the words of the ballad.

Old Jack Riley

Postscript

There was actually no one Man from Snowy River. Nobody has ever been able to identify this mythical mountain horseman. Paterson always refused to name the man upon whom his hero was based: the character was very likely a composite. When pressed on the subject not long before he died in 1941, he said: 'To make any sort of job of it I had to create a character, to imagine a man who would ride better than anybody else, and where would he come from except from the Snowy? And what sort of horse would he ride except a half-Thoroughbred pony?'

'But I let my pony have his head, and he chased them down the mountain like a torrent down its bed.'

Clancy of the Overflow, otherwise known as Thomas Michael McNamara, told Brisbane's *The Courier-Mail* in 1938 that the real Man was Jim Troy, of Wagga Wagga. Other plausible contenders include Owen Cummins of Dargo, Victoria, who was buried at Wave Hill Station and whose tombstone reads 'The [Northern] Territory's Own Man From Snowy River'; 'Hellfire' Jack Clark of Jindabyne; Lachie Cochran, of Adaminaby; Jack Spencer of Excelsior; and an Aboriginal tracker named Toby.

Nevertheless, the headstone on the grave of Jack Riley, who was buried in Corryong in 1914, reads: 'In Memory of the Man from Snowy River.'

1895

BANJO PATERSON AND CHRISTINA MACPHERSON CREATE 'WALTZING MATILDA'

'But Barty, wait a moment—how do you know everyone will understand what waltzing Matilda means?' Christina Macpherson asked, stopping mid-tune and turning around on her stool to give Andrew Barton 'Banjo' Paterson a disarming look.

'Well they understand out bush, don't they, Christina?' Paterson replied, looking up from the table where he was drafting a ballad. 'And I'm writing this story to go with the lovely tune you have just played for our bush friends right here on Dagworth station,' Paterson said, pointing out the sitting-room window to a paddock full of rain-sodden sheep huddled under coolibah trees. 'So let's keep going till we finish putting words to your tune.'

'All right. Anyway, there's not much else to do now the Wet has arrived and the river is up,' Christina said, smoothing her long, flowing skirt with one hand. 'We certainly can't leave the property, let alone get into Winton.'

'The paddocks need the rain, of course. But back to the ballad,' Paterson said. 'You're the great musician—let's hear that catchy tune again and I'll see if I can write more words to fit it.'

'I'm only playing it by ear, but I'll try it again,' Christina said, turning back to her zither and starting to play. 'Listen carefully, but don't use any more mysterious words.'

'They're not mysterious,' Paterson murmured, getting up and walking over to her. He listened patiently for a few minutes, pen and manuscript still in hand.

After playing for a few minutes, Christina looked up at Paterson and asked, 'What do you think? Can you put your words to that?'

'Yes, but where did you get that tune from?' Paterson said. 'It's such a happy, rollicking rhythm. This fast-moving narrative will go with it perfectly.'

'I don't know where the tune comes from, but I first heard it played in Warrnambool, in Victoria,' Christina said. 'Let's hear your first verse, Barty. I'll play my tune as you read to see if your words fit. One, two, three . . .'

'Oh there once was a swagman camped in the billabong, under the shade of a coolibah tree. And he sang as he looked at the old billy boiling, Who'll come a-waltzing Matilda with me?'

'Very good,' Christina said excitedly. 'The first verse matches the tune well. And I think audiences will be able to deduce what a billabong is. But how does that chorus go?'

'It's pretty simple, I am afraid,' Paterson said, 'but here it is:

Waltzing Matilda, waltzing Matilda,
Who'll come a-waltzing Matilda with me?
And he sang as he sat and waited till his billy boiled,
Who'll come a-waltzing Matilda with me?

'Bravo, bravo!' Christina said, standing up and clapping. 'Though I think you will still have to explain what "waltzing Matilda" means. But I love the main story,' she said. 'I can just picture the swagman at the billabong singing by the fire. But what's next?'

'Now we get to the real drama,' Paterson teased. 'The swaggie commits a crime—are you ready to play your tune?'

Down came a jumbuck to drink at the billabong
Up jumped the swagman and grabbed him with glee
And he said as he put him away in the tucker bag
'You'll come a-waltzing Matilda with me.'

'Bravo, Barty. It fits my tune beautifully' Christina said, looking adoringly at her bush poet. 'Your words are delightful. People will easily understand that jumbuck means sheep—Aboriginal word, isn't it? I can't wait to hear what's next.'

'Are you ready?'

She flicked the page of her home-made musical score.

'Now the plot really thickens,' Paterson said.

Down came the squatter, a-riding his thoroughbred
Down came the policemen, one, two and three
Whose is the jumbuck you've got in the tucker bag?
You'll come a-waltzing Matilda with me!

But the swagman he up and he jumped in the waterhole
Drowning himself by the coolibah tree
And his ghost may be heard as it sings by the billabong
Who'll come a-waltzing Matilda with me?

'Wonderful, Barty—but what a sad ending,' Christina said as she played the last note.

'Thank you, Christina,' Paterson said, rewarding her enthusiasm with a hug, 'but it's your tune that brings it to life.'

'Well let's try it out next time we go into Winton and see what the crowd at the North Gregory Hotel think—they have a piano there.'

'That's exactly what we'll do when the rain stops,' Paterson said, putting the manuscript into his satchel. 'And if the drinkers like it, I will ask *The Bulletin* to publish it—then Lord knows what will happen.'

IT WAS A GREAT MOMENT because between them that wet afternoon at Dagworth Station in far west Queensland, Banjo Paterson and Christina Macpherson had created what would become Australia's favourite song. The tune she had picked up in Victoria had inspired one of the poet's greatest ballads. They tried it out on an audience at the North Gregory in Winton on 6 April 1895, and it was a great success. It became more popular every time it was performed around the district, and once the words and music were revised and published, the song's popularity spread across the country.

Historical background

Paterson enjoyed a lifelong love affair with the bush, through which he travelled widely, gathering stories that he wrote into his poetry. In 1895, the same year 'The Man from Snowy River' appeared in book form, he wrote the words to 'Waltzing Matilda'. Recalling Paterson's visit to Dagworth, Christina later wrote:

The gifted pianist Christina Macpherson, who played the tune that inspired Banjo Paterson to write 'Waltzing Matilda', had hoped to win the heart of the handsome bush poet as they collaborated on their masterpiece, but the footloose and fancy-free balladeer was dating other women back in Sydney.

One day I played (from ear) a tune which I had heard played by a band at the Races in Warrnambool . . . Mr Patterson [*sic*] asked what it was—I could not tell him, & he then said he thought he could write some lines to it. He then and there wrote the first verse. We tried it and thought it went well, so he then wrote the other verses. I might add that in a short time everyone in the District was singing it . . . When Mr Patterson returned to Sydney he wrote and asked me to send him the tune.

'Your words fit the tune like a glove and the story fits the outback perfectly.'

Paterson probably based 'Waltzing Matilda' on the story of an out-of-work shearer who was found dead near Dagworth in 1894 during a failed strike. In the prolonged economic depression of the 1890s, wool prices fell and station owners tried to cut shearers' pay. But the strikers were readily replaced by 'scab' workers drawn from the masses of unemployed. Many shearers became itinerant labourers, walking from station to station with their belongings rolled up in a swag, or 'matilda'. Those who did so were said to be 'waltzing their matilda'. Nor was it unheard-of for hungry swagmen, as they were called, to steal and butcher a sheep.

The uniquely Australian 'Waltzing Matilda' certainly struck a chord. After performing it in Winton, Christina and Paterson tried it out more professionally at nearby Oondooroo station, where there was a good piano and where the baritone Herbert Ramsay sang the song. Five years later, Ramsay performed it at the request of the Queensland Governor. In 1902 the first published version of the lyrics appeared in the Hughenden (Queensland) *Observer*.

The song was used to advertise Billy Tea, and was a favourite with Australian servicemen in the First and Second World Wars. Popularised by country singers like Slim Dusty, it is today an unofficial national anthem, sung at overseas sporting events including Olympic Games. Not a bad afternoon's work for a bush poet and an amateur musician marooned by the Wet.

Postscript

The origins of 'Waltzing Matilda's tune have been the subject of controversy for decades. Scholars believe it was influenced by the English song 'The Bold Fusilier', which includes the refrain 'Who'll be a soldier for Marlborough and me?', or alternatively the Scottish lover's lament 'Thou Bonnie Wood of Craigielea'. Initially Paterson did not think much of either the tune or the words: he said he

sold the copyright, along with 'a lot of other old junk', to a publishing company for a negligible sum. The gifted but little-known Christina Macpherson never received the recognition she deserved for her tune—nor did she win the heart of her bush poet.

Despite the song's appeal, voters in a 1970s referendum rejected it as a possible national anthem. It received a fresh boost in 1995, its centennial year, when this author organised a celebratory performance at the North Gregory Hotel to help establish the Waltzing Matilda Centre in Winton. The legend of the song is now commemorated with an annual festival there.

1901
BARTON USHERS IN NEW NATION OF AUSTRALIA

'It's not as big a crowd as I thought it would be, Alfred, for such a great and important day,' Edmund Barton said, walking down a red carpet between spectators towards the Federation Pavilion, a gleaming white rotunda rising above the lawn in Sydney's Centennial Park. 'You'd think more people would have turned out to see the Governor-General proclaim the Commonwealth of Australia.'

'I wouldn't have expected any more, Edmund,' Alfred Deakin said, following uneasily behind the provisional Prime Minister, who'd been sworn in the previous day. 'For many Australians it is neither a great nor an important day.'

'Surely you are mistaken,' Barton said, nodding automatically at spectators who caught his eye as he drew closer to the spot chosen for the ceremony. 'All the colonies have passed the referendum to form the Commonwealth. Everyone now wants us to become a nation.'

'Do face facts, Ed,' Deakin said. 'A great many people didn't want us to federate. The first referendum here in New South Wales failed, and although the last one passed, more than 100,000 people still voted No.'

'But the colonies were always going to federate, my dear Deakin,' Barton said, pausing to bow to a pretty lady with a white parasol.

'Rubbish. It's taken more than ten years of bickering since old Sir Henry Parkes set things in motion with his speech in Tenterfield,' Deakin said. 'No, there has always been strong opposition from radicals, trade unionists, the industrial working class and, of course, Tocsin—the so-called alarm bell.'

'Tocsin is just a group of Melbourne lunatics . . . and anyway, we federationists have beaten them and all the other anti-Federation madmen. Nothing can stop us now.' Barton bowed again at another pretty woman as he approached the pavilion.

'You are wrong, Ed. As I just wrote in an article for my London newspaper, the Tocsin radicals still claim that Federation is a plot by businessmen to control the unions and workers,' Deakin said, 'and the workers don't trust a powerful unelected Governor-General with reserve powers that could be used against the Labour Party.'

'But that's just Labour paranoia!' Barton said.

'Not at all: Tocsin says a hostile Governor-General could one day dismiss a Labour Prime Minister,' Deakin insisted.

'That's a bit far-fetched, Alfred,' Barton said, kissing the white-gloved hand of an admiring woman.

'Let's face it, a lot of the people only voted Yes because they believed a national government would be better able to defend them in the event of war and keeping out the Chinese,' Deakin said. 'We've only become a nation by the skin of our teeth'.

'I do know that smaller colonies feared the bigger ones would dominate them—and that's why Western Australia only joined at the last moment,' Barton said, as they neared the red-carpeted steps of the rotunda, 'but that's why we've given all states equal representation in the Senate.'

'But that does not help the women. Don't underestimate the problems looming there. Women like Catherine Spence from South Australia are now demanding the federal vote,' Deakin said, following Barton up the stairs and taking a seat beside him.

'Poppycock, Alfred! Politics is a man's world,' Barton muttered out the corner of his mouth.

'You wait, Ed. Things will change!' Deakin warned. 'And sooner than you think.'

'Hush, Mr Deakin,' Barton said. 'Here comes the Governor-General to inaugurate the Commonwealth of Australia.'

IT WAS A GREAT MOMENT because on 1 January 1901, the first day of the new century, the Governor-General, Lord Hopetoun, proclaimed the brand-new Commonwealth of Australia. Despite Deakin's fears, the ceremony at Centennial Park in Sydney went off without a hitch. The 3.75 million people in

Overleaf: The Commonwealth of Australia was proclaimed in Sydney's Centennial Park on 1 January 1901 when the colonies were forged into the one nation to the cheers of thousands of spectators and distinguished guests, including incoming prime minister Edmund Barton, who said, 'This is the first time in history where there has been a continent for a nation and a nation for a continent.'

the six colonies could now call themselves Australians, as Matthew Flinders had always hoped they would. Along with other 'Fathers of Federation', Barton and Deakin had helped create a union formed from New South Wales, Queensland, Tasmania, Victoria, South Australia and Western Australia. The proclamation that day paved the way for the first federal elections and the opening of the first Federal Parliament, on 9 May 1901. As Barton said: 'This is the first time in history where there has been a continent for a nation and a nation for a continent.'

Historical background

Edmund Barton (1849–1920) was an appropriate choice as Australia's first Prime Minister. Born and educated in Sydney, he was a leading lawyer, a member of the New South Wales Parliament, and leader of the Protectionist Party, and had carried the baton for Federation since the death of Sir Henry Parkes in 1896. Alfred Deakin (1856–1919), a Melbourne lawyer who had served in the Victorian Parliament, had also worked long and hard on Federation but was more left-wing than Barton. A deeply religious philosopher and journalist (for London's *Morning Post*), he often sided with the working classes. After Barton's retirement, he served three terms as Prime Minister.

Both Edmund Barton (as the first Prime Minister) and his political colleague Alfred Deakin (as Attorney-General) were in the Cabinet of the new nation, which also included, left to right: (standing) Senator J. Drake, Senator R. O'Connor, Sir P. Fysh, C. Kingston and Sir John Forrest; and (seated) Sir W. Lyne, Barton, Lord Tennyson (Governor-General), Deakin and Sir George Turner.

When voters in the colonies finally agreed to federate, Queen Victoria signed the Constitution Bill passed by the British Parliament in 1900 and ordered that the new nation be created on New Year's Day, 1901. A grand procession of people from all walks of life and horse-drawn vehicles representing the various colonies, political, industrial and social organisations started the day's events by travelling from the Domain to Centennial Park.

After a choir of 15,000 sang the hymn 'O God Our Help in Ages Past', the Anglican Archbishop of Australia recited the prayers prescribed for the occasion. The former clerk to the federal conventions of 1897–98, E.G. Blackmore, then administered to Lord Hopetoun the oaths of office as Governor-General, whereupon Hopetoun proclaimed the Commonwealth of Australia. The new flag was hoisted, the crowd of 60,000 cheered, and artillery fired a series of salutes. Hopetoun then read messages from Queen Victoria and the British Government.

There were no protests, despite the discontent of Tocsin and other radical groups, though as a precaution trade union representatives were admitted to the inner sanctum set aside for 7000 invited guests only in limited numbers. But Deakin was right: the nation had federated by the skin of its teeth. After decades of debate and negotiations, political leaders had only just managed to unite the extremely far-flung colonies of Australia into a single political entity. These colonies had all been started at different times, some as convict prisons and some as free settlements. Some had prospered, some had not, and most had survived only by protecting their fledgling industries and trade with tariffs. Some colonies were hotbeds of labour radicalism, full of resentful unionists; others were conservative to the core. Some had already fought hard to secure independence from each other or from Britain, and now they had to surrender it all to central control. That they federated at all was a minor miracle.

'Let's face it, a lot of the people only voted Yes because they believed a national government would be better able to defend them in the event of war.'

Postscript

The Commonwealth may have united the colonial political structures, but it was not quite a union of all Australians. The voting rights of women were not clearly established, and those of Aborigines even less so. Barton once said he believed in the equality of man, but he never thought such equality should include blacks. And the first laws passed by the Federal Parliament were designed to expel non-whites already working in Australia (the kanakas who had been

Many working class Australians opposed creating a Federal Parliament because they feared the young nation would be shackled by expensive and bureaucratic parliaments at both federal and state level. Cartoon by Marquet for *Table Talk*.

brought in as semi-slaves from the Pacific Islands) and stop others (mainly Chinese) from coming in. The Commonwealth Immigration Restriction Act and the Pacific Island Labourers Act formalised a 'White Australia' policy. From then on immigrants faced hurdles, such as being required to pass a dictation test in any European language, which could be applied at whim to keep out 'undesirables'.

The Commonwealth soon enfranchised women, as some states had already done, and they were able to vote in the elections of 1902. But the situation with Aborigines was far more complex. As the Australian Electoral Commission explains:

Legally their rights go back to colonial times. When Victoria, New South Wales, Tasmania and South Australia framed their constitutions in the 1850s they gave voting rights to all male British subjects over twenty-one, which of course included Aboriginal men. And in 1895 when South Australia gave women the right to vote and sit in Parliament, Aboriginal women shared the right. Only Queensland and Western Australia barred Aborigines from voting.

However, 'very few Aborigines knew their rights, so very few voted, although some eventually did—Point McLeay, a mission station near the mouth of the Murray, got a polling station in the 1890s. Aboriginal men and women voted there in South Australian elections and voted for the first Commonwealth Parliament in 1901.'

Although the Tocsin group accepted the new nation, they were proved right in one respect: Governor-General, Sir John Kerr did indeed use his reserve powers to dismiss Gough Whitlam's Labor Government in 1975. In the late twentieth century, a further campaign began to replace the constitutional monarchy declared in 1901 with a republic.

The new nation was lucky to get that goodwill message from Queen Victoria, as she died later that month. The far-flung latecomer Western Australia voted to secede from the Commonwealth in 1933, but it failed to get enough support from Britain to go it alone.

1904

JOHN WATSON FORMS WORLD'S FIRST LABOUR GOVERNMENT

'Look at these numbers, Billy,' said the incoming Labour Prime Minister, John Christian Watson, handing over a sheet of paper listing MPs' voting preferences. He walked to the window of the Labour Party office in downtown Melbourne. 'This is going to make people take our party seriously.'

'What an understatement! Mr Watson, this is a momentous event for Australia!' Billy Hughes said, hardly glancing at the figures on the page. 'I remember when we founded the Labour Party in Balmain back in 1891—it's not much more than thirteen years old!'

'So you think it's historic, Billy?' Watson asked, absent-mindedly scanning the street below.

'Of course! The Members of Parliament have just voted in Australia's first national Labour Government,' he said, waving the page in the air, 'and you will be its leader.'

'Well, perhaps you have a point,' Watson said, watching a road gang downing tools at the end of their day and scurrying down the street to catch horse-drawn trams. 'I suppose it could help boost the morale of the working classes.'

'Chris, you are far too modest. Not only will ours be Australia's first national Labour Government, it will be the first such government in the world.'

'What about Great Britain?' Watson asked, watching traffic bank up behind a cart as its horse stopped to drop a load of manure. 'Or Canada, for that matter—they have federated too.'

'No, Chris. We are the first!' Hughes said, approaching the window to see what was fascinating Watson so much. 'Remember how, when we created the

Not only was John Watson an unlikely candidate to become Australia's first leader of a national Labour Government—he was born in Chile, brought up in New Zealand and left school at thirteen—but he also later turned his back on Labour and went into business.

119

The world's first national Labour Government Cabinet, formed under the leadership of John Watson, second from left, front row, included two future prime ministers, Andrew Fisher, at left standing up, and Billy Hughes, front row centre.

Labour Party, it was just to give a voice to the unions in New South Wales? We never dreamed we would soon win control of a state, let alone the blooming Federal Government.'

'You never expected the working classes and unions to support a new political party created for them?' Watson asked, watching the horse and cart start up again.

'Not to this extent. Anyway, there was no Commonwealth of Australia back then. Old Sir Henry Parkes had only just made his Tenterfield speech calling for Federation,' Hughes said.

'Do you think women will help us, Billy, now that they are going to vote thanks to Catherine Spence?' Watson asked, his eyes following a pretty woman into a haberdashery.

'They're sure to,' Hughes predicted.

'I hope you're right—Labour needs all the votes it can get to beat the conservatives, both the Protection and Free Trade parties.'

'That's a nice umbrella she's carrying, eh—exactly the sort I used to manufacture before I got into politics,' Hughes said with a laugh.

'You've done well, Billy—from brollies to bashing ears in Parliament,' Watson said, also laughing.

'Now you've beaten that old Protectionist Alfred Deakin! Fancy him resigning in a fit of pique just because we wanted to stop him punishing the workers with his anti–trade union bill,' Hughes said. 'That'll teach him. Now Labour is the only party with the numbers to form government.'

'So we can call the shots,' Watson said, returning to his desk. 'We can do something for the working classes.'

'Of course. And I want a ministerial portfolio—External Affairs will do,' Hughes said.

'Better for you to have your love affairs overseas than at home, Billy,' Watson teased.

'Enough of that,' Hughes said. 'Let's just make sure Labour is here to stay, Mr Watson. Govern well—the world will be watching you.'

'Right. Let's reply to the Governor-General's invitation to form a government,' he said, sitting down and picking up his pen. 'Thanks, Billy. I'll remember this moment for years to come.'

IT WAS A GREAT MOMENT because Watson was indeed about to form Australia's and the world's first national Labour Government. It was 21 April 1904, and Labour's leader in the House of Representatives had just earned the Prime Ministership in fine political style by persuading enough non-Labour Members to vote against the draconian Conciliation and Arbitration Bill introduced by the Protectionist leader and Prime Minister, Alfred Deakin. Watson and his group had voted against a hostile amendment that undermined Deakin's plans, forcing the humbled leader to resign. With the backing of twenty-four Labour Members and other MPs who'd supported his anti-Deakin campaign, Watson was now invited by the Governor-General to form his history-making government.

'You never expected the working classes and unions to support a new political party created for them?'

Historical background

John Christian Watson (known as Chris) was born in Valparaiso, Chile, in 1867. He went to school in Oamaru, New Zealand, before joining the local newspaper as a printer's helper at the age of thirteen. Moving to Sydney, he became active in the typographical union and was elected President of the Sydney Trades and Labour Council and, by age twenty-four, President of the Labour Party

When the trade unions created the Labour Party in the early 1890s to give the working man a political voice against 'fat cat capitalists', they did not expect their new party to become the first in the world to win national government the following decade.

Conference, where he helped pioneer the Caucus solidarity system. One of the first Labour Members of the New South Wales Parliament, he was elected to the first national Parliament in 1901 and appointed Labour's leader in the House of Representatives.

As both conservative parties needed Labour's support to pass bills, Watson was in a strong position to challenge Deakin's draconian Conciliation and Arbitration Bill. Seeing the successful challenge as an insult to his leadership, Deakin resigned, leaving Watson with the numbers to form a minority government.

Watson served as Prime Minister and Treasurer, Billy Hughes (later to become Prime Minister) as External Affairs Minister; and Andrew Fisher (also a future Prime Minister) Minister of Trade and Customs. Deakin graciously praised Watson's 'soundness of judgement, clearness of argument and fairness to opponents', saying that when his rival became Prime Minister 'his simple dignity, courage and resource' earned him 'hosts of admirers and many friends' and 'the confidence of the House of Representatives'.

Postscript

Although the Australian Labor Party (it dropped the 'u' from its name in 1912) celebrates Watson as its first Prime Minister, he was the only Australian Prime Minister not to have been born in either Britain or Australia. Despite some worthwhile legislative initiatives, Watson's historic government lasted only four months. When he tried to introduce his own Conciliation and Arbitration Bill, favouring unionists, an unsympathetic House amended it to undermine the privileges Watson wanted to guarantee to unionists. When the Governor-General refused his request for a dissolution of Parliament, Watson resigned and the arch-conservative Free Trade leader George Reid took over as Prime Minister. Labour's moment in the sun was over—for now.

Watson resigned from Parliament in 1907 and was expelled from the Labor Party in 1916 for voting in favour of conscription for the First World War. To everyone's surprise, the pioneering Labour leader then went into business, becoming a director of several big companies and eventually chairman of the board of the petroleum giant Ampol. He died in 1941.

1912
MAWSON SURVIVES ANTARCTIC BLIZZARD FOR AUSTRALIA'S SAKE

'Take care, Ninnis!' Douglas Mawson yelled above the howl of the Antarctic wind at his exploring partner, Lieutenant Belgrave Ninnis, trudging behind him, and Dr Xavier Mertz, the third man of Mawson's team.

'Mertz and I are testing the ice and keeping our eyes open for any sign of a crevasse, but you be careful too.'

'Yes, Doug, I'm watching every step,' Ninnis said. 'You blokes are just worried because I'm pulling the sled with most of our supplies, aren't you,' he joked.

'But do take care, Ninnis,' Mertz called back to his friend as the trio trudged on. 'We'll never make it back to base unless we all stick together.'

They battled on for a while, bent double against the wind, Mawson and Mertz nearest to each other when suddenly something made Mertz look back behind him. There was nobody there. 'Where the hell is Ninnis?' he called out to Mawson.

'God knows!' Mawson replied, looking back in horror. 'We'll have to go back quick smart,' he ordered, and the pair turned around and began retracing their steps.

Before long, Mawson and Mertz could see clearly from tracks where Ninnis had disappeared. The snow cap Ninnis had been creeping across had cracked and collapsed into a crevasse opening up below—taking Ninnis and the precious sled and dog team with it.

'Ninnis!' Mawson screamed out looking down the crevasse, but keeping a safe distance from the gaping chasm: 'Ninnis! Ninnis!' He couldn't see anything apart from an injured dog lying on a ledge about a hundred and fifty feet below, and there was no reply—only the echo of Mawson's call and the sound of the dog whimpering.

'My God,' he said, turning to Mertz. 'What a price we are paying to explore this godforsaken land. Scott was right: this is an awful place, for sure.'

'Poor bastard,' Mertz said.

'Here, help me untie this rope and we'll throw down a line. If he's still alive he might grab it and we can try to pull him up,' Mawson said. 'But be careful, the lip of the crevasse could give way under us.'

Mawson and Mertz lowered a line as far as it would reach. But it was no use. The crevasse seemed bottomless. There was certainly no tug on the rope from Ninnis, and even the dog had stopped whimpering.

'Well, there's no chance of getting him back now,' Mawson said shaking his head desperately, after fruitless hours had gone by. 'We both risk dying if we stay much longer, so I'll just say a prayer for his soul and let's go. We've got to head for base camp as fast as we can.'

'What supplies have we got left to share between us?' asked Mertz. 'Do you think we'll make it?'

'Well we've got very little now, apart from a few bars of chocolate and some biscuits. Most of our food, our tools and the food for the dogs was on that sled. We'll have to kill the remaining six dogs for fresh meat to make it back,' Mawson replied. 'May God help us.'

It was 14 December 1912, and the two survivors were more than 500 kilometres from base camp with ten days' worth of food. In these frozen wastes, they could cover only a few kilometres a day. Yet on they trudged, day after day, growing ever weaker.

'Focus on your feet,' Mawson kept yelling at Mertz above the wind. 'Just put one foot in front of the other. Don't stop, man.'

'I can't lift my feet, Doug . . . I'm done for,' Mertz kept saying.

'Here, this will give you more energy,' Mawson insisted, feeding Mertz a chunk of dog's liver.

But it was no use. 'I've got to lie down, Doug. I can't even stand any more. Leave me here and go on to the base camp on your own,' Mertz finally said, sinking to the snow.

After one of his expedition members fell into a crevasse and the other died from malnutrition, Antarctic explorer Douglas Mawson was forced to battle back to base camp alone.

Mawson described blizzards with 'Herculean gusts' of up to 320 kilometres an hour, especially around his hut at Cape Denison.

Three weeks after Ninnis's death, Mertz succumbed to illness, leaving Mawson alone with only scraps of dog meat and his iron will to keep him going.

For a while he pulled the sole remaining sled, which held his tent and other necessities, talking to himself to keep awake and sane. But on 17 January the snow beneath him suddenly gave way and he tumbled into a crevasse. Fortunately, his sled got stuck at the top. Mawson was left dangling at the end of the rope that harnessed him to it. 'My God,' he said, looking into the chasm. His only hope was to pull himself back up the rope without dislodging the sled. 'I'll wait till Providence gives me strength to do it,' he said. He made it, panting and puffing, pulling himself up the rope inch by inch. Then, just as he thought he was safe, the edge of the chasm collapsed and he fell again to the end of the rope.

'I owe that sledge everything,' he whispered to himself, for it hadn't budged. Knowing he had strength for only one more climb, he rested awhile. 'Please don't let me die in this icy coffin,' he prayed. Again he inched up the rope and, with a final Herculean effort, heaved himself over the top and crawled away from the edge as fast as he could.

'This is it,' he said to himself after a brief sleep. 'I'm not going to stop now till I get there. I don't want to die like Scott's men, frozen to death in their tents.'

Mawson missed the departure of his ship *Aurora* by a few hours but it could not have waited any longer. Ships had to leave before winter set in and the sea froze over, trapping them in the ice and crushing their hulls.

Harnessing himself to his sled, he resumed his struggle towards the base. By now the soles of his feet were peeling off, exposing raw and tender flesh, and he had stomach cramps from the dog meat. Fuelled by will power alone, he dragged himself and his sled across a great glacier of broken ice, waded through kilometres of soft snow that he prayed—calling out loud to Heaven—would not hide more crevasses, crossed a vast ice plateau and climbed 1000 metres of steep crags.

He battled through blizzards and white-outs during which he could barely see his compass. His aching body crying out for a sleep that would have ushered in certain death, he repeated over and over 'No, no, no, I will not go to sleep.' Then came the miracle: he saw the base hut ahead and three men outside. He waved and they hurried to meet him, anxious to know who had survived.

IT WAS A GREAT MOMENT because, by making it back to camp against almost impossible odds, Douglas Mawson became Australia's greatest polar explorer. It was 8 February 1913, at the Australian expedition's base at Cape Denison in Antarctica. As an individual achievement Mawson's feat rates alongside that of Ernest Shackleton, the British explorer who a couple of years later would bring his crew back from the dead after their ship *Endurance* sank in the icy Weddell Sea. Leaving his men on a rocky islet, Shackleton sailed for sixteen days in an open lifeboat to South Georgia Island and returned with a rescue ship.

Over the next two decades, through expeditions and research, Mawson helped establish Australia so firmly in Antarctica that by 1933 Britain had transferred most of her Antarctic territories to Australia, making it one of the largest territorial stakeholders on the icy continent.

Historical background

Born in Yorkshire, England, in 1882, Mawson became a geologist and joined Shackleton on a 1907 expedition to Antarctica. This was the age of heroic polar exploration. In 1911, the Norwegian explorer Roald Amundsen reached the South Pole—the first man to do so—just ahead of Britain's ill-fated Robert Scott.

Mawson, who had declined an invitation to accompany Scott as a geologist on the 1910 Terra Nova Expedition, had achieved his own first in 1909 along with Edgeworth David and Forbes Mackay, reaching the South Magnetic Pole. Mawson and Edgeworth David were also the first to climb Mount Erebus, in Antarctica.

In 1912, Mawson led his own Australian Antarctic Expedition to King George V Land and Adelie Land, the sector of the continent immediately south of Australia, which at the time was almost entirely unexplored. Sailing from Hobart, the team landed at Cape Denison on Commonwealth Bay on 8 January. They built a hut on the rocky cape and wintered through nearly constant blizzards, with what Mawson described as 'Herculean gusts' of up to 320 kilometres an hour.

Ten months later, he set off with Xavier Mertz and Belgrave Ninnis to explore King George V Land to the east. When Ninnis and his dog team and sledge, loaded with most of the provisions, were lost, Mawson and Mertz had little hope of survival. Short of food, they slaughtered and ate their remaining sled dogs, unwittingly putting their survival ever further at risk: dog liver contains so much vitamin A that its consumption can be toxic. Mertz soon became incapacitated and died, leaving Mawson to struggle on alone. So ghastly did he look when he reached the base that the first person to greet him asked, 'My God, which one are you?'

The expedition's ship, the *Aurora* had left just a few hours before—a piece of unfortunate timing to rival that of Burke and Wills on their return to Cooper's Creek in 1861. The ship was recalled by radio, but ice prevented it from reaching the base, so Mawson and the six men who had remained behind to look for him were forced to stay for another ten months.

Finally, on 26 February 1914, Mawson arrived back in Adelaide. He had explored large areas of the Antarctic coast, describing its geology, biology and meteorology, and more exactly determined the location of the South Magnetic Pole. His achievements were promoted by fellow Antarctic explorer and film-maker Frank Hurley, who had survived with Shackleton and who produced a documentary film on the Mawson expedition called *Home of the Blizzard* (Mawson wrote a book by the same name). Mawson, who served in the First World War, led more expeditions to Antarctica, conducting important research in geology and marine science. His portrait appears on Australia's $100 bill.

> 'I can't lift my feet, Doug . . . I'm done for.'

Postscript

Despite his scientific achievements, his role in securing a claim over a large area of Antarctica for Australia, and his extraordinary story of survival, very few Australians know of Douglas Mawson—perhaps because so few have visited Antarctica.

1914

HMAS SYDNEY, ROUND 1: CAPTAIN GLOSSOP SINKS GERMANY'S *EMDEN*

'Tell me when we get close enough to open fire on the Germans, please, Lieutenant,' Captain John Glossop, the English skipper of HMAS *Sydney*, ordered, his eyes glued to his binoculars. 'We're probably about 11,000 yards from *Emden* now, aren't we, and still out of range?'

'No, sir, we are steaming so fast we're only 10,500 yards from the Germans now,' the navigation officer said, checking his coordinates repeatedly on the chart laid out on the table.

'But still out of their range,' Glossop said, still focusing on the enemy raider.

'Probably, Sir,' the gunnery officer chipped in, 'but you never know.'

'Rubbish! You should know Jerry can't reach beyond 10,000 yards,' Glossop said, scanning *Emden* for any sign of activity, 'and our ship's guns are bigger and have the greater range.'

'But Captain, since the Germans are already within our range, why don't we fire now?' the gunnery officer asked apprehensively. 'We don't *have* to wait till we can see the whites of their eyes, do we?' He looked at the navigation officer nodding his head impatiently and the gunners poised ready to fire.

'At 10,000 yards our salvos will be more accurate,' Glossop said. 'Actually, I may wait until we are closer than that so we won't waste a shell. Navigator, tell me when we close to 9500 yards and then we will fire.'

Before the lieutenant had a chance to reply, a shell screamed in to strike *Sydney* amidships, sending metal splinters and sparks flying and starting a fire among some cordite charges. Sailors jumped out of the way, officers shouted orders, and all hell broke loose.

Australia's famous light cruiser HMAS *Sydney* (which later sunk the German cruiser *Emden*) was the pride of the new fleet when it first arrived in Sydney Harbour in 1913 along with battle cruiser *Australia*, light cruiser *Melbourne*, and destroyers *Parramatta* and *Yarra*.

'Good God,' Glossop gasped, staggering away from the rail and dropping his binoculars. 'How did they do that? They must have increased their range.'

'Yes, indeed they must,' the gunnery officer yelled, picking himself up from the deck. 'Now can we fire, Sir?'

'Yes!' Glossop called out, recovering his composure 'Put out those flames and fire!'

'We can't fire, Sir!' the gunnery officer called back.

'Why the hell not?' Glossop demanded. 'We can't waste a second, man!'

'That first salvo has killed the range-finding officer, sir.'

'Well, replace him and start firing!' Glossop ordered.

'Our range-finder is destroyed too, Sir!' came the reply.

Rushing to the bridge rail to see for himself, Glossop shouted; 'Set the guns manually and start firing back!'

By now *Emden* was firing a salvo every six seconds. Lacking range-finders, Glossop ordered his ship full steam ahead so his gunners would have a better chance of landing some hits. Seeing *Sydney* coming, *Emden*'s captain, Karl von Müller, began weaving his ship from side to side, but Glossop's gunners soon hit home.

Sydney's 45-kilogram shells struck *Emden*'s wireless room, the captain's voice pipes (used to give instructions to the gunners) and the command transmission system. Now the tables had turned: the German captain was unable to direct his crew. HMAS *Sydney* then destroyed *Emden*'s steering gear. Glossop's gunners hit the *Emden*'s fore funnel and foremast, which crashed onto her deck. Then they struck the final blow, holing *Emden*'s hull below the waterline.

The *Emden*'s second torpedo officer, Franz Joseph, Prince von Hohenzollern, reported:

> On deck a terrible picture of wreckage met my eyes. Everything was lying tossed together; what was destructible destroyed, two funnels completely demolished and the foremast thrown over the port side by a full hit, lying across the railing with its point in the water. Everywhere lay the dead and the wounded and the groaning and cries caught at one's heart and filled one with the bitterest regret, for first aid materials were lacking and the best will in the world could do little to help because it was impossible to get into the first-aid room and the whole stern deck and sides of the ship were red-hot with fires burning everywhere.

Müller had no alternative but to run his wrecked raider aground on the rocks off North Keeling Island and surrender.

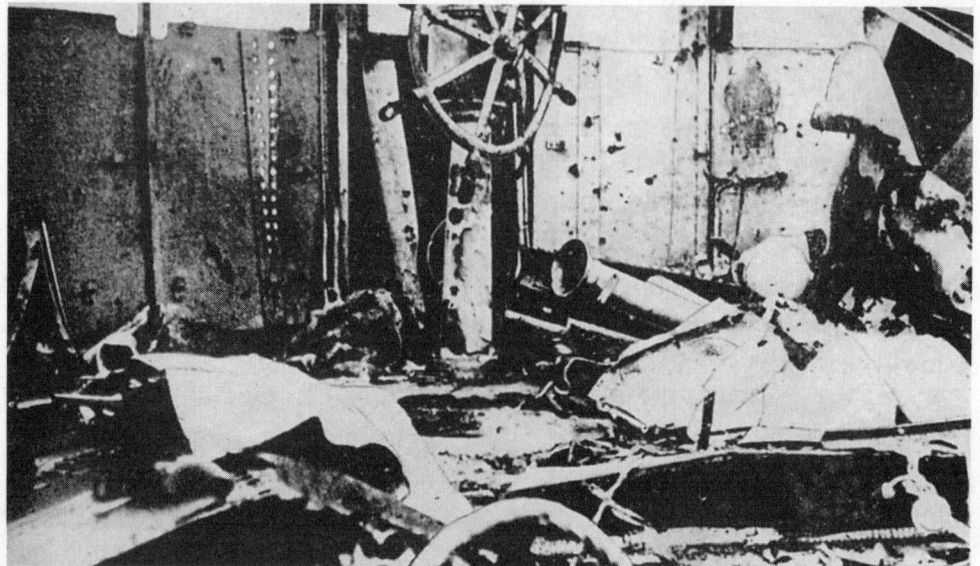

HMAS *Sydney* claimed one of the first scalps of the First World War when they shelled the deadly German cruiser *Emden* off the Cocos Islands. The *Emden* was wrecked, but some of the crew escaped in a small boat back to Germany.

1914

IT WAS A GREAT MOMENT because the Royal Australian Navy's first flagship, HMAS *Sydney*, had won the new nation's first sea engagement. It was 9 November 1914, off the coast of Cocos Island, north-west of Western Australia. Glossop had sailed *Sydney* out from Britain only the year before, but she had succeeded in destroying the experienced German merchant-shipping raider *Emden*, which had sunk at least sixteen British ships. *Sydney* had claimed her first victory as part of a convoy carrying Anzac troops to the Mediterranean. She had been ordered to steam off to deal with *Emden* after officers in the convoy overheard suspicious radio messages coming from the Cocos Islands. The cocky *Emden* had been informing a sister ship that she planned to land men at Direction Island and destroy an Allied radio station there.

Historical background

Captain John Glossop (1871–1934) was born in England and in his late teens started serving on British ships in the Australian squadron. After commanding HMS *Prometheus*, a protected cruiser sailing the Pacific Islands, in mid 1913 he was chosen to captain Australia's new light cruiser HMAS *Sydney*. In the early months of the First World War *Sydney* searched for enemy warships off northern New Guinea and helped capture Rabaul from the Germans. She then helped escort the first Australian and New Zealand troop convoy to Egypt. The convoy was some 80 kilometres off the Cocos Islands when the wireless station there reported the presence of a German ship and *Sydney* was detached to investigate.

The light cruiser SMS *Emden* engaged *Sydney* at extreme range, killing four sailors and destroying the ship's range-finder before *Sydney* opened fire. However, *Sydney*, with the advantage in speed and armament, thereafter stayed out of *Emden's* range, reducing her to a blazing shambles and driving her aground. *Sydney* sailed away to pursue the fleeing collier *Buresk*, took off her crew and watched her sink, then returned to *Emden* to find her ensign still flying. When Glossop's demands for surrender were ignored, he fired two salvos. The ensign came down and white flags were shown. Assistance could not be given to *Emden* immediately, as the German landing party on Direction Island had to be dealt with. Glossop was unaware that they had escaped after destroying the wireless station, but *Sydney's* diversion to the island meant that medical aid was not given to *Emden* until late next day. With the last survivors, including Müller, transhipped, *Sydney* made for Colombo to rejoin the convoy.

'Everywhere lay the dead and the wounded and the groaning and cries caught at one's heart and filled one with the bitterest regret.'

Emden had cut a swathe through British and Allied shipping in the Indian Ocean, and the news of her end was received with jubilation. Glossop was congratulated by the Australian Naval Board, though he has been criticised since for being caught by *Emden*'s first salvo (in fact, he was unaware that her guns had been modified to increase their range). He correctly fought the remainder of the action out of his enemy's reach.

The battle was a baptism of fire for the Australian sailors who manned the flagship along with Royal Navy counterparts. As Glossop reported: 'The hail of shell which beat upon them was unceasing, but they paid as little heed to it as if they had passed their lives under heavy fire, instead of experiencing it for the first time.' Winston Churchill, then Britain's First Lord of the Admiralty, wrote:

'Warmest congratulations on the brilliant entry of the Australian Navy into the war, and the signal service rendered to the Allied cause and to peaceful commerce by the destruction of the *Emden*.'

It was fortunate for *Sydney* that *Emden* failed to disable or sink the ship—and lucky for Australia that *Emden* did not manage to intercept any of the vessels transporting 30,000 Anzac troops to Egypt en route to Gallipoli.

Glossop commanded *Sydney* till 1917, then served as Captain-in-Charge of Naval Establishments and presided over the controversial court-martial of mutineers from HMAS *Australia*. Described by *The Bulletin* as a 'suave, bald, soft-voiced little man who looked the antithesis of a fire-eater', he was to his officers 'the embodiment of the true English gentleman'. For destroying the *Emden* he was made a Companion of the Order of the Bath and awarded the Japanese Order of the Rising Sun and the French Légion d'Honneur. He was promoted to Rear Admiral in 1921 but retired next day.

Postscript

Although Glossop was well rewarded for his victory, he was naive to have supposed that his ship was beyond range of *Emden*'s guns. (A similar error was made in the Second World War by a later HMAS *Sydney* captain.) Glossop also made the mistake of not trying to round up the remaining *Emden* crew members on Direction Island till the next morning. Overnight, the Germans escaped on a schooner, making it back home in one of their nation's great escape stories.

1915

CHARLES BEAN LANDS WITH THE ANZACS AT GALLIPOLI

'It is a perfect moonlight night, just what we need for the landing.' Charles Bean scribbled in the gloom as he sat on the upper deck of the darkened *Minnewaska*. It was some time in the early hours of 25 April 1915, and the ship, with thousands of Anzac troops aboard, was heading towards the Gallipoli peninsula, on the Turkish coast.

'Quiet,' a nearby officer hissed over the rail at the soldiers chatting on the deck below.

'And put out that bloody cigarette, you fool!' Bean whispered under his breath, seeing a light among the dark figures packed together like sardines.

'It's not a fag—it's a pipe,' the soldier hissed back.

'Even worse, you prize idiot,' Bean retorted, leaning over the rail. 'Do you want us all killed? Put it out or I'll report you.'

'That's fine, that is, coming from a bloody journalist,' the private shot back.

'I may not be a combatant, but I don't want to be reporting your death, do I?' Bean said.

'I was only smoking it for me bloody nerves—the wait is killing me,' the soldier said, knocking out his pipe on the heel of his boot.

It *was* taking a long time, thought Bean. He read over his diary entry of the evening before: 'Of course some people have been a little thoughtful tonight, because we know what a tremendous job it is, this assault on a strong fortress . . . One is inclined to think of the utter hopeless wastefulness of this whole war.' As he thought of the troops below, he wrote: 'The Turk does not realise what is in store for him during the next few hours.'

When journalist Charles Bean saw how brave the Anzacs were at Gallipoli he started writing colourful newspaper articles that celebrated their courage and founded the Anzac legend.

On the battleship up ahead, the first troops chosen to go ashore were already lined up on the decks. They belonged to the 3rd Brigade, an all-Australian unit led by the British Colonel Ewen Sinclair-MacLagan that comprised four battalions of 1000 men—the 9th, from Queensland; the 10th, from South Australia; the 11th, from Western Australia; and the 12th, mainly from Tasmania. Their officers repeated their orders—to climb into the landing boats, sit tight, then dash ashore when the boats arrived and force the Turks back from the beach before climbing the cliffs to capture Turkish positions on the closest hilltops. Fortunately, nobody knew how difficult this would turn out to be. At 3 a.m. they collected their kits and climbed as quietly as possible over the sides of the ships, down rope ladders and into the boats, where they sat waiting for a few minutes before oarsmen pushed off for the fatal shore.

'It is well past four,' Bean scribbled in his notebook after walking up to the bow to get as close as possible to the action, 'and the dawn is slowly growing'. A little later, peering towards the shore in the dim light, he wrote: 'for the first time listening eagerly I heard the distant echo of rifle firing—the first few shots, then heavy and continuous firing which is going on in the hills. Our men must have landed and the battle must have begun.'

The boats carrying the first wave of Anzacs had scraped onto the rocky beach. The Turks fired on them as they neared the shore, and several were killed before they landed. On the beach they came under even more intense fire. Their only choice was to scramble up the steep hillsides towards the Turkish positions on the heights.

IT WAS A GREAT MOMENT because the Australian and New Zealand soldiers succeeded in establishing a foothold on Gallipoli in the face of murderous fire from Turkish soldiers well placed atop the cliffs that rose steeply from the narrow strips of sand. That beach—just south of the headland of Ari Burnu—was the wrong one, thanks to blunders by Royal Navy commanders who landed the troops about 1.5 kilometres north of their intended destination, Gaba Tepe. At Anzac Cove, as the landing site became known, steep, scrub-covered slopes hemmed the Anzacs into what amounted to a shooting gallery. Hundreds of Australians were killed that first day, but 12,000 of them, and some 4000 New Zealanders, got ashore in the first twenty-four hours. It was a tough test for the men of the new nation and their comrades-in-arms, but the

The Anzacs were off-loaded from ships just short of Gallipoli early on 25 April 1915, and transported in open boats to the beach. There they scrambled ashore, facing deadly fire from the Turkish defenders.

Australians passed it with flying colours and soon forged a reputation as brave and resourceful fighters.

Historical background

Charles Bean (1879–1968) was selected by ballot to serve as Australia's official war correspondent and given the honorary rank of captain. He landed at Gallipoli on the first day and stayed until the evacuation in December, tirelessly covering the whole campaign. He then followed the Australian Imperial Force to the Western Front, where he covered the war until it ended in 1918.

Back home, he helped establish the Australian War Memorial and, with a team of researchers, started the formidable task of writing the definitive history of Australia's part in the First World War.

Bean was born in Bathurst but educated largely in England. He became a reporter on *The Sydney Morning Herald* and travelled widely in the bush. His war reports and his history were a tribute to the bushman–soldier, that resonated powerfully in Australia. Through these writings, Bean almost single-handedly created the Anzac legend.

After naval assaults on Constantinople (Istanbul) failed, the British hoped to defeat Germany's ally, Turkey, by landing Allied forces on the Gallipoli peninsula, then marching north to take the capital. British troops would land on the southern tip of the peninsula and the Anzacs on the western side. With more than 200 troop ships, it was the largest invasion fleet yet to attempt an opposed landing. Lieutenant General Sir William Birdwood, commander of the Australia and New Zealand Army Corps, warned: 'We are about to undertake one of the most difficult tasks any soldier can be called upon to perform. Lord Kitchener [British Minister for War] has told us he lays special stress on the role the army has to play in this particular operation—the success of which will be a severe blow to the enemy.' There would be plenty of obstacles:

> The country whither we are bound is very difficult, we may not be able to get our wagons anywhere near us for some time and so you must carry enough food and water for three days and take the greatest care with ammunition and only fire when you find the Turks in their trenches. It will be difficult but it will go down in history to the glory of the soldiers of Australia and New Zealand.

'It will be difficult, but it will go down in history to the glory of the soldiers of Australia and New Zealand.'

Unfortunately, the Turkish commanders had anticipated the invasion and were thoroughly prepared. The local defenders were commanded by Mustafa Kemal, later Atatürk, founder of the modern Turkish state.

Postscript

Though Bean's dispatches (and those of Britain's Ellis Ashmead-Bartlett) elevated the Anzacs to hero status, the invasion force was defeated. It made no permanent capture of enemy territory, achieved little and was eventually withdrawn. The soldiers' bravery and skill sustained the Gallipoli campaign for eight months, but the effort cost Australia 8709 dead and New Zealand 2701. The news reports were of course censored in an attempt to make readers think the war was going well. But Bean's personal diary revealed how badly he thought the campaign was going. Poorly planned, in impossible terrain and against a well-established enemy, it was doomed from the outset. The reason the Anzacs are today celebrated for their role in this misadventure is that they were all volunteers and fought with great courage in a hopeless situation. General Birdwood suggested that they be evacuated the day after they landed, but his recommendation was refused.

By December 1915, when the evacuation finally took place, a total of 50,000 Australians had served on the peninsula. The death toll had horrified the nation, which—not surprisingly—voted against conscription the following year and again in 1917. The Gallipoli campaign also killed more than 21,000 British troops, 10,000 from France and 86,000 Turks. But it paled beside the slaughter of the Western Front battlefields of France and Flanders, where more than 46,000 Australians would lose their lives.

1915
ALBERT JACKA WINS AUSTRALIA'S FIRST GALLIPOLI VC

'What happened, Private Jacka?' Lieutenant Keith Crabbe fought to catch his breath after sprinting to the edge of the trench in which Albert Jacka stood. 'Are you all right?'

'I managed to get the beggars, Sir,' Jacka said, looking up. His finger was still on the trigger of the rifle—its bayonet dripping blood—with which he'd just killed seven Turks.

'My God, Jacka, how did you take back this trench on your own?' Crabbe asked, looking at all the bodies at Jacka's feet.

'Well, Sir, some of our men threw bombs at the other end so I could jump in, then I shot five of the beggars because I wanted to get rid of as many as I could before they came for me,' Jacka explained nonchalantly, nodding his head at the bodies lying further up the trench. 'Then I had to bayonet those two quick smart because they got to me before I could reload,' he said, indicating two corpses lying at his feet. 'The rest dropped their guns and ran.'

'Good work, Private Jacka, absolutely capital,' Crabbe exclaimed. 'But why were you on your own?'

'Four of us were attacked but the other three were shot,' Jacka said. 'So I carried on alone.'

'How many Turks were in the trench when you arrived?' Crabbe asked, looking around for other enemy bodies.

'Not sure, Sir—maybe a dozen altogether.'

Crabbe grunted in astonishment. 'You must be exhausted . . . let's get you back to the beach.'

JOIN TOGETHER
TRAIN TOGETHER
EMBARK TOGETHER
FIGHT TOGETHER
LIEUT. JACKA V.C
Enlist in the Sportsmen's Thousand
SHOW THE ENEMY WHAT
AUSTRALIAN SPORTING MEN CAN DO.

'But sir, will you send reinforcements to hold the trench before the Turks counterattack?'

'Of course. Absolutely,' Crabbe said, blowing his whistle to summon troops into the trench.

'And the bodies, Sir?' Jacka asked.

Crabbe turned to the new arrivals. 'Lance-corporal! Order a burial detail immediately. Now, Jacka, you must return to your dugout and clean up.'

'Thank you, Sir, I would like that,' Jacka said, as the enormity of his achievement began to sink in.

'And do you know what?' Lieutenant Crabbe said just before Jacka walked off. 'I'm going down to our beach HQ to report your splendid work and I will be recommending you for a Victoria Cross, man—the highest award there is.'

'Thank you, Sir, thank you,' Jacka replied, 'but I was only doing my duty.'

IT WAS A GREAT MOMENT because Jacka had just won Australia's first Victoria Cross at Gallipoli and its first of the Great War. It was 19 May 1915, at a section of trench known as Courtney's Post. Not surprisingly, Crabbe's recommendation was accepted, and Private Albert Jacka of the 14th Infantry Battalion was decorated by King George V the following year. It was a great moment for Australians back home, who were reeling from news of the slaughter of the Anzacs since their landing a month before. When his story was told, Jacka became a national hero overnight, inspiring the army to use his photo on recruiting posters. His efforts also earned him the £500 and gold watch promised for the nation's first Victoria Cross winner by the Melbourne business and sporting identity John Wren.

Historical background

The son of a rural labourer from near Geelong in Victoria, Jacka worked as a labourer before enlisting in September 1914, a month after war broke out. After training in Egypt he landed at Gallipoli on 26 April 1915, at the age of twenty-one. On May 19 the Turks launched a massive counterattack along the entire Anzac line in hopes of pushing the invaders back into the sea. Courtney's Post was rushed at about 4 a.m. leaving only Jacka alive and captured after bitter fighting. While other Anzacs opened fire and lobbed two bombs at the Turks

The Army used this picture of the gallant Albert Jacka to inspire young sportsmen to enlist after he won the first Victoria Cross at Gallipoli, but enlistments were still so slow the government organised referendums to try to introduce conscription.

It was not easy for Albert Jacka to kill five Turks and capture an enemy trench single-handed at Gallipoli because the trenches were deep, strongly fortified and well defended—like this captured Turkish trench manned by five Australians.

to create a diversion, Jacka ran into no man's land and re-entered the trench further down to charge the enemy. (That same day, John Simpson Kirkpatrick, 'the man with the donkey', was killed by Turkish marksmen as he led his donkey towards the front line to bring back another wounded soldier.)

Jacka was quickly promoted to corporal, then second lieutenant. After receiving his officer's commission he was posted to the Western Front. At Pozières, in August 1916, German troops overran a part of the line outside Jacka's dugout and rolled in a bomb, killing two men. Jacka charged up the steps firing and came upon a large number of enemy rounding up forty Australians as prisoners. Rallying the seven men of his platoon still able to fight, he led a charge against the enemy, some of whom immediately threw down their rifles. Furious hand-to-hand fighting erupted as the prisoners also turned on their captors. Fifty Germans were captured and the line was retaken. Journalist Charles Bean described the counterattack as 'the most dramatic and effective act of individual audacity in the history of the [Australian Imperial Force].' Jacka, who was gravely wounded and had to be sent to hospital in London, was awarded the Military Cross. Rejoining his unit, he was promoted to captain and appointed the 14th Battalion's intelligence officer.

On 8 April 1917 Jacka led a night reconnaissance party into no man's land near Bullecourt to inspect enemy defences before an Allied attack against the new German line. He penetrated the wire at two places, reported back, then went out again to supervise the laying of tapes to guide the infantry. A two-man German patrol saw the tapes, so Jacka drew his pistol. It malfunctioned, but he was still able to capture the Germans, a feat that added a Bar to his Military Cross.

Wounded by a sniper's bullet a few months later, Jacka spent several weeks out of the front line. In May 1918 he was badly gassed at Villers-Bretonneux and declared unfit for further combat.

'It was the most dramatic and effective act of individual audacity in the history of the Australian Imperial Force.'

Postscript

In Australia, Jacka became the face of Gallipoli and the Great War. Bean named him 'Australia's greatest frontline soldier' because of his fighting ability, bravery and tactical sense. Despite the adulation, however, Jacka was one of many Diggers who found it hard to fit back in to civilian life. There was no post-traumatic-stress counselling for the many returned soldiers who suffered from nightmares, depression or alcoholism.

The Man with a Donkey

There were many heroes apart from Albert Jacka at Gallipoli, but none caught the imagination of Australians more than Simpson and his donkey. Simpson of the 3rd Field Ambulance, a larrikin whose real name was John Simpson Kirkpatrick, became a hero soon after landing at Gallipoli when he broke ranks, captured a donkey from the Turkish defenders and began rescuing wounded soldiers from the front line high up on the cliffs above. Most stretcher-bearers worked in teams of two—running up to the front line, picking up a wounded soldier and bringing him back on a stretcher to the casualty stations down on the beach. But Simpson thought he could collect more wounded if he used the donkey to carry them. It was a good initiative, efficient because they were short of stretcher-bearers, and brave. It was also dangerous, because the Turks shot at any target. Simpson got away with his mercy mission for a few weeks but, inevitably, on 19 May, a Turkish marksman who saw Simpson leading the donkey up Shrapnel Gully, shot the enterprising ambulance man in the heart just 25 days after they landed.

Ironically, Simpson was not an Australian. He was an Englishman, a Geordie from South Shields, who had jumped ship in Australia and worked his way around the country with a swag. He enlisted when war broke out to get a free ride back to England, where he imagined the troops would be put ashore for training and where he may have jumped ship again. However, the convoy took a different route. Although fans of Simpson have tried to get him a posthumous Victoria Cross, the government has refused because he was acting without orders. Nevertheless, this independently minded maverick won the hearts of Australians back home, who built statues to Simpson around the nation—including a life-size 'man with a donkey' outside the Australian War Memorial in Canberra.

Things went well for Jacka at the start: when his ship reached Melbourne, he was greeted by the Governor-General and escorted to the Town Hall at the head of an eighty-five-car convoy to meet the men of the 14th Battalion. Demobilised in January 1920, he teamed up with two fellow veterans in an electrical-goods business. He married Frances Carey, a typist from his office, and they adopted a daughter. Jacka was elected to the St Kilda (Melbourne) Council and, after becoming mayor, concentrated on helping the unemployed. But his company collapsed during the Depression and his wife left him for a richer man.

Jacka died in 1932 of chronic kidney inflammation. At least 6000 people filed past his coffin when it lay in state in Melbourne's Anzac House, and 1000 returned soldiers led his funeral procession before thousands of onlookers. His pallbearers were eight Victoria Cross winners.

1917
SIR JOHN FORREST RIDES FIRST TRANSCONTINENTAL TRAIN

'**T**his great train should silence the people who still attack me because I led Western Australia into the Commonwealth,' Sir John Forrest said, lowering his great weight onto the seat and looking out the window at the flat landscape of the vast Nullarbor Plain speeding past.

'Why is that, dearest?' his wife, Margaret, asked absent-mindedly as she sketched the scene on a white artist's pad. 'How could a train stop those beastly secessionists attacking you?'

'Once this first transcontinental train arrives in Kalgoorlie, they will see with their own eyes that it was worth joining the Federation,' Forrest said, turning to look at his wife's sketch.

'Of course—no Federation, no east-west railway,' she replied, looking up momentarily from the landscape she was sketching for one of her water-colours.

'Exactly. If those wretched secessionists had had their way, we in the west would be a different nation. And if those gold miners at Kalgoorlie and Coolgardie had broken up our state to create their own colony, we wouldn't have got federal help to build a railway linking Perth to the eastern states. Forrest said. 'It's only because we joined up and I negotiated hard—it didn't hurt that I was Treasurer, of course—that I got the money to build this vital railway.'

'It's certainly a lot better than sailing backwards and forwards across that terrible Great Australian Bight,' Margaret said. 'I hated that, getting seasick all the time. This is so smooth and fast. Look at all those kangaroos, they look as if they're chasing the emus, don't they?'

'I led Western Australia into the Common-wealth.'

'The people of Kalgoorlie had better appreciate it,' Forrest said, still focused on politics. 'After all, it's cost £5.8 million and taken more than 3500 workers five years to build—almost as long as we've been fighting this wretched war.'

'Well, dear, it's yet another jewel in the crown of your achievements,' Margaret said.

'Joking aside, Margaret, I do see this great railway as the best thing I have done for Western Australia,' Forrest said, gazing at the scenery. 'When I think of walking across this wilderness with horses—we lost sixteen horses on my 1874 expedition alone.'

'If anybody has earned the right to ride across the continent in comfort it is you, dear, after all your exhausting exploration,' Margaret said, engrossed in her picture. 'I'm so glad you've lived long enough to see your dream realised—and they'd better give you a hero's welcome when we arrive.'

The towering political leader John Forrest, who persuaded the Western Australian colony to join the new nation in 1901, had also led a series of inland desert expeditions as a younger man searching for new grazing and the lost explorer Ludwig Leichhardt.

IT WAS A GREAT MOMENT because the Forrests were in the first train to travel on the Trans-Australia Railway that now spanned the continent of Australia. It was 22 October 1917, and they were en route from Adelaide to Perth. The train made the journey safely and in good time, and the giant of Western Australian politics, who had first won fame by crossing these deserts as an explorer, did get a warm welcome. From that day on, Australians were able to travel between east and west quickly and in comfort, and the nation was united as never before.

Historical background

John Forrest (1847–1918), born into a large Scots family near Bunbury, Western Australia, was a self-made man of action and a giant in colonial Australia—in stature as well as achievement. He was 183 centimetres tall, weighed 127 kilograms, and had a 137-cm waistline. Trained as a surveyor, he had opened up the Outback with a series of expeditions. He became the first man to travel from the west coast to the centre of the continent, and also searched in vain for the lost explorer Ludwig Leichhardt. After publishing books on his expeditions and observations of Western Australia, he served as Surveyor-General and in 1890

became Western Australia's first Premier—once Responsible Government was granted in 1890. He thereupon helped the colony join the Commonwealth, and was elected to the House of Representatives in Canberra. Between 1901 and 1918 he served as a minister in a range of portfolios. An arch-conservative, he supported conscription in the First World War. He was also the first Australian raised to the British peerage (as Baron Forrest of Bunbury).

The construction of the transcontinental railway, which spanned 1691 kilometres between Port Augusta and Kalgoorlie, was in its day a remarkable feat. Surveying work began in 1909, and the first sod was turned in Port Augusta on 14 September 1912, and in Kalgoorlie four months later. Labouring in the scorching heat of the treeless Nullarbor desert, the 3500 workers lived in moving tent cities, with most of the supplies shipped in on camels and horses. It was difficult and dangerous laying large sleepers and steel track, and operating heavy equipment: there were more than 900 accidents, and thirty men were killed. The track includes the longest straight stretch of rail in the world, 478 kilometres.

It was a great relief when the first steam train left Adelaide for Western Australia in 1917; it took 3500 workers five years to complete at enormous financial cost, and thirty workers died in the scorching desert heat.

Postscript

Although Forrest had dragged Western Australia into the Commonwealth and united the nation with the transcontinental railway, many of the 'sandgropers'—as Western Australians were called by people back east, who in turn were known as 't'othersiders'—resented being forced to join a nation conceived and administered thousands of kilometres away. Forrest had many enemies among the secessionists, who campaigned until 1933, when their last attempt to break out of the Federation was vetoed by the British.

Having become Baron Forrest, he set sail for Britain, where he hoped to receive treatment for cancer and perhaps also take his seat in the House of Lords. But he died at sea, less than a year after his great train ride. Although he was officially told of the peerage in February 1918, no letters patent were issued before his death, so the barony was never created.

1917
LIGHT HORSE CHARGE CAPTURES BEERSHEBA

'If Lawrence of Arabia can conquer Turkish outposts like Aqaba and capture so many Turkish prisoners with his Arab forces,' the commander of the Desert Mounted Corps, Lieutenant General Harry Chauvel, said, shifting in the saddle as he stared across the desert, 'our Australian Light Horse should be able to capture Beersheba, Bill.'

'Do you reckon we can, Harry?' replied Brigadier General William Grant, commander of the 4th Australian Light Horse Brigade, as he followed Chauvel's gaze towards Beersheba, in the far distance: 'Mind you, Lawrence knows the desert backwards—all the villages and their wells—and he can get the Arabs to do anything on their camels. And of course he speaks their language.'

'That may be so—but our blokes are the best horsemen in the desert,' Chauvel shot back. 'Anyway, General Allenby wants us to take Beersheba so we can advance further north, capture Jerusalem and expel the Turks from the Holy Land.'

'I agree it's a great idea, but there cannot have been many cavalry charges as ambitious as the one you're proposing, Harry. It will be a long, dusty and dangerous ride over miles of open desert,' Grant warned.

'Don't forget our 10th Light Horse successfully assaulted the enemy defences at Magdhaba last December,' Chauvel said.

'But wasn't that against a smaller force? Beersheba is so strategically important— with the only water for miles—that it will be stoutly defended by thousands of Turks and the German big guns,' the cautious Brigadier-General replied.

'But Bill, our horsemen are at their peak now and can ride long distances at full gallop. As you know, they're bushmen. Like me, they grew up on horses,'

The charge of the Australian Light Horse on 31 October 1917, which captured the Turkish stronghold of Beersheba, turned the tide of the war in the Middle East, and was history's last successful cavalry charge.

Chauvel said. 'And they are pretty handy with the bayonet as well, once they reach the trenches, especially the boys who were at Gallipoli.'

'What about the artillery?' Grant asked.

'I believe our Allied artillery can silence theirs,' Chauvel said, patting his horse's head, 'and our men will ride so fast they'll get to Beersheba before the batteries can lower their sights. Right now they are calibrated for long-range firing.'

'And how will we get across the trenches surrounding Beersheba?' Grant asked.

'Bill, our men are country blokes used to jumping wombat holes—they'll just jump the blooming trenches,' Chauvel reassured his earnest subordinate, 'and they'll also jump in with bayonets to fight the Turks in the trenches hand to hand.'

'How will you get through the barbed wire in front of the town?' Grant asked, looking down as Chauvel dismounted to stretch his limbs.

'We'll attack from the left flank, where our observers tell us there is no wire. So Bill, what do you think? Can we take Beersheba?' Chauvel said.

'You've convinced me, Harry. But what's the urgency?'

'It's days since our horses have had a decent drink. We've got to take those wells by nightfall before they start to die of thirst. And we don't want any Turkish reinforcements sneaking in overnight, either,' Chauvel explained.

'How many of my 4th Brigade's regiments will you use?' asked Grant, giving way at last.

'Two, the 4th and the 12th,' Chauvel said. 'We'll follow them with the 11th Regiment and the 5th Mounted Brigade.'

'Well, I'll start briefing my men, then,' Grant said, turning his horse towards headquarters.

'Tell your men we must take Beersheba at all costs,' Chauvel called, remounting and urging his horse in the direction of his tent. 'If we do, our charge will go down in history—and I want you to give the order to charge, Bill!'

Grant briefed the regimental commanders, who assembled their men behind rising ground seven kilometres south-east of Beersheba. They all knew the fate of this battle—and perhaps the entire Middle East campaign—depended on them. Grant gave the order and the Light Horse leapt into action, starting at the trot, spreading out to five-metre intervals, then breaking into a gallop by the time they reached the top of the rise. They galloped like a wide, breaking wave over the ridge and down the gentle slope towards the Turkish trenches in front of the town.

As soon as the surprised Turks saw the Australians, their artillery opened fire, sending shells high into the air. But the Light Horsemen rode like the legendary Man from Snowy River, 'down the mountain like a torrent in its bed', and the gunners could not adjust their sights fast enough to keep up with them. Even the Turkish machine-gunners failed to stop this brown and khaki wave, because British batteries shelled them before they could do much damage. The Turkish infantry in the trenches then opened fire with their rifles, but in a matter of seconds the first Australians had reached the outer trenches and jumped over them, as Chauvel said they would.

Some of the Australians dismounted to attack the Turks from behind. Others rode straight through to the town centre to secure the wells. When his horse was wounded by Turks as he approached a trench, one officer, Major Cuthbert Fetherstonhaugh of Coonamble, drew his revolver and shot first his suffering horse and then the enemy soldiers in the trench. Some horsemen in the first wave captured whole trenches full of Turks single-handed. Overpowered and shocked, the Turkish garrison 'threw up their hands quick smart', as one Light Horse trooper reported.

'Our men are country blokes and used to jumping wombat holes they'll just jump the blooming trenches.'

Some country boys who enlisted in the Australian Light Horse, such as Troopers Gerald Digby and Colin Bull, were so keen to enlist they put their ages up to meet the minimum age requirement of eighteen.

IT WAS A GREAT MOMENT because it was one of the greatest cavalry charges in history, and the last successful one. It was also the first time the Light Horse had charged armed only with rifles and bayonets. Normally mounted infantry rather than full cavalry, they were not equipped with swords like British cavalrymen. It was 31 October 1917, and the men of the 4th and 12th Regiments had captured Beersheba—and its vital wells, where, after thirty dry hours, their horses had a well-earned drink. They lost only thirty-one men killed and thirty-six wounded. And they had charged just in time: the Turks and their German masters, preparing for the worst, were about to poison and blow up all the wells before retreating to a safer position. The Australians had not only won the day and the water but broken through the front line of the Turkish eastern defences, which the enemy never managed to repair.

Historical background

Lieutenant General Sir Harry Chauvel was the first Australian to achieve that rank in the First World War. An Army officer, he had served with distinction in the South African (Boer) War as a Major in the 1st Queensland Mounted Infantry, after which he was decorated. From 1901 he helped establish the

Australian Army and the Royal Military College at Duntroon. He commanded the 1st Light Horse Brigade at Gallipoli and, from 1916, the Anzac Mounted Division in actions at the Suez Canal, Romani, Rafa and Magdhaba. After these successes he was given command of the Desert Mounted Corps, becoming the first Australian to lead such a large body of troops.

At Beersheba, Chauvel attacked from the east at sunset, seizing all but two of the wells intact. The capture of Beersheba and of Gaza the following month unlocked the Turkish position in southern Palestine. After Jerusalem was taken in December, the Allies invaded Syria and Lebanon and finally seized Damascus. This too was thanks largely to the Australian Light Horse—even though Lawrence of Arabia claimed the credit, as Harry Chauvel had predicted.

After Beersheba, Chauvel went from strength to strength, commanding the Light Horse at Megiddo in one of the most completely successful operations of the war, and at Damascus and Aleppo before the war in the Middle East theatre came to an end. In the five weeks since the opening of the final offensive, the divisions of the Desert Mounted Corps had advanced from 480 to 800 kilometres, taking more than 78,000 prisoners.

Returning to Australia, he became Chief of the General Staff and in 1929 was made a General, the first Australian to attain that rank. His retirement the following April was almost a national occasion.

Brigadier General William Grant, the commander of the 4th Australian Light Horse Brigade, gave the order for the legendary charge.

Postscript

Beersheba helped turn the tide of war in the Middle East, effectively neutralising the Turkish cavalry and pushing the Turks back to Damascus, which the Australians reached ahead of Lawrence. If it was galling to see Lawrence hailed for this feat, worse was to come. At the end of the Middle East campaign, military authorities claimed they could not transport the Light Horse mounts back to Australia, so the men had to either give their horses away or shoot them. This was a blow not only to the horsemen, but to the senior officer who had tended their horses during the campaign—none other than the bush poet A.B. 'Banjo' Paterson.

Despite Chauvel's victories at Beersheba and elsewhere, some British officers slighted him as a mere colonial. He was criticised for a lack of resolve in some battles, but this reflected his unwillingness to accept heavy casualties for prizes he did not value. Unlike the British officers, he also joined his men in battle and in the field lived simply, sleeping in his greatcoat on the sand when his force was on the move.

Some of Chauvel's men damaged the reputation of the Australian Light Horse in December 1918 when, just after the end of the war, they reputedly massacred locals in an Arab village known as Surafend. The war-weary Australian and New Zealand men of the Light Horse, who were camped on the Philistine Plain close to the Mediterranean Sea, had become increasingly irritated by local Arabs stealing from their camp while they waited to return to Australia. When an Arab thief shot dead a New Zealander who had caught the thief in the act, a large number of New Zealanders, accompanied by Australians, retaliated by storming the thief's village, where they killed or wounded as many Arabs as they could and set fire to their houses before also taking out their anger on a nearby Bedouin camp. Their Commander-in-Chief, General Allenby, condemned their brutality and accused them of being 'a bunch of murderers'. So-called 'official inquiries' were conducted into the incident, but no concrete details were published and no charges were ever laid.

Despite this black mark, the Light Horse charge at Beersheba remains unrivalled. Although Polish horsemen charged advancing German tanks and Italians charged the Russians in the Second World War, both failed, making this history's last successful cavalry charge.

1918
GENERAL MONASH WINS TURNING-POINT BATTLE OF HAMEL

'I do not care what the British say,' Lieutenant General John Monash said, lighting another cigarette as he stared at his campaign map by candlelight in a French chateau on the Western Front. 'I know we can turn the tide against the Germans if we only start attacking instead of defending our front line—it's high time we took the offensive.'

'But the British orders are to continue defending our trenches,' his chief of staff, Brigadier General Thomas Blamey, cautioned as he placed a fresh candle on the map where the village of Hamel was marked. 'You cannot defy those orders.'

'Apart from being commander of the Australian Army Corps, I am an engineer in civilian life,' Monash said. 'I know we now have the technology to defeat the Germans—if only we could use it. If I deploy the new fighter planes, latest Mark V tanks and heavy artillery in a coordinated strike ahead of the infantry advance, I can capture this village with minimal infantry casualties,' he added, pointing at a spot on the map.

'A promising strategy, Sir, but why pick Le Hamel?' Blamey asked.

'Because German prisoners I interviewed recently confirm my belief that it is the enemy's weakest link,' Monash said, pacing around the map table and puffing impatiently at his cigarette. 'They are short of men and supplies . . . it should be an easy target.'

'But do we have enough soldiers ourselves to attack Hamel?'

'We will have more than enough if the American generals let me give some of their fresh troops real battle experience,' Monash said.

Although General John Monash was the first Allied commander to harness the technological resources to win breakthrough battles like Hamel, and was knighted in the field by King George V, he was not fully accepted by Australian peers because he was a civilian soldier and Jewish.

'Surely American generals would never let an Australian lead untested troops into their first battle,' Blamey said.

'Why do you think I've chosen July 4 for the battle?' Monash asked with a wry smile. 'We've already discussed using several hundred Americans in the attack. I'm just waiting for confirmation.'

Blamey turned back to the map. 'So how long do you think the battle will take?'

'Ninety minutes, according to the plan I have developed,' the commander said, tossing his cigarette butt into an empty shell case.

'What about casualties?' Blamey dared to ask.

'Not as bad as all these defensive battles we've been fighting,' Monash said. 'You know I hate to suffer casualties unnecessarily. If I attack the Germans now, I can achieve the first breakthrough. So pray that High Command approves my plan.'

Monash soon got the go-ahead—and US approval to use four companies of the American soldiers training with the Australians. After a few hours' sleep, he finalised preparations and ordered his troops into position.

IT WAS A GREAT MOMENT because the battle-hardened Australian troops broke through the German lines and easily captured the German-occupied village of Le Hamel. Although a limited action, it was the first successful offensive of 1918 and substantially altered the Allies' defensive mindset. The battle went largely according to the civil engineer's detailed plan. Instead of sending in foot soldiers after a preliminary artillery bombardment, as the British usually did, Monash kept up a bombardment of the kind the Germans took as routine while bringing up heavy artillery. This was held back until the day of the attack to avoid forewarning the enemy. Noisy bomber aircraft helped cover the sound of tank movements, and later Australian Flying Corps aircraft dropped ammunition to forward troop positions by parachute—the first use of such tactics. The new tanks were a great success, smashing down barbed wire and protecting the infantry following closely behind. The battle was over in ninety-three minutes.

1918

Ever since the big German offensive at the start of 1918, British commanders had ordered Allied forces to defend their positions. Monash introduced a new kind of 'all-arms' warfare that was studied by the German military in preparing its Blitzkrieg tactics of the Second World War. British Great War commanders also sent copies of his orders to other generals as a blueprint for future battles. An Australian had arrived as a world-class military commander.

Historical background

John Monash (1865–1931) was born in Melbourne to Prussian Jewish parents, who brought him up to speak German as well as English. In 1874 the family moved to Jerilderie to manage a general store. Monash later claimed that Ned Kelly had given him a shilling to mind his horse during the Kelly gang's raid on the local bank in 1879. A star student, Monash graduated from Melbourne University as an engineer. He served as an officer in the militia, then became a full-time Army officer when war was declared in 1914. He landed at Gallipoli on the first day, and led troops in the field from then to the end of the war. Married with children, he kept a mistress during the war.

Australian troops were sent to the Western Front—a line of trenches snaking through France and Belgium—in April 1916. They fought in many major battles,

The Germans never stood a chance at Hamel; General John Monash used the latest planes, modern tanks and heavy artillery in an all-encompassing attack that caught the defenders by surprise, defeating them in ninety-three minutes.

159

including Fromelles, Pozières, Messines, Menin Road, Polygon Wood and Passchendaele. In 1918, Monash was appointed Commander-in-Chief of the Australian Army Corps, which by the time of Hamel comprised five divisions—about 100,000 men.

The Australians were well equipped to win at Le Hamel, as for the previous three years they had fought some of the toughest battles on the Western Front. They and the Americans—whose country had joined the war only in 1917—inflicted 2000 casualties on the Germans and captured 1500 prisoners, at the cost of 1062 Australian and 176 American casualties.

Monash was unimpressed with British battle tactics on the Western Front. At Hamel he was able to combine modern aircraft for reconnaissance and ammunition drops; the relatively new tanks, to blaze a trail for the infantry, protect the soldiers and bring back the wounded; and the latest heavy artillery. He also made sure his infantry, both the Australian and American, were well fed and rested before they went into battle. Visiting the battlefields, Prime Minister Billy Hughes praised Monash for being so careful with the lives of his troops. Monash's conduct of the battle of Hamel became a template that helped the Australians—ten per cent of the total Allied force—capture about twenty-five per cent of all the German territory, prisoners, arms and ammunition taken by the Allies.

> 'I hate the business of war, the horror of it, the waste, the destruction, and the inefficiency.'

Postscript

Although US commanders had asked Monash to lead some of their troops into their first major battle of the war, General John Pershing got cold feet when he realised the scale of the assault and ordered Monash to withdraw them. Monash refused, because by then American soldiers were right up in front-line trenches and the Germans would have seen them retreating. So they fought with the Australians and acquitted themselves well.

King George V was so impressed with Monash after Le Hamel and the battle of Amiens that he drove onto the battlefield and knighted him—the first time a monarch had knighted a warrior in the field for more than a century, and the last time. Yet Australia's most successful warrior wrote in his memoirs: 'I hate the business of war, the horror of it, the waste, the destruction, and the inefficiency ... my only consolation has been the sense of faithfully doing my duty to my country.'

General John Monash took newly arrived American troops into their first battle at Hamel on their Independence Day, 4 July 1918, ordering his Australian soldiers to show 'the Yanks' how to fight in the trenches.

Charles Bean and Keith Murdoch, Australia's two best-known war correspondents, disliked Monash, and the Melbourne Club declined to admit him as a member because he was Jewish. Monash was offered the position of Governor-General on the condition that he give up his mistress, but he refused. Britain's wartime Prime Minister, Sir Lloyd George, said Monash was 'the most resourceful General in the whole of the British Army', and the British historian A.J.P. Taylor described him as 'the only General of creative originality produced in the First World War'.

The final assessment of Monash came at his funeral in 1931, when more than 100,000 former servicemen (the equivalent of five army Divisions) turned out to say goodbye to a leader who had always tried to protect the lives of his men.

1919
SMITH BROTHERS FLY FROM ENGLAND TO AUSTRALIA

'I reckon we're in the lead now, Keith, we haven't seen Poulet's plane or any other contenders for days,' Captain Ross Smith shouted over the roar of the Vickers Vimy bomber, looking away from the instruments to the Indonesian islands far below.

'Too right. Out of five, maybe six planes eligible for the prize, we must have the best chance,' said the pilot's brother, Lieutenant Keith Smith. He took his eyes off the map to search the skies around them.

'So that £10,000 could be ours,' Ross said, giving his brother the thumbs-up. 'That would be bonza. But first we've got to get across this Arafura Sea—our biggest water crossing so far.'

'I don't know what happened to those Frenchmen, Poulet and Benoist, but they were my main worry. Even if they won't qualify for the prize, I didn't want them to beat us,' his brother Keith replied.

'We haven't seem them since Burma, when they took off heading for Rangoon,' Ross said. 'But I reckon we are well ahead of them anyway.'

'They must be keen—after all, they know only Aussies can take the money,' Keith said, checking the course again. 'Our Prime Minister Billy Hughes wouldn't put up a prize for anyone else.'

'I wonder how the other war vets are going. You know, Ray Parer and John McIntosh. Wonder if they'll ever get that Airco DH9 off the ground.'

Keith laughed. 'They'd have to be way behind us, Ross.'

'Pity old Charles Kingsford Smith wasn't allowed to compete, just because he can't navigate well enough,' Ross said, tightening his leather helmet against the cold.

'Keep listening. We don't want any unplanned landings in the drink.'

During the first flight from England to Australia the Smith brothers (in uniform immediately to the right of the two white-suited dignitaries in the centre), had many receptions as locals inspected their Vickers Vimy aircraft and met the two heroes and their engineers (standing to the left of the two white-suited dignitaries.)

'It was bad enough cutting Smithy out, but what about Bert Hinkler?' his brother said. 'Fancy being dropped just because he wanted to fly solo. Strewth, what a loner he must be.'

'Terrible that both Lieutenants Douglas and Ross were killed back at Hounslow at the start of their flight, wasn't it?' Ross said, shaking his head. 'It's a dangerous business, this—as we've proved on this blooming flight ourselves. It's just a miracle we got through all that bad weather from England to Cairo.'

'Not to mention having to fly blind up to 11,000 feet through those thick clouds to cross the mountains in Burma.' Keith replied, turning back to the engineers. 'That was our worst moment.'

'Well, both engines seem to be going strong, don't they, Jimmy?' Sergeant Wally Shiers said as he checked his Rolls-Royce technical manual.

'So far, so good—touch wood,' his fellow engineer Sergeant Jim Bennett replied, tapping a wooden stringer with a grin. 'But keep listening. We don't want any unplanned landings in the drink—even though we've got our escape kit tied to the tail.'

'Well Alcock and Brown got right across the North Atlantic in one of these Vimys,' Ross said. 'So these Rolls-Royce engines should get us there. Righto, navigator, how far are we from Darwin now?' He turned to his brother, who was peering through the windscreen to the south-east.

'Not long now. I think that's Bathurst Island lighthouse on the horizon, so we'll certainly make it by mid-afternoon. That will put us well within the thirty-day limit. It's only Day 27 now,' Keith said excitedly.

'Well, crew, fingers crossed for this last stretch,' Ross said, scanning the control panel instruments yet again, 'For once it looks like the weather is on our side. Let's hope luck is too.'

IT WAS A GREAT MOMENT because these air aces did land ahead of their rivals, becoming the first men ever to fly from England to Australia. They landed in Darwin at 3 p.m. on 10 December 1919, well before the cut-off date of 13 December 1920. The trip had taken only 124 hours' flying time. The four airmen shared the £10,000 between them. Suddenly, thanks to them, the world had shrunk for Australians.

Despite severe storms, the Smith brothers covered more than 11,300 miles (18,200 kilometres) on board their open-cockpit Vickers Vimy in just twenty-seven days and twenty hours—well under the thirty-day time limit set by the government.

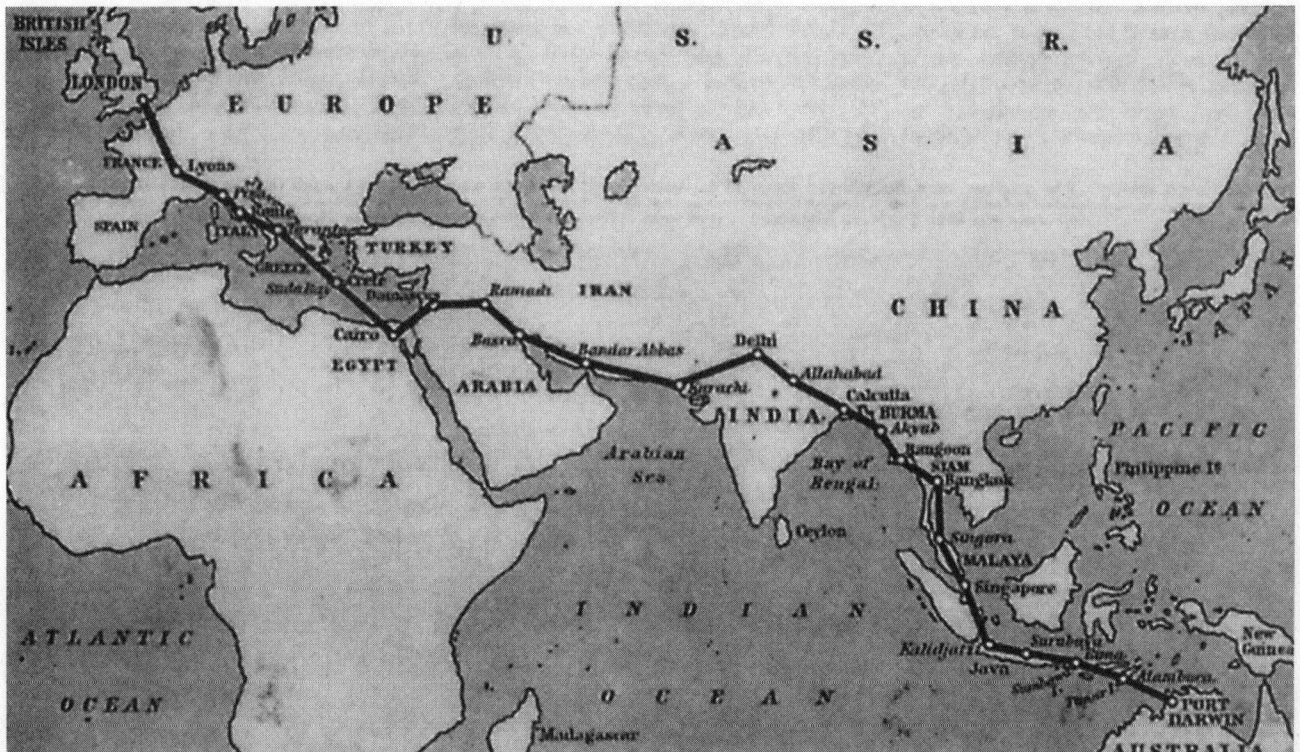

Historical background

The First Fleet in 1788 had taken eight months to reach Australia. The Smiths' 11,300-mile (18,200 kilometres) journey, including stops, took twenty-seven days, twenty hours. Ross and Keith Smith, both from South Australia, were knighted, and Shiers and Bennett were awarded bars to their Air Force Medals. Knowledgeable people now speculated that, with relays of crews and planes, the trip from England to Australia could be reduced to five days despite the fact that the second-place getters—Parer and McIntosh—took 206 days. Within a couple of years Qantas (Queensland and Northern Territory Air Service) was established for domestic flights, and by the early 1930s there was a regular airmail service between Australia and England. But it would be another quarter-century before a regular passenger service began on that route.

Ross Smith (1892–1922) served in the 3rd Light Horse Regiment at Gallipoli before joining the Australian Flying Corps—he became the personal pilot of Lawrence of Arabia. He won the Military Cross, and the Distinguished Flying Cross three times. He was also among the first group of aviators to fly from Cairo to Calcutta in 1919. His brother, Keith (1890–1955), who had been a combat instructor with the Australian Flying Corps during the war, agreed to be Ross's navigator.

Prime Minister Billy Hughes, seeing the promise aviation held for Australia, sponsored the England to Australia race, offering £10,000 to the first Australian crew to fly the 11,300 miles in thirty days or less before the end of 1920. The safest and most logical route was a land hop across Asia to Darwin.

Despite having no chance of taking the prize money, French pilot Etienne Poulet and his mechanic, Jean Benoist, were determined to win the race. Theirs was the first plane to take off, almost a month before the Smiths got under way in their Vickers bomber. Poulet had been grounded in Persia with engine trouble, but the Smiths battled through cloud cover all the way to Cairo. They had nearly frozen to death in their open cockpit over France and almost crashed over the Apennines in Italy. When they reached Delhi, they learned that Poulet had left earlier the same day, but they caught up to him in Burma. Forced to use paddocks as airstrips, they kept getting bogged, and Bennett had to climb down to the tail in mid-air to add enough weight for them to land on the Singapore racecourse. Expecting to crash into the Arafura Sea, they asked HMAS *Sydney* to patrol below and tied emergency rations to the plane's tail, which would have sunk last. But they made it to Darwin, and Frank Hurley—who had made *The Home of the Blizzard* with Douglas Mawson, climbed on board for the last leg to Sydney and filmed their epic arrival.

Several months later Poulet and Benoist, who had been having mechanical problems, crash-landed and finally abandoned their attempt. Parer and McIntosh were the only other team to make it to Australia, and Parer was henceforth known as 'Battling Ray'.

Postscript

Ross Smith and engineer Bennett were killed while testing a Vickers Viking amphibian aircraft in 1922; Smith was given a state funeral. Charles Kingsford Smith and Bert Hinkler would also die in plane crashes in the years to come. As Ross Smith had always said, flying was a dangerous business. Less than eighty years after the Smiths' trip, an aircraft flew from London to Sydney non-stop in less than twenty-four hours.

1921
WOMEN BREAK NEW GROUND AS EDITH COWAN ENTERS PARLIAMENT

'You won't do it, Mum—you'll never beat Mr Draper,' Dircksey said, placing a ladder against a telegraph pole in West Perth. 'You are a woman—and, if you don't mind my saying it, unmistakably so!'

'The electorate will not be voting for me as a woman,' Edith Cowan answered, securing the ladder against the pole. 'They'll be voting for the political ideals I represent.'

'Well, I may be young, but I do know T.P. Draper is the state Attorney-General!' Dircksey said, holding the ladder steady as her mother started to climb the rungs.

'I have already been officially endorsed by the Nationalists as the candidate for West Perth, so I have the party behind me,' Cowan said, reaching the top of the ladder.

'Nationalist or no Nationalist, you're still a female,' Dircksey said.

'And not the only one standing for election—there are five of us now,' Cowan called down. 'Pass up one of my campaign posters.'

'You think five will confer strength in numbers?' Dircksey asked, handing up a rolled poster.

'Don't forget that women are now a majority of voters in this electorate,' Cowan retorted. 'They care about law and order, and education, and child welfare—and women's rights. We are standing because we think these are things men sometimes need to be reminded about. Hammer, please.'

1921

'But the men in Parliament won't listen to a woman Member,' Dircksey said, passing up the hammer. 'They'll just see it as nagging. Anyway, no woman has even been elected to Parliament—think about that, Mum.'

'Well, it's about time. It's nearly twenty years since Catherine Spence over in South Australia persuaded the federal politicians to let women vote and serve in Parliament,' Cowan said. 'And now our state Parliament has done the same. Please pass me a nail.'

'But do you really think a woman could win a seat in the government of Sir James Mitchell?'

'I'm certainly not the first to try. Over in Victoria, Vida Goldstein stood for Parliament back in 1903, well before the war,' Cowan said.

'But she was defeated,' Dircksey warned, as her mother banged in the first nail.

'She got more than 50,000 votes, though!' Cowan said. 'Another nail please. Anyway, somebody has to stand up for issues like migrant welfare, and child health and other things men don't much care about.' She hammered away. 'I'm also convinced of the need for motherhood endowment and a housewives' union—and I have a proven record of diligent community service. And we also need sex education in our state schools.'

'Goodness, Mum! Here's the last nail, and I'll hold the ladder steady as you come back down. All I can say is, you'll have your hands full if by some miracle you are elected.'

The first woman elected to any parliament in Australia, the passionate social reformer Edith Cowan overcame a disastrous childhood when her mother died in childbirth and her father was hanged for murdering his second wife.

IT WAS A GREAT MOMENT because Edith Dircksey Cowan did become the the Member for West Perth in the state Legislative Assembly—and the first woman elected to any parliament in Australia. It took a while for others to follow her, but within thirty years Enid Lyons was elected to Federal Parliament and some sixty years after that, Anna Bligh was elected Premier of Queensland in her own right (Joan Kirner and Carmen Lawrence had been Premiers in Victoria and Western Australia after taking over their party's leadership while it was in government) and from 2007 Julia Gillard became Deputy (and, at times, Acting) Prime Minister of Australia.

Australian women who had campaigned successfully for political equality from the late nineteenth century won the right to vote in federal elections in 1902, fielded a candidate in 1903 and succeeded in getting their first female politician, Edith Cowan, elected in 1921.

Historical background

Edith Cowan's mother, a teacher, died in childbirth and her father, a pastoralist, was hanged for murdering his second wife. Those experiences left her determined to improve conditions for others, especially women and children. She was staunchly supported by her husband, James Cowan, a Perth police magistrate who had served as registrar of Western Australia's Supreme Court, and by her five children, including Dircksey, who would also enter public life.

Cowan was amply qualified for parliamentary service at a time when most Members of the Legislative Assembly were elected on the basis of social and political connections rather than practical merit. She had served the North Fremantle Board of Education, the Ministering Children's League, and the House of Mercy and been a founding member of the Children's Protection Society. She had pioneered day nurseries, helped establish the Children's Court, and served on its bench as well as being a Justice of the Peace. She helped set up the Women's

Service Guild, King Edward Memorial Hospital for Women and Western Australia's National Council of Women, of which she became president. By the time she entered state Parliament she had also travelled widely in Britain and Europe and been admitted to the Order of the British Empire for her social work during the First World War.

In Parliament, she worked tirelessly to improve the lot of women, introducing a bill that allowed women to break through another barrier and practise law.

Postscript

Despite her track record as a social reformer and an MLA, Edith Cowan was defeated at the next election. The businessmen of West Perth ganged up against her and her female supporters and put their money behind the strongest male candidate they could field, Thomas Davy. Cowan lost none of her activist zeal and helped plan the state's centennial celebrations in 1929. She died in 1932 aged seventy-one. Friends and admirers erected a clock tower at the gates of King's Park in Perth to salute 'one of Australia's greatest women'; her portrait appears on the reverse of the $50 note.

'Somebody has to stand up for issues like migrant welfare, and child health and other things men don't much care about.'

1927

DAME NELLIE MELBA HELPS OPEN NATION'S NEW PARLIAMENT

'**P**rime Minister, I do not want anybody joining in when I sing,' Dame Nellie Melba said emphatically, looking around the stage, which was lavishly set for the opening of Parliament the following day. 'There is nothing worse than having untrained, out-of-tune voices spoiling the performance—is that clear?'

'Absolutely, Dame Nellie,' Prime Minister Stanley Bruce said, rather taken aback: usually all present joined in when 'God Save the King' was sung. But, nodding meekly, he added: 'We're very lucky to have our celebrated diva back from England, so it will be as you ask.'

He turned to his private secretary at the edge of the stage: 'Please make a note to inform all the guests of Dame Nellie's request.'

'No! That will not suffice, Prime Minister. I want everyone advised in writing.'

'But the program is printed,' Bruce said, holding up a copy.

'Then please type up a special notice and hand it to the guests on arrival,' Melba said.

'Very well,' Bruce agreed, and turned again to his aide. 'See that a notice demanding silence is prepared by tomorrow.'

'And Prime Minister, make sure your notice confirms that I will sing both "God Save the King" and "Land of Hope and Glory".'

'The program already confirms your performance of both, in the presence of the Duke and Duchess of York,' Bruce said, bending to flick a spot off his gleaming white spats.

'The Duke of York . . . opened the Parliament, unlocking the huge doors with a large gold key.'

'And of course we must all address their Royal Highnesses as "Your Royal Highness", just as their loyal subjects do back home in England,' Dame Nellie said.

'We shall, Dame Nellie, and I wish you the best of British luck for tomorrow's performance.'

'And to you, too, Prime Minister. I am pleased you will be reading the Proclamation from His Royal Highness King George V,' she added, 'because you are the only politician out here who speaks the King's English.'

'Apparently so, Dame Nellie,' Bruce said, 'but my humble efforts will pale beside your renditions.'

'Most gracious of you, Prime Minister. Now, if you would kindly leave, I wish to rehearse once more for tomorrow,' Melba said, moving towards centre stage.

Taking his cue, Bruce spun on his heels and disappeared with his aide down the steps as the first notes of the national anthem rang out.

Having performed around the world since her youth, the prima donna Dame Nellie Melba was at the peak of her career when she sang at the opening of Federal Parliament, one of her last big public performances.

IT WAS A GREAT MOMENT because the next day, true to form, Dame Nellie Melba embellished the opening of the new Federal Parliament in Canberra with her renowned voice. The Duke of York also literally opened the Parliament, unlocking the huge doors with a large gold key. In the speeches that followed, the Duke said King George V wished the nation well and hoped it would advance and be prosperous, and the Prime Minister said the new Parliamentary building was timely, since Australia had now developed a national consciousness. But it was the soaring soprano voice of Australia's greatest opera singer that was best remembered by the guests.

Historical background

The nation had been waiting for its new Parliament House ever since the Commonwealth was proclaimed in 1901. The Federal Parliament met in the meantime in the Colonial Parliament building in Melbourne, at the top of Bourke Street.

It had also taken many years to select a site suitable for the national capital, which—owing to fierce rivalry between Melbourne and Sydney—the Constitution

Thousands of spectators came to watch the Duke of York, later George VI, open the new Federal Parliament buildings in Canberra on 9 May 1927, then inspect a 2000-strong guard of honour and review an air force fly-past.

stipulated had to be more than 100 miles (160 kilometres) from Sydney. Canberra was eventually chosen—one reason being that its inland location would protect it from naval bombardment, and the Federal Capital Territory (renamed the Australian Capital Territory in 1938) came into being in 1911.

The foundation stone was laid two years later for what was intended to be a provisional Parliament House—expected to serve the purpose for about fifty years. It was officially opened on 9 May 1927 by the Duke of York, later George VI, and the Duchess of York, later Elizabeth, the Queen Mother. The Duke inspected a 2000-strong guard of honour and reviewed an Air Force fly-past. Prime Minister Stanley Bruce, a Toorak-born businessman who now led a coalition Nationalist–Country Party Government, had played a key role in transferring the Federal Parliament to Canberra and wanted to be remembered for the achievement.

Dame Nellie Melba was by then a world-renowned prima donna, so she could afford to call the shots. She was the world's finest coloratura soprano, with a voice of rare purity that spanned two and a half octaves and enabled her to command a huge repertoire of twenty-five operas. Her popularity was unprecedented, and attendances at her Australian performances broke all records.

After war broke out in 1914, Melba had devoted herself to raising money for war charities, singing unpaid at dozens of patriotic concerts. She raised more than £100,000 and was created a Dame of the British Empire.

In 1924 she gave a farewell performance that proved to be only the first of many. In some of her later 'farewells' Melba, aged sixty-three, sang in *La Bohème*,

Faust and *Otello* alongside much younger performers. 'It was really wonderful to see how all classes were swept up in the wave of enthusiasm,' she said. 'People cheerfully waited in the streets for hours to obtain seats.' A gala charity matinée of *La Bohème* at Her Majesty's in Melbourne was broadcast live to an estimated audience of 150,000.

Melba's final 'farewell' tour, in 1927 included concerts in small town halls to raise funds for local charities. Melba was paid £3000 a week, though she had to cancel several performances owing to illness. She sang on the operatic stage for the last time in October 1928, in a program in Adelaide that combined parts of *La Bohème* and *Otello*. That was it for the great diva, who had always said: 'I must sing or I will die.' She died just over a year later.

Her funeral was one of the biggest ever seen in Australia. Mourners remembered her farewell message: 'I have done my best. For all that Australia has done for me, for all the beauty she has shown me, for all the love she has offered, I wish to say "thank you" from the bottom of my heart.' Her grave in Lilydale, Victoria, bears the inscription '*Addio senza rancor*' (farewell without bitterness), a line from her most famous role, that of Mimi in her beloved *La Bohème*.

Postscript

Grand though it was, the opening of the Australian Parliament was not open to all the King's subjects. An Aboriginal visitor, King Billy, was turned back and led away by police on the ground that he was 'inadequately dressed'.

A bust of Melba graces the foyer of the Royal Opera House in Covent Garden, but there is no equivalent monument to her in Australia. There are collections of Melba memorabilia in the Victorian Arts Centre in Melbourne and at the Lilydale and District Historical Society Museum, but no significant national tribute. Today her name is most commonly spoken by people ordering *pêche Melba*—a dessert based on peaches and ice-cream. She deserves a better memorial: not only did she give Australia one of its greatest historical moments, but she was very likely the first Australian to be world famous *as* an Australian.

The dapper Stanley Bruce, who was determined to be remembered as the prime minister who transferred Federal Parliament from Melbourne to Canberra, invited Dame Nellie Melba to sing at the opening because he wanted the world's best opera singer to embellish the event.

1930

MELBOURNE CUP WONDER HORSE PHAR LAP WINS AUSTRALIAN HEARTS

'Now, Jim, the race starts in an hour and the float's ready, so we'll make a dash for it,' Phar Lap's trainer, Harry Telford, whispered into the jockey's ear in the quiet of the stables at their secret hideaway.

'What about the gunmen?' Jim Pike asked, standing nervously beside the horse known as Bobby and, stroking his long neck for comfort.

'Those thugs don't know where we are, lad, and I've got armed guards out the front of these stables who will travel with the float to Flemington,' Telford said, patting the jockey on the back. 'Just remember, Jim, this is the ride of your life—you've got to push him hard.'

'Yes, Mr Telford,' Pike said with a nod. 'I'll do me best, but Bobby's nerves may still be a bit rattled by the shooting.'

'Don't worry, son. Now that we've escaped that bookie's gunman we can do anything,' Telford said, grabbing the jockey by both shoulders and staring into his worried face. 'Forget it, Jim, will you? The bookmakers just had to try something when they realised "the people's horse" was gunna be such a favourite— probably about 11-8 on. They'll lose an awful lot of money if he wins, so they hired an assassin. But he missed, didn't he?'

'Yes, Mr Telford,' Pike said with a sigh.

'Money's tight in this Depression, Jim,' Telford said. 'Never forget I'm training this horse for nothing. That tight-arsed Yank Davis refused to pay me, so the only hope I have is to get some of the winnings.'

'Well, I'm doing me best, Mr Telford,' Pike said, stroking Phar Lap's neck. 'I'll try and win for ya.'

Although the champion Phar Lap emerged as the darling of Australian race-goers after winning 'a rich purse' at the 1930 Melbourne Cup, he was actually from New Zealand and was owned by an American, who bought the wonder horse for just 160 guineas.

'I know you will, son . . . Bloody Davis forgets my brother bought this beauty for just 160 guineas, 30 less than Davis expected him to sell for—so I deserve a big win,' Telford said, moving towards the stable door. 'And not just me. The whole of Melbourne's betting their hard-earned dough on Phar Lap, so make sure you win, Jim.'

'But Mr Telford—you know Phar Lap is going to be handicapped with one of the top weights ever for the Cup, nine stone twelve,' Pike said as he tightened his grip on the reins and led the horse towards the open door and the waiting float.

'Yes, Jim, but he's got a very big heart,' Telford said, dropping the float's ramp to let Phar Lap walk in.

'I'll just say, Mr Telford,' Pike said, leading the horse up, 'that if any horse can win against such odds, I know in me bones it's our Bobby.'

'That's the spirit, boy,' Telford said, closing the float on Phar Lap. 'Now let's go and make some history.'

IT WAS A GREAT MOMENT because—against heavy odds—the horse that had gripped Australian hearts like none before or since won the 1930 Melbourne Cup. It was, of course, the first Tuesday in November, the 5th. Telford and Pike got the horse safely to Flemington, where the big-hearted wonder horse won by four lengths—even though many people had tried to stop him. Bookmakers' assassins had shot at him; gangsters had threatened his minders; he had been hidden until an hour before the race and then rushed to the start, where armed police guarded the barriers; and the handicappers hit him with a big weight penalty for his successes in the Spring Carnival—but he still won.

Amid the hardships of the Great Depression, with about a quarter of the workforce unemployed, Phar Lap's victory was a great tonic for the public. Small-time punters who backed him won some badly needed money. Australians love a winner, and Phar Lap was almost unbeatable. Between 1930 and 1932 he won thirty-two of his thirty-five races.

Historical background

Telford's brother, Hugh, had bought Phar Lap in New Zealand for 160 guineas for the American-born David Davis. The horse's name was based on the Thai for 'lightning flash'. But Davis did not like Phar Lap when he arrived in Australia,

claiming he was 'gangly, his face was covered with warts, and he had an awkward gait', so he refused to pay to train the horse. Telford agreed to train him for nothing in exchange for a two-thirds share of any winnings. He needed patience, because Phar Lap finished last in the first race he entered and in his next three races did not place at all.

He won his first race on 27 April 1929, and when he took second in the Chelmsford Stakes at Randwick a few months later, the racing community started treating him with respect. In 1930 and 1931 he won fourteen races in a row, and in the four years of his racing career he failed to win only fourteen of the fifty-one races he entered. He won £66,000, placing him among the greatest racehorses of his time.

Phar Lap caught the imagination of people battling the Great Depression when, despite great odds, carrying a heavy weight and eluding an assassination attempt, he won the Melbourne Cup in 1930 by four lengths.

Postscript

Phar Lap had to carry even more in the 1931 Melbourne Cup—68 kilograms—which would have made him the all-time top weight carrier if he'd won; in the event, he finished eighth. It was partly in response to these near-impossible handicaps that Phar Lap's owner shipped him to the US in 1932 to compete in the country's richest race, at the Agua Caliente track in California. Phar Lap won in track-record time while carrying 58.5 kg, creating a sensation. He was then sent to a private ranch near Menlo Park, California, for a spell, but on April 5 strapper Tommy Woodcock found him with a high temperature, in pain and haemorrhaging. The great horse died soon after.

When news of Phar Lap's death reached Australia, millions grieved. Sporting champions paid tribute, including Australia's leading cyclist, Hubert Opperman, who said: 'I am not a follower of horse-racing, but like every Australian with red blood in their veins I have followed with close interest Phar Lap's gallop to world fame. He was truly a great boost for Australia and, like every other Australian, I mourn his passing. In my opinion, there is nothing maudlin in a nation mourning the loss of a racehorse when that horse is Phar Lap.'

Phar Lap's heart was donated to the Institute of Anatomy in Canberra and his skeleton to the New Zealand National Museum in Wellington. His hide was placed in the Melbourne Museum after being preserved by a New York City taxidermist. Phar Lap's heart, which weighed 6.2 kilograms—an average horse's heart weighs about 3.2 kg—was taken to the National Museum of Australia, where it is the object visitors most often ask to see.

When an investigation revealed that the horse's stomach and intestines were inflamed, many believed he had been poisoned either deliberately or by insecticide. But in the 1980s an infection was formally identified, and a later study found that Phar Lap died of an acute bacterial gastroenteritis. However, in 2006 two Australian scientists analysed some hairs from the horse in a synchrotron and concluded that he was poisoned with a single large dose of arsenic thirty to forty hours before he died. This seemed to support the theory that Phar Lap was killed on the orders of US gangsters who feared the champion would inflict big losses on illegal bookmakers. A follow-up study, in 2008, confirmed the finding.

Other horses have won the Melbourne Cup by greater margins and more often, notably three-time winner Makybe Diva, but none has claimed a more significant place in Australian history than Phar Lap.

'There is nothing maudlin in a nation mourning the loss of a racehorse when that horse is Phar Lap.'

1932

JACK LANG AND CAPTAIN DE GROOT OPEN SYDNEY HARBOUR BRIDGE

'To Hell with the English banks,' New South Wales Premier Jack Lang shouted above the din of construction work. 'I won't pay them a penny of the interest owed on their loans. We are in the middle of a Great Depression, in case they'd forgotten!'

'But the New South Wales Government is bound by law to repay that interest as long as you have the loans, Mr Lang!' said the newly arrived State Governor, Sir Philip Game, clutching at a piece of scaffolding to steady himself in the wind.

'That may be the law of Great Britain,' Lang said, leading Game up onto a viewing platform, 'but I have to finish building this bridge here, and I need those funds. The work you can see all around you is creating badly needed jobs.'

'But the British banks also need those interest payments to help the Mother Country recover from that dreadful war,' Game said, climbing the stairs behind Lang.

'Don't mention that bloody war, Sir Philip!' Lang said, turning from the rail. 'You British took all of our best young men and millions of pounds to fight it. More than 60,000 Diggers died for the Old Country—and now, when we are down and out, you tell me we have to make those crippling interest payments ahead of everything else?'

'The Mother Country is deeply grateful for your gallant war effort,' the diminutive Game said, stepping away from the 'Big Fella'. 'But debts must be repaid before you embark on any new public works projects—including this bridge.'

'Yet Britain has repudiated her own war debt to the United States, Sir Philip—explain that,' Lang said, looking up at workers on the newly completed

Labor Premier Jack Lang was confident of fighting off political opponents and the British banks themselves to fund the building of his harbour bridge—but had no idea he would be dismissed by New South Wales Governor Philip Game for failing to pay interest on British loans. Cartoon by George Finey.

steel arch, which had been built simultaneously from both sides of the harbour. 'Do as I say, not as I do, eh? You should practise what you preach.'

'That war cost us dearly,' Game said.

'And this bridge costs a lot, too—but it is all going to plan. See how perfectly the two sides of the arch have joined in the middle,' Lang said with a note of triumph. 'It is the greatest project ever started in Australia—the people's project— and we will finish it on time despite the Depression. And neither you nor anyone from Britain can stop us.'

'Perhaps you could spare some of the funds for interest payments that I hear you have been sinking into your excessively generous welfare programs,' Game persisted.

'No! I will not take pensions from widows and the families of Diggers killed in that war we fought for you, just to help balance the books of British bankers!' Lang said. 'Nor will I stop making sustenance payments to the unemployed in the middle of this dreadful Depression.'

'What shall I report to London then, Mr Lang?' Game asked.

'Tell your Prime Minister in Westminster, and your King at Buckingham Palace for that matter,' Lang shouted, putting his hands on his hips, 'tell 'em all that Jack Lang—the Big Fella, the leader of the people of New South Wales—has collected all of that cash and locked it up in his Treasury and won't give 'em a penny till after he's built his mighty bridge and the Depression is over!'

'I don't believe it,' Game said, stepping back against the safety rail. 'That's criminal!'

'You're in my territory now,' Lang said, turning to leave the platform. 'If you want your dirty money you can get it from Canberra!'

'Wait—Great Britain may now take action against you,' Game said, blocking the stairway, 'even before I am called upon as His Majesty's representative to open your dashed bridge!'

'I don't care,' Lang spat back. 'And you won't be opening the people's bridge, Sir Philip: I will open it! The ribbon will be cut by a man of the people, not an upper-class representative of the King of England.'

True to his word, Lang, finished the bridge and organised the great opening ceremony for 19 March 1932. After delivering a fiery speech, with Governor Game in attendance, the Big Fella, brandishing a pair of ceremonial scissors, led the official party off the dais and over to the ribbon stretched across the southern end of the bridge. Suddenly there were shouts from the crowd and the sound of a galloping horse.

'Look out—a horse has bolted!'

'Get out of the way, the horseman's waving a sword!'

'The rider must have gone mad!'

Lang looked up, Game stepped aside, and a uniformed rider galloped towards the gleaming white ribbon, wildly waving a sword. Unopposed by the shocked onlookers, the horseman reached the ribbon and, leaning over, sliced it in two, yelling: 'I open this bridge in the name of all the decent people of New South Wales.'

Representing the right-wing New Guard, Captain Francis de Groot took everyone by surprise when he galloped through the crowd and cut the ribbon ahead of Premier Jack Lang to open the Sydney Harbour Bridge 'in the name of all the decent people of New South Wales'. Cartoon by Frith.

It was over in a flash. The long-anticipated opening had been turned on its head. Police grabbed the horse's bridle, forced the rider to dismount and arrested him. He was Captain Francis de Groot, and he represented an anti-Lang, anti-socialist group called the New Guard.

Lang, unflappable to the last, ordered the cut ribbon to be rejoined, then stepped forward and cut it again, officially opening the bridge in the name of all the people of New South Wales.

'I open this bridge in the name of all the decent people of New South Wales.'

IT WAS A GREAT MOMENT because thanks to Jack Lang, Australia's largest city got its long-awaited harbour crossing, an essential connection now used by hundreds of thousands of people each day. It was also a great moment because a Labor leader had stood up to Britain and got away with it—for long enough, a least, to build his vital bridge in the world's worst Depression. Jack Lang is still remembered as the man who got the bridge built. As for De Groot and the New Guard they may have upstaged the Premier, but their political movement was soon consigned to history's dustbin.

Historical background

Born in 1876 to poor Catholic parents, Jack Lang trained as an accountant and worked his way up through the Labor movement. He entered the New South Wales Parliament in 1913 and served as Premier from 1925–27, then again from 1930–32. Although stubborn and combative, he became increasingly popular with the party's left wing and the working class. He was a hero to many during the Great Depression, when he managed to keep the state going despite the near collapse of the national economy and soaring unemployment rates. Lang's admirers on the far left publicly proclaimed him 'Greater than Lenin'.

One of his main achievements was supervising the completion of the Sydney Harbour Bridge, which cost £9 million. The project employed 1400 workers, feeding many families. Lang accepted money from the Federal Government to pay the interest due on British loans, but confiscated the funds and refused to pay up. He sent government cars to Sydney banks to withdraw all the money from State Government accounts in case Canberra or British bankers tried to take it.

Sydney had been trying to build a bridge across its great harbour for a long time. The architect Francis Greenway had suggested one as early as 1815, saying he 'proposed to build a fort on Observatory Hill, with an advanced redoubt on Dawes Point and to construct a bridge thence to the northern shore of the Harbour'. But the government never had enough money and the authorities could never make up their minds how to go about such a project. Finally, they committed to a design espoused by Chief Engineer John Bradfield, and the first sod was turned in July 1923.

Bradfield had to build an unprecedented structure for Australia, the largest single-span bridge in the world at the time, amid the financial constraints of the Depression. It was he who decided to build both sides of the arch together: despite all the challenges, they met perfectly on 19 August 1930, and Bradfield finished the bridge in time for the 1932 opening.

Postscript

Lang may have put the desperate workers and his bridge ahead of his legal obligations for a while, but his government's refusal to pay the interest on British loans cost him dearly. Conservative forces ganged up on him, the appointed Upper House repeatedly blocked his legislation, and 400,000 people signed a petition protesting against his high-handed approach to government. In 1932 Lang was dismissed by Governor Sir Philip Game.

Game later expressed regret for having taken that step, but in the ensuing election Lang and his Labor Party were easily defeated. A continuing thorn in the side of his own party, Lang was subsequently expelled from the ALP in whose name he had fought and governed so passionately.

The vice-regal dismissal of a Labor Premier was seen as an enabling precedent in 1972, when Governor-General Sir John Kerr dismissed Labor Prime Minister Gough Whitlam, another 'Big Fella' who governed in a similar style to Lang.

1934
BRADMAN CONQUERS WORLD CRICKET

'**K**eep a straight bat, Bill,' Don Bradman said, meeting fellow batsman Bill Ponsford in the centre of the pitch while they waited for a replacement umpire to come out during the Fifth Test against England at The Oval.

'With any luck we'll go for a Test record here today. That'll show the Pommies we can fight back after their dirty bodyline bowling in the last series in Australia.'

'Do you think we can do it, Don?' Ponsford asked, looking around at all the English faces in the crowd. 'What if the Poms get desperate and try more of that bodyline stuff?'

'They wouldn't dare after the outcry they caused last time, Bill—anyway, all we'd have to do is keep our heads down and look for balls we can hit,' Bradman said, searching for any sign of an Australian flag in the crowd.

'Do you reckon they could get away with playing dirty in their own country?' Ponsford asked, trying a few practice swings.

'I'm not sure, but if they do we must play on as if nothing is happening,' Bradman said, taking his gloves off. 'We have to show, with our partnership today, that we are the better sportsmen.'

'And we won't forget poor old Bill Oldfield,' Ponsford said. 'The stretcher-bearers had to carry him off at Adelaide in the last series when Larwood fractured his bloody skull. So much for Jardine's "leg theory" bowling!'

'If they bowl any bodyline just duck, Bill. Keep your wits about you and play the game as it should be played,' Bradman said. 'Forget last time in Australia and concentrate on hitting a top score today.'

'Look at the crowd—they know what's going on,' Ponsford said, waving his bat around the English ground. 'I reckon even these spectators would want you

Don Bradman would have averaged a century, after playing Test cricket for two decades—had he not gone out for a duck in his last innings.

to complain if their own English bowlers try any more bodyline. You're their hero, after all, even in the home of cricket.'

'Well, the Marylebone Cricket Club has banned "direct attack" bowling since last year, but if it happens I refuse to get angry,' Bradman said. 'I'll remain silent and uphold the spirit of the game by just playing as a good sportsman should.'

'But did you see that newspaper poster in the high street—"Bradman versus England", it said,' Ponsford laughed.

'Well, today let's make sure it's "Ponsford and Bradman versus England",' Bradman said, bending to adjust his pads.

'All right, Don, I won't let you down,' Ponsford said, as the next English bowler started warming up. 'We'll go for that record you want.'

'Come on, Bill, here comes the new umpire . . . back to the crease,' Bradman said firmly. 'We'll try for 450. That'll show the Poms that we Aussies can bounce back better than ever, even after something like bodyline.'

Bat on the pair did, with straight bats and playing the game as it should be played until between them Bradman and Ponsford scored 451 not out—a partnership record that still stands for England–Australia Ashes matches.

IT WAS A GREAT MOMENT because Bradman and Ponsford had achieved a Test record and laid to rest the fears generated by the bodyline series of 1932–33. Bradman had already established himself as cricket's greatest batsman, having hit enough world records to secure his crown. Now, in this Fifth Test, he led a triumphant Australian comeback after the infamous English bodyline attack of the previous Test series in Australia. (In 1934 a London daily newspaper did indeed devote its whole front page to proclaiming 'Bradman versus England'.)

It was certainly a great moment for the working people back in Australia. For years Bradman had helped distract them from the problems of the Great Depression. By fighting back after the bodyline scandal, Bradman had the same effect that the heavily weighted Phar Lap did with his great Melbourne Cup win in 1930, lifting the nation's spirits by winning against the odds.

Historical background

In 1928–29, Donald Bradman scored the highest number of runs in a season in Australian cricket history—1690, including seven centuries. He kept up the pace the following season, when he made the highest score then recorded in Australian (and world) first-class cricket—452 not out for New South Wales in a match against Queensland at the Sydney Cricket Ground, a record that stood until 1958. In doing so he broke the world record of 437 runs set by Bill Ponsford of Victoria. He continued to break records, scoring 334 against England in a Test Match at Leeds later the same year.

After the controversial 1932–33 bodyline series that gave the English side such a bad name in Australia, Bradman was seen to be restoring the integrity of the game when he set the Test record partnership with Ponsford. He also captained the Australians when they won the Ashes in 1937, and after the war led them back to England in 1948, for a 4–0 Ashes sweep. Completing the tour unbeaten, the team earned the title of The Invincibles.

'What if the Poms try more of that bodyline stuff?'

Postscript

To stop the 'unbeatable' Bradman, in the Ashes Tests in Australia in the early 1930s British cricket authorities decided to use bodyline bowling, which had begun to infest English county cricket. This tactic was pioneered by the English captain Douglas Jardine and executed by his most aggressive bowler, Harold Larwood. Bradman and the Australians believed bodyline lowered the traditional standards of cricket, but Jardine claimed the English were only practising 'leg theory' bowling. English bowlers struck increasing numbers of Australian batsmen, including Bill Oldfield, who had to be taken to hospital with a fractured skull. The bodyline scandal was the last straw for Australians, who were battling the Great Depression and, having sacrificed 61,000 lives for Britain in the First World War, had been told to pay the operational costs of their Army's participation. They vented their fury at the cricket grounds, in the newspapers and on radio. Australian officials appealed to cricket's highest authority, the Marylebone Cricket Club, to have the bodyline bowling stopped. In 1933 the MCC ruled that batsmen should not be 'directly attacked', but did not specifically rule out bodyline.

In a cruel twist of fate, in 1948, the world's greatest batsman went for a duck in his last Test innings. He had wanted 'to retire before the umpire gives me out', but it was too late—and it also cost him his chance for a Test average of 100 (it became 99.94).

1934

'SMITHY' FLIES THE WORLD TO CONQUER THE SKIES

'So far, so good—the *Lady Southern Cross* is flying beautifully at this height, don't you reckon, Bill?' Charles Kingsford Smith said to his second pilot and navigator, Patrick Gordon 'Bill' Taylor, as he checked the instruments on the panel in front of him.

'She'd better be—there's a lot of water down there,' Taylor said, looking down at the Pacific Ocean far below. 'It's a lot bigger than the Tasman—and it's a lot further to America than to New Zealand. Let's just pray *Lady Southern Cross* makes it without any engine trouble or fuel blockages like we had crossing the Tasman,' Taylor said. 'Or that if she does play up, it will be near one of our island stepping-stones to the US.'

'Have faith, Bill. We have the wind behind us—we'll be in California before you know it,' said the ever-optimistic Kingsford Smith.

'Don't you ever consider the possibility of crashing, Smithy?' Taylor asked. 'I mean, it does happen.'

'I've done that before—went down in the Australian desert back in 1929 and waited nearly two weeks to be rescued,' Kingsford Smith said. 'But given the number of successful flights I've made in different parts of the world, I'd say Lady Luck's on my side—she's probably in the cockpit with us. That's why I called this bird *Lady Southern Cross*.'

'Yeah, but we lose good pilots all the time,' Taylor said as the plane droned on. 'Ross Smith died in that crash in the Twenties after winning the England-to-Australia prize, and even Bert Hinkler, one of the best, was killed on his England–Australia flight last year.'

'We'll make it to California, all right—and be the first to fly the Pacific from west to east!'

The great pioneer aviator Charles Kingsford Smith, left, set more records than any other early airman and seemed invincible, until his plane crashed into the Bay of Bengal on a flight to England.

'It's a risky business, sure, but the *Lady Southern Cross* is the best plane I've ever flown,' Kingsford Smith said. 'We'll make it to California, all right—and be the first to fly the Pacific from west to east!'

IT WAS A GREAT MOMENT because Kingsford Smith and Taylor became the first to fly west to east across the world's largest ocean in their single-engined Lockheed Altair, *Lady Southern Cross*. They flew from Brisbane to San Francisco in thirty-three days, making fuel stops on the way. It was a crowning moment for Kingsford Smith, topping a stellar career as one of the world's leading pioneer aviators.

Historical background

Brisbane-born Charles Kingsford Smith, known affectionately as 'Smithy', flew in the First World War before achieving more in the air than any other pioneer aviator. He was the first to fly across Australia and first to fly across the Tasman Sea to New Zealand (when co-pilot Taylor saved both their lives by climbing out on the wings and transferring oil from one engine to another). Later that year Smithy was also first to fly the Pacific from the United States to Australia. In 1929 he flew from Australia to England in twelve days, despite a first attempt resulting in an unscheduled landing in the desert. He had also circumnavigated the world.

Smithy was one of a band of pioneer aviators who were contemporaries of Ross and Keith Smith. They included Bert Hinkler, Charles Ulm, G.V. 'Scotty' Allan, and, of course, P.G. Taylor. These men helped put Australia at the forefront of world aviation, inspiring John Flynn of the Inland Mission to take medical services to the Outback with his Flying Doctor Service. Smithy himself taught several of the first female pilots, including Maude Rose Bonney, New Zealander Jean Batten, and the first woman to obtain and use a commercial pilot's licence, Nancy Bird (who later changed her name to Nancy Bird-Walton).

Charles Kingsford Smith, known affectionately as 'Smithy', towers over his father and mother as he prepares for yet another record-breaking flight; his parents were born in the age of the horse and cart.

Postscript

Despite Kingsford Smith's bravado, the hero of the skies crashed, almost certainly into the Andaman Sea west of Burma and Thailand, on another England-to-Australia flight in 1935. Although a wheel and strut that washed up on an island were identified as belonging to *Lady Southern Cross*, neither he nor co-pilot J.T. Pethybrige was heard of again. His wife had pleaded with him not to go on this last flight because he was exhausted and depressed by financial worries.

But Smithy was lucky even to have lived long enough to take to the skies, because he almost drowned as a young boy. He was saved from a violent surf at Bondi in the early 1900s by a member of the newly formed Bondi Surf Life Saving Club.

Although Charles Kingsford Smith flew a number of different planes, his best-known aircraft was the *Southern Cross*, named after the useful navigational stars in the southern hemisphere.

1941
HMAS SYDNEY, ROUND 2: GERMANS SINK AUSTRALIAN FLAGSHIP

'Take her in closer, helmsman,' Captain Joseph Burnett ordered, gazing through his binoculars from the bridge railing on HMAS *Sydney*. 'I want to speak to this "Flying Dutchman" now we are catching up to her.'

'Are you sure, Captain?' asked Commander Edmund Thrushton of the Royal Navy, deep concern showing on his face. 'That's likely to bring us within firing range.'

'Firing range?' Burnett said, lowering the binoculars and turning towards the worried commander. 'She's a bloody Dutch trader!'

'But how can you be so sure, Captain?' Thrushton said as respectfully as possible.

'She's plainly flying the Dutch flag—look!' Burnett said.

'I can see the Dutch colours, Captain, but why has she been steaming away from us ever since we first sighted her? In British waters enemy ships often disguise themselves in wartime, especially German raiders.'

'But these are Australian waters,' Burnett said, 'and there are no known German raiders off Western Australia right now. We're only about 110 nautical miles [200 kilometres] out from Shark Bay. Besides, even if she were armed, we can outshoot a vessel this size.'

'Let's not forget what happened to the first *Sydney* in this very ocean in the First World War,' Commander Lionel Dalton, of the Royal Australian Navy, chipped in. 'That smaller German cruiser *Emden* took her by surprise and fired first as HMAS *Sydney* approached.'

The ill-fated HMAS *Sydney* chalked up a distinguished track record in the early part of the Second World War.

'Completely different circumstances, Lionel,' Burnett said, raising his binoculars again. 'It is standard practice to sail up close to confirm the identity of unknown ships and this is not a German vessel, it's Dutch. Let me prove it to you,' he added, turning to his signals officer. 'Signal the Dutch ship to identify herself.'

'Aye, aye, Sir,' he replied, immediately making the lamp blink out its Morse message.

'What's her reply?' Burnett asked, as he saw the other ship responding.

'She says "I see your signal but cannot make out what it is", Sir.'

Captain Joseph Burnett had served in the First World War but didn't command a ship until 1941 when he took over HMAS *Sydney*. He may not have realised the disguised German raider *Kormoran* was luring him into a trap.

'Well, that confirms our need to get closer so she can read our signals,' Burnett said, feeling vindicated. 'Catch up to her. The old girl is travelling about six knots slower than us, anyway.'

'I still don't like it, Captain,' Thrushton insisted.

'Doubting Thomas, aren't you?' Burnett said as *Sydney* closed the distance. 'Now we're only about 9000 yards off. Tell her to signal her name.'

'Aye, aye, Sir.'

'We can't be sure she'll tell the truth, Joe. Should we ask her to confirm her secret sign as well?' Thrushton said.

The signals officer interrupted: 'Reports her name as *Straat Malakka*, Sir.'

'Sounds pretty Dutch to me,' Burnett said, turning to Thrushton. 'Now sail in closer and we'll say hello.'

'But Sir,' interrupted RAN Commander Thomas Maynard, looking up from some paperwork. 'According to the intelligence reports of the Vessel Area Indicator that we received today, the only Dutch ship in the Indian Ocean is the *Jepara*.'

'Maybe the VAI has not picked up all shipping, Tom,' Burnett said, moving towards the chart table, with doubt at last creeping into his voice. 'Here, show me.'

'And that ship is three times *Jepara*'s size and has a totally different profile,' Maynard said, gaining confidence as he eyed the now clearly visible vessel ahead of them.

'Hmm. Why hasn't the VAI tipped us off about the *Straat Malakka*?' Burnett asked anxiously, looking up from the report. 'How far off is she now?'

'About 1000 yards, sir,' his navigator replied.

'We should not be approaching with our port side exposed, Captain; that's certainly against British naval policy,' Thrushton warned. 'It would be far safer if we had only our bow exposed.'

'I'm the captain of this ship,' Burnett retorted. 'But demand she show us her secret sign. I must have confirmation that she is *Straat Malakka*.'

'Aye, Sir,' the signals officer replied.

'She'll not tell us,' Thrushton shouted, 'because she doesn't have one—look at that!'

Across the narrowing stretch of dark blue heaving sea, Burnett watched in horror as the 'cargo ship' pulled down the Dutch flag and hoisted the unmistakable and dreaded German battle ensign. 'Action stations!' he shouted, turning back from the enemy ship with a look of utter desperation.

But it was too late. Even as Burnett's order rang around HMAS *Sydney* and the crew responded, he saw the Germans clear the camouflage from their guns. A deadly barrage began within seconds, sending shells straight into Burnett's ship.

IT WAS A GREAT MOMENT in the worst sense, because what happened next created the greatest naval loss in Australian history, and Australia's worst all-hands loss in the Second World War. On 19 November 1941, the *Sydney* and its crew of 645 were destroyed. The disaster ranked alongside that of Fromelles, in the First World War, when nearly 2000 Australian soldiers were killed in twenty-four hours. But because *Sydney* managed to fatally cripple the German *Kormoran* (the real identity of the mystery ship), Prime Minister John Curtin was able to claim the loss as a great example of the upholding of naval tradition.

'The Australian cruiser HMAS Sydney, which carried a complement of 645 officers and men, is missing and presumed lost.'

Historical background

Captain Joseph Burnett had graduated from the Royal Australian Naval College in 1917, he served on HMAS *Australia* in the First World War, on HMAS *Adelaide* in the 1920s, and on HMAS *Canberra*, as executive officer, until the Second World War broke out. But he did not get his first command till May 1941, when he took over HMAS *Sydney*, a ship with a distinguished war record in the Mediterranean. In November 1941 *Sydney* was ordered to escort the troopship *Zealandia* to Sunda Strait. En route back to Fremantle, on a latitude between Carnarvon and Geraldton, she sighted what appeared to be a merchant ship about 20 kilometres (11 nautical miles) away and challenged it. It was the raider *Kormoran*, disguised as a Dutch freighter.

According to later reports by *Kormoran* crew members, *Sydney* chased the raider while exchanging signals to verify her identity. The Australian ship closed to within 1000 yards and demanded a secret password from the captain of the *Kormoran*, at which point the Germans opened fire.

Hit several times, *Sydney* caught fire. But she was better armoured and more heavily armed than the German ship, and eventually returned its attack, hitting *Kormoran* in the funnel and engine room and severely disabling the raider.

With both ships badly damaged, *Sydney* turned south and, having disappeared from *Kormoran*'s view, sank with all hands. *Kormoran* was scuttled by her captain.

The battle was probably all over for Burnett in an instant, because the Germans' first salvo, delivered at 5.30 p.m., scored a direct hit on the bridge. When the wreck was found sixty-six years later the bridge was destroyed. That first salvo also wiped out the command equipment, the gunnery direction tower and the wireless aerials. At least forty-five shells slammed into that port side Commander Thrushton had been so reluctant to expose. The machine-gunners on *Kormoran* followed up the shells by raking *Sydney*'s crew as they rushed to their action stations. Thousands of shrapnel splinters flew around the decks, fires started all over the ship, and further shelling destroyed the two forrard gun turrets, leaving *Sydney* only the aft turrets to fight with. *Sydney* got some torpedoes away, but all missed. As the ships turned, *Kormoran* also slammed forty-eight shells into *Sydney*'s starboard side.

The shells and machine-gun bullets, fires, smoke and heat probably crippled about three-quarters of the crew or stopped them from fighting back. The battle

In the biggest naval disaster in Australian history, all 645 crew of HMAS *Sydney* died after the German raider *Kormoran* shelled their ship, setting it on fire and destroying their lifeboats and rafts.

raged for about fifty minutes, until *Kormoran* delivered the killer blow, firing a torpedo into *Sydney*'s bow, which gaped and broke away, sending the ship and her crew to a watery grave.

They could not escape because the lifeboats had been damaged or destroyed. Some of the crew might have jumped into the sea wearing life vests, but they could not have survived for long. One sailor who escaped on a Carley float washed up on Christmas Island three months later, dead from a shrapnel wound to the head.

Shells from HMAS *Sydney* had started fires on *Kormoran* that were spreading to holds containing 320 mines, so Captain Theodore Detmers ordered his crew to abandon ship and fired a scuttling charge to sink her. *Kormoran* sank at 12:30 p.m. and Detmers and 317 of his 393 crew escaped in lifeboats. They made their way east towards the Western Australian coast; some were picked up by ships and others after landing.

The HMAS *Sydney* became a favourite with armed forces, who never dreamt their beloved naval flagship would be sunk by a German raider in 1941.

The ships' armaments were quite evenly matched: *Sydney* had eight 15-centimetre guns, four 10-centimetre guns and eight torpedo tubes. *Kormoran* also had eight 15-centimetre guns, two anti-tank guns, five anti-aircraft guns and six torpedo tubes. The German ship won the battle because she had the advantage of surprise, opened fire first and from point-blank range, and quickly destroyed *Sydney*'s command and control systems.

Postscript

Although the Federal Government knew HMAS *Sydney* had been lost, Prime Minister John Curtin did not tell the public for almost two weeks. The *Sydney Morning Herald* reported on 1 December 1941 that the cruiser was 'presumed lost'. It said *Sydney* 'had been in action with a heavily armed merchant raider which she sunk by gunfire. No subsequent communications had been received from the Sydney, the information of the Australian Naval Board having come from the survivors of the enemy vessel who were picked up some time after the action.' Curtin told Australians that an extensive search by air and service units was being continued and that next-of-kin had been informed. 'While regretting the loss of the *Sydney* and her gallant complement,' he said, 'the people of Australia will be proud that she and they upheld the traditions of the Royal Australian Navy and completed her glorious career in successful action against the enemy.'

Curtin could not have known then what a disaster that action had been. Nobody would know for another sixty-six years. There were uncanny parallels with the case of the earlier HMAS *Sydney* in the First World War. Both ships were in the Indian Ocean, had been on escort duties, had foolishly approached the enemy ship and were attacked before they could fire their guns. In both cases, the enemy crew escaped. Both incidents occurred in November—one in 1914, the other in 1941. The second *Sydney* might not have been lost, however, if Burnett had recalled how his *Sydney* 1 counterpart had been caught out after sailing too close to the German *Emden*.

Once HMAS *Sydney* defeated the German ship *Emden* in the first year of the First World War, the disabled vessel ran aground on North Keeling Island off Western Australia. 'Emden Beached and Done For', by Arthur Burgess (1920), Australian War Memorial

The Australian journalist Charles Bean, who was appointed the official Commonwealth Correspondent for the First World War, not only covered the landing at Gallipoli but also helped to create the Anzac legend with his colourful reports which turned the soldiers into heroes. Portrait by George Lambert (1924), Australian War Memorial

As the cliffs were so steep above the main beach at Gallipoli and the well-armed Turks were entrenched above, the Anzacs trapped below had to make the best of a crowded situation.
'The Beach at Anzac', by Frank Crozier (1919), Australian War Memorial

As they fought their losing battle at the beach head on Gallipoli, where they had to withstand continual Turkish counter-attacks, the Anzacs were romanticised in both words and pictures.
David Barker (1915), Australian War Memorial

The Western Australian Premier John Forrest, who fought long and hard to keep Western Australia from breaking away from the rest of Australia, managed to persuade the people of the west to join the Federation in the nick of time. Cartoon by Hop, *The Bulletin*

Lieutenant General Harry Chauvel who commanded the Desert Mounted Corps in the First World War was the first Australian to become a Lieutenant General and also oversaw the legendary Australian Light Horse charge at Beersheba. Portrait by W.B. McInnes (1938), Australian War Memorial

The Australian exploits in the Middle East campaign were legendary. Australian airman Frank McNamara made a plucky escape when he took off just before mounted enemy Turkish forces reached his plane after he had landed to scoop up a wounded comrade, Douglas Rutherford, whose plane had been shot down. 'The Incident for which Lieutenant F.H. McNamara was Awarded the V.C.', by H. Septimus Power (1924), Australian War Memorial

New South Wales Premier Jack Lang officially opened the Sydney Harbour Bridge in 1932 by cutting the ribbon, but the New Guard officer Captain De Groot had actually just beaten him to it by galloping along the bridge on his horse and slashing through the ribbon with his sword—as a protest against Lang's socialist policies.

For nearly two decades from the late 1920s to the late 1940s the great batsman Don Bradman, affectionately known as 'Our Don', won the hearts of Australian cricket fans by hitting century after century. National Library of Australia

Salvage operators retrieve one of the three Japanese midget submarines that crept into Sydney Harbour in the dead of night on 31 May 1942. A torpedo loosed by one sub was fired at the USS *Chicago*, but missed and killed nineteen servicemen on the *Kuttabul*.

Australia's top military commander, General Sir Thomas Blamey, on the left, watches with great relief as the Japanese sign the papers confirming their surrender at the end of the Second World War—a war that had claimed millions of lives, including those of 39,000 Australians.

Green bans leader Jack Mundey attended an emotional 25-year reunion in Sydney in 1996 with the women who had led the successful campaign to save Kellys Bush. The campaign had paved the way for future green bans which protected heritage buildings and the environment around Australia. Fairfax Photos

From the moment they established their Aboriginal Embassy in 1972 to lobby for better treatment, Aborigines continued to maintain a presence outside the parliament, refusing to be expelled. Fairfax Photos

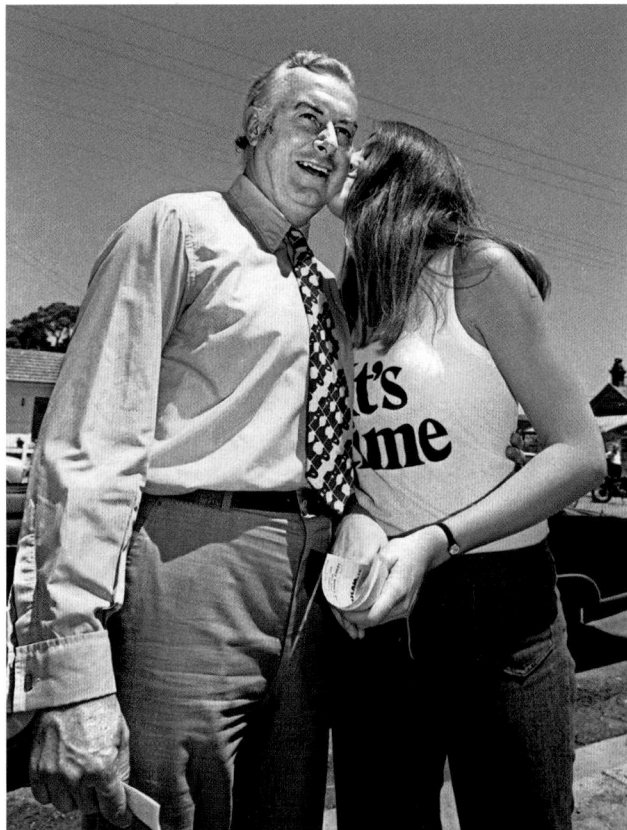

Labor leader Gough Whitlam, who won the federal election in 1972 on the slogan 'It's Time', was a great hit with women, who idolised the tall, good-looking maverick who had just broken a 23-year drought for Labor. Fairfax Photos

The people of Sydney had waited for so long for their controversial Opera House to be finished that they crowded into every available space on land and took to the water in their boats to celebrate the great day when the Queen finally opened this wonder of the world. *Fairfax Photos*

Bob Brown on the Franklin River in 1980. Photo by Les O'Rourke/Fairfax Photos

1941

FEARFUL PRIME MINISTER SWITCHES ALLEGIANCE FROM BRITAIN TO USA

'This is terrible news. And how do I know Australia won't be next?' Prime Minister John Curtin said to his personal secretary, Gladys Joyce, as he scanned the telegram she had just handed him. 'If they've got the gumption to bomb Pearl Harbor and take on the Yanks, the Japs could conquer the whole Pacific, couldn't they?'

'I imagine so, Sir,' she said.

'Well, I'm not going to be the first prime minister to allow Australia to be invaded,' Curtin said, pacing up and down his office. 'And I certainly can't send all my troops to defend England from the Germans now—I need them here!'

'Yes, Sir, of course.'

'Especially now we've just lost HMAS *Sydney* somewhere off Western Australia,' Curtin said, shaking his head. 'Who knows? The Japanese might have helped the Germans sink her.'

'I thought we were keeping that quiet,' Joyce cautioned.

'Of course. The nation's not ready to hear that 645 of our boys have been killed just yet,' a sombre Curtin acknowledged.

'But you are right, Prime Minister. As you've said before, we're in danger of running out of men, let alone ships for home defence,' Joyce ventured.

'Damn it!' Curtin said. 'Get me the Defence chief immediately! Shedden must stop our troops leaving for England!'

'Yes, Sir,' she said, dashing for the telephone.

It was 8 December 1941—an unusually dark and cloudy summer's day—and Curtin had just received confirmation that the Japanese had attacked the US

Despite traditional links with far-flung Britain, Prime Minister John Curtin, right, switched Australia's allegiance to the more powerful USA after the Japanese attacked Pearl Harbor and invited America's General Douglas MacArthur, left, to establish his fight-back headquarters in Australia, knowing he would also defend Australia.

Pacific Fleet at its Hawaiian base. The Japanese had been belligerent for years, conquering large areas of China, but nobody had expected them to attack the British in Hong Kong and Malaya, let alone the United States. Singapore could be next, and Australia would surely follow. It was time to act.

'Come in, Shedden. I suppose you've heard the news?' Curtin ushered his Defence chief into the office and pointed to a chair.

'About the Japanese attacking Pearl Harbor?' Shedden replied. 'Yes, I heard through military intelligence. Certainly changed the focus of the war, hasn't it?'

'Indeed. I want to discuss with you our best possible response—independent of Britain,' Curtin said.

'Well, it could be just a matter of time before the Japs attack Australia,' Shedden said, sitting on the edge of his chair, notebook and pencil in hand.

'That's why I think we should get in first and declare war on Japan,' the Prime Minister said.

Shedden cocked his head. 'You mean even before Britain responds?'

'Too right. This is no longer about Britain, it's about America and us,' Curtin said. 'We should show the Japs we mean business.'

'I agree, Prime Minister, and I would urge you and your Cabinet colleagues to issue the declaration today,' Shedden said.

'Good. But we have to go further than that,' Curtin said, walking over to the world map on his wall. 'This is a new theatre of war, the Pacific. It's our home patch, and our main ally is inevitably going to be the US, not Britain. The UK is too far away, and it's history in this region. That's why it's time to change horses.'

Hours later, after a War Cabinet meeting, Shedden was to tell Curtin that the information Cabinet had received from the military chiefs of staff was 'scrappy and meagre . . . the Government must press it right home that this is a new war'.

Curtin handed Shedden an order he'd just finished typing. 'This instructs the military to recall all our troops presently heading for Europe and redeploy them up north for the defence of Australia.'

'All our troops?' Shedden took the sheet of paper. 'What about Churchill's demand for the maximum number of Australian soldiers to stop a German invasion of England?'

'Damn Churchill. We don't owe him a thing. We have our own war to fight now,' Curtin said, starting to pace the floor again. Curtin gazed out the window at the unsuspecting Canberra citizens going about their business.

'Very well. I will order the troops back. We'll never rely on the British again,' Shedden said. 'They will be lucky if they can hang on to Singapore, let alone help us in our hour of need. No, we'll have to go it alone.'

'Not alone,' Curtin said. 'I'm going to invite the Americans to set up their headquarters here. They will want to punish the Japanese for Pearl Harbor, and they can do that most effectively by using Australia as a base. In the meantime, they will defend us from attack.'

'A brilliant strategic move, Prime Minister,' Shedden said.

'Listen to this,' Curtin said. 'It's a New Year statement I have been working on. In this blackest of hours, I want to give our people hope.'

He read:

Without any inhibitions of any kind, I make it quite clear that Australia looks to America, free of any pangs as to our traditional links or kinship with the United Kingdom. We know that Australia can go and Britain can still hold on. We are therefore determined that Australia shall not go, and we shall exert all our energies towards the shaping of a plan, with the United States as its keystone, which will give our country some confidence of being able to hold out until the tide of battle swings against the enemy.

'Australia looks to America, free of any pangs as to our traditional links or kinship with the United Kingdom.'

'Bravo, Prime Minister,' Shedden said, aware he was witnessing a historic moment. He leapt to his feet to shake Curtin's hand.

'We'll have American forces here by early next year,' said Curtin, 'and I am going to get General Douglas MacArthur from the Philippines to lead them. But first recall our 6th and 7th Division troops from the Middle East and pull back any who were heading for Europe.'

IT WAS A GREAT MOMENT because Curtin had the vision and courage to publicly switch Australia's allegiance from Great Britain to the United States in the nick of time. On 29 December 1941, he broadcast his turning-point speech in a New Year radio message. Within weeks, he was proved right. On 3 February 1942, Japanese planes bombed Port Moresby. Twelve days later the Japanese forces seized the British stronghold of Singapore, capturing thousands of British and Commonwealth troops, including Australia's 8th Division. Now Australia was really on its own. The Japanese bombed Darwin on February 19, but MacArthur would soon set up the base in Australia from where much of the US-led campaign against the Japanese would be coordinated.

Once the Japanese attacked Hawaii's Pearl Harbor in December 1941, Australian Prime Minister John Curtin knew it was only a matter of time before they attacked Australia— which they did in February 1942, bombing Darwin.

Threat from the North

The Second World War was much more frightening for Australians than the First, because the Japanese actually attacked Australia itself. The nation may have lost 61,000 soldiers in the First World War, which was nearly twice the 39,000 killed in the Second, however the battlefields of the First World War were far away and now Australia itself was threatened—for the first time. Australians feared the Japanese would invade, and some Japanese military leaders did propose invasion. In 1942 Japanese planes bombed Darwin 60 times, killing over 200 people; they also bombed Broome, killing 70 people, and Wyndham, Port Hedland and Townsville. With Japanese midget submarines also attacking Sydney Harbour, claiming nineteen lives, and submarines shelling Sydney and Newcastle, many Australians were so frightened they evacuated major cities and headed inland. These fears inspired the government to invite the United States to establish its headquarters in Australia, from where the US helped to defeat the Japanese.

Historical background

Having lived in Western Australia before moving to Canberra, Curtin knew how vulnerable the vast Australian continent was. Not only did he switch the nation's primary allegiance to the US at a crucial moment, but he was also lucky that it suited the Americans to send their former commander in the Philippines, General Douglas MacArthur, to Australia, where he was made Supreme Commander of all Allied forces in the South-West Pacific. Churchill and the British Government became increasingly preoccupied with the European theatre and lost interest in Australia, which they saw as expendable. Curtin refused to send any of Australia's 46,000 returning Middle East veterans to Burma to help the British there, and this break with Britain and his later announcement of the US alliance was a historic turning point. There would be no return to the old order.

Postscript

The stresses of wartime leadership took their toll on Curtin, who was often seen walking around Parliament House late at night. By 1945 his health had collapsed and he died, on July 5—a month before the the war in the Pacific ended.

8 Dec 1941. Japs attack Pearl Harbour.
29 Dec 1941. Aust declares war on Japan. & allies with USA.
3rd Feb recalls Aust troops from Overseas.
3rd Feb 1942 bombed PT Moresby.
15th Singapore captured.
19th Feb Darwin bombed

205

1942

WATCHMAN SPOTS JAPANESE MIDGET SUB ATTACKING SYDNEY HARBOUR

'**I** think I just saw something move in the water out there,' Sydney Maritime Services Board watchman James Cargill whispered excitedly to his fellow watchman, William Nangle, as they chatted on a floating pile driver moored in the dark harbour. 'I know it's pretty hard to see, but I saw some kind of disturbance lit up by the moon.'

'Are you sure, Jimmy?' Nangle asked. 'The sea's choppy tonight . . . you might be seeing things. You haven't been drinking, have you, mate?'

'Not a drop, Bill. I haven't had a beer all day,' Cargill said. 'But I know this harbour like the back of my hand, and there's never any ripples out there. I think I'd better row over and have a look—I'm on watch, after all.'

'Wait a sec, mate—where is it?' Nangle said.

'Right over where the anti-torpedo boom net is strung between Georges Head and Watsons Bay,' Cargill said. 'It could be a bloody Japanese sub for all I know.'

'Oh, the Japanese would never come down here, Jimmy. Australia's too far and too big for them Nips to invade.'

'What about Pearl Harbor, Bill?' Cargill said, getting binoculars out of his kitbag. 'They bombed that last year—in Hawaii, thousands of bloody miles from Japan—and just by the by, they sailed midget submarines in there.'

'Well, yes, they did, too. But Japan's still a mighty long way from Australia.'

'Orright, what about bloody Singapore? They invaded there earlier this year,' Cargill said. 'And what about Darwin? There might be wartime censorship, but

He may have been just an ordinary watchman for Sydney's Maritime Services Board, with a rowing boat as his main defence, but in 1942 James Cargill, pictured here with his proud wife, nevertheless spotted a Japanese midget submarine sneaking into Sydney Harbour.

everyone knows the bastards have bombed it. That close enough for you, Bill?' Cargill asked, fixing his binoculars on the spot where the ripple was. 'Since February they've killed more than 200 Aussies.'

'The bastards! I didn't know that,' Nangle said, suddenly convinced of the threat. 'Maybe you should row over there. I've got to stay here watching this pile driver. What's the time?'

'Just after 20:15. Make a note of the time of my first sighting, Bill, in case we find something and we have to make a report,' Cargill said grabbing the oars and starting to row. 'I'll do some investigating.'

'You think it'll be safe to go so close? I mean, if it is a Jap sub you could be a goner,' Nangle said, as Cargill rowed towards the ripple zone.

'It's my duty, Bill. I'm on watch, mate, I've been asked to help defend Sydney Harbour, and if it's the Japs then maybe I can stop the buggers.'

As Cargill reached the ripples above the boom net, he saw a violent disturbance in the water, with water jets and rising bubbles, and a metallic object. He couldn't see clearly enough to be certain it was a Japanese midget submarine, but he rowed over and reported the sighting at 9.30 p.m. to the nearby naval patrol boat *Yarroma*, commanded by Lieutenant H.C. Eyers, which was on duty in the vicinity of the boom. Cargill said he had seen 'a suspicious object caught in the net'.

Twenty minutes later Eyers reported the sighting to his superiors and was ordered to do a follow-up check, which confirmed that the suspicious object was a submarine. Just one hour after Cargill's report, Eyers messaged the office of the Rear-Admiral Gerard Muirhead-Gould: 'Object is submarine. Request permission to open fire.'

'Object is submarine. Request permission to open fire.'

IT WAS A GREAT MOMENT because an alert Australian, James Cargill, had spotted the first enemy attack on Australia's largest city in time to stop the Japanese midget submarines from doing too much damage. It was 31 May 1942, and despite his companion's scepticism he used his common sense and raised the alarm. Lieutenant Eyers did not have to fire on the sub, however: five minutes after he requested permission to do so, the Japanese detonated explosives on board, destroying themselves and their submarine.

But it was just as well that the commander of the Sydney Harbour defences, Rear-Admiral Muirhead-Gould, had decided to issue a general alarm, because two other midget subs had sneaked through the boom nets and were still lurking inside the harbour. The alarm raised, Royal Australian Navy craft sprang into action, quickly destroying one of the submarines and driving the other from the harbour.

While that submarine fired a torpedo which hit a naval depot vessel, *Kuttabul*, killing nineteen men sleeping on board, it missed its main target, the American cruiser USS *Chicago*. The Japanese raid had ended in failure.

Historical background

The three midget submarines, each crewed by two men, had crept into the harbour under cover of darkness. The first sub (No. 14), piloted by Lieutenant Kenshi Chuman, was caught in the defensive net and spotted by Cargill. The second, No. 24, piloted by Sub-Lieutenant Katsuhisa Ban, surfaced near Garden Island and then dived before firing its two torpedoes, missing *Chicago* but sinking *Kuttabul* (a disused ferry being used for accommodation). This sub escaped to a position off Long Reef on Sydney's northern beaches, where it stopped and sank; its wreck was only discovered in 2006. The third sub (No. 21), piloted by

Lieutenant Keiu Matsuo, was intercepted deeper in the harbour and destroyed with depth charges. A salvage operation found that Matsuo and his partner had shot themselves. They and the men of No. 14 were given military funerals.

An unknown plane had been seen flying low over Sydney the day before the attack, but authorities thought it was American. It was a Japanese light spotter plane from one of the mother submarines, piloted by Lieutenant Susumo Ito. He had flown over Sydney Harbour unopposed on a reconnaissance flight to identify ship locations before he returned to the mother sub 11 kilometres out to sea. His plane capsized on the water, but he and his observer got safely on board and delivered a report that initiated the attack.

As if that brazen assault were not enough, before they disappeared back out to sea the Japanese mother submarines shelled Sydney and Newcastle on June 8,

One of the Japanese midget submarines that entered Sydney Harbour fired a torpedo at American warship USS *Chicago* but missed and hit the *Kuttabul*, killing nineteen servicemen who were sleeping on the disused ferry.

damaging houses in Sydney's Bellevue Hill, Rose Bay and Bondi, but in each case only one shell detonated and nobody was killed or even badly injured.

As Cargill had reminded Nangle, the attack on Sydney followed a long line of Japanese air and sea attacks—those on Pearl Harbor and Singapore, and the surprise bombing of Darwin on 19 February 1942, by 188 carrier-borne bombers, dive bombers and fighters from ships in the Timor Sea and airfields in Ambon. They killed 243 people, sank two ships at sea and destroyed eight in the harbour and damaged twelve more, and wreaked havoc in the town. The Japanese also bombed the airport, wrecking hangars, aircraft maintenance facilities and the runways. The post office was destroyed, along with the postmaster's residence and many offices and homes. The bombs also set fire to oil tanks beside the harbour. Many residents evacuated, immediately heading south.

It was the first of sixty-three raids on Darwin up to November 1943. Japanese planes also bombed Broome in Western Australia, killing at least seventy people and destroying twenty aircraft and flying boats. They then turned their attention to Wyndham, Townsville, which they bombed three times, and Port Hedland.

Postscript

Despite James Cargill's early sighting of the midget submarine and the speedy raising of the alarm, Sydney was nevertheless very lucky to escape with so little damage that night. Defence personnel should have acted after the sighting of the unidentified spotter plane. The response to Cargill's sub sighting should also have been faster: it took two and a quarter hours for a general alarm to be raised, by which time the other two midget submarines were well inside the harbour. It also took seven and a quarter hours for all the patrol boats to go into action. Fortunately the torpedo aimed at USS *Chicago* missed its mark.

Watchman James Cargill never received the recognition he deserved.

1942
CHOCOLATE SOLDIERS STOP 'JAPS' ON KOKODA TRACK

'We've gotta stop the bloody Japs coming down this Kokoda Track, boys,' said Lieutenant Colonel Ralph Honner, Commanding Officer of the 39th Battalion. As his men rested on the ground, he pointed at a muddy track winding its way up a steep hill through the jungle.

'How close are the bastards now, sir?' asked Private Kevin Surtees, a Victorian carpenter serving with the militia battalion.

'They're still a fair way up, but if they get through to Port Moresby they could attack Australia itself,' Honner said.

'What are we gunna do then?' asked Private Dick Secker, a Victorian slaughterman.

'We're going to a village called Isurava, where we have to stop them,' Honner said. 'Now grab your kitbags and fall in, boys.'

'Strewth, Dicky,' Surtees said, turning to Secker as they started climbing the narrow track in loose formation. 'Do you reckon we've got much of a chance against these bloody Japs?'

'God knows, Kev,' Secker said. 'We didn't get much training, most of us have only got .303s and they reckon we're short of ammo—in fact the bloody newspapers are calling us "chocolate soldiers".'

'Why chocolate?' asked Surtees, lifting his leg with both hands to extract his foot from the mud.

'Oh, the press reckon Australia should have sent tough Anzac diggers instead of just us militia, 'cause like chocolate soldiers we'll melt in the sun,' Secker said, breathing hard and breaking off a branch to use as a walking stick.

Many soldiers fighting in New Guinea were wounded far from casualty stations; they depended on mates to escort them from the front line to be 'patched up' behind the lines.

'The ratbags.' Surtees spat on the muddy track, now huffing and puffing. 'Well I'm not gunna bloody well melt, are you, Dicky boy? Let's show those reporters they're bloody wrong.'

1942

'We might be militia, but we're still Aussies, still got the Anzac spirit, mate,' Secker replied, slipping in the mud. 'So we'll stop the Japs till the regular army blokes arrive, eh?'

'Too right. Bugger those Japs,' Surtees panted as he crawled over a rotting tree trunk lying across the track.

'Anyhow, what would those pen-pushers back in Brisbane know about fighting?' Secker said.

Surtees looked at his 39th Battalion mates struggling up the track ahead. 'There may not be many of us, but we'll show the bloody Japs we're no pushover.'

When the 39th reached Isurava they dug in ahead of the Japanese arrival. They did stop the invading forces and, despite the press's scepticism, refused to budge, holding the position until the first of the regular AIF reinforcements arrived. Then, after falling back a little to regroup, they stayed in the line to help the regulars battle the Japanese to a standstill.

IT WAS A GREAT MOMENT because, for the first time, Australians had successfully defended their own back door from enemy attack. It was also the first time in the war in the Pacific that a Japanese advance had been stopped on land. Given that Papua was an Australian Protectorate, the 39th had technically repelled an invader on Australian soil—and, as Prime Minister John Curtin had foreseen, they had done it without the material presence or support of the United Kingdom. This citizens' 39th Battalion had stepped into the breach because there were not enough Australian troops available, as so many had been fighting in the Middle East and North Africa.

Historical background

The 39th Battalion—a militia unit of relatively poorly trained and equipped citizen soldiers that had been organised in case of an invasion of the Australian mainland—was shipped to New Guinea and ordered to stop the Japanese from advancing down the Kokoda Track until regular AIF soldiers, recalled by Curtin from Middle East service, could arrive. The press, clamouring for 'real' troops in the face of the Japanese threat, dismissed the untested militia as inadequate.

213

The Japanese planned a full-scale overland assault against Port Moresby with at least 8500—and perhaps as many as 10,000—seasoned troops commanded by Major-General Tomitaro Horii.

To begin with, the Japanese won the battles on the track and the 39th retreated from Awala, where they were outgunned and heavily outnumbered, falling back to Kokoda village, where they were also defeated after their commanding officer was killed in action. Under Lieutenant Colonel Ralph Honner, the Australians then withdrew to Isurava, where, on 14 August 1942, they dug in using their bayonets to await the Japanese onslaught. There were only about 400 Australians, some of whom were sick or already wounded. But their AIF reinforcements had only just arrived in Port Moresby (the Australian base in Papua) and the first reinforcements, troops of 2/14th Battalion, would still take some time to reach the 39th.

At dawn on August 26 the Japanese attacked the 39th at Isurava. The 'chocos' held on gallantly, but were on their last legs when the first companies of the

The Japanese advancing down the Kokoda Track were no match for jungle fighters like John Hannan, determined to stop the enemy capturing Port Moresby. From this port it was just a brief hop to Australia.

2/14th arrived at the front next day. Yet the battered Diggers of the 39th refused to leave because they knew the Australians were outnumbered about five to one. So 'these ragged bloody heroes', as they were later to be called, remained in the line against the Japanese: the 'chocos' had refused to melt, either in the hot sun or the heat of battle. The Japanese, bolstered by reinforcements, launched a final assault on the Australian positions, from sunrise to sunset attacking in overwhelming numbers.

The regulars of the 2/14th Battalion fought very hard alongside the 39th. Lieutenant Harold Bisset's platoon fought off eleven consecutive attacks, killing at least 200 enemy troops, until he was killed by machine-gun fire. Private Charlie McCallum, with a Bren gun in one hand and a Tommy gun in the other, shot about forty charging Japanese soldiers, a feat that earned him the Distinguished Conduct Medal. Also clutching a Bren gun and 'with his blood up', Private Bruce Kingsbury stopped a fresh Japanese assault by rushing the enemy, firing from the hip, through a storm of machine-gun fire. He cleared a path 100 metres long before being shot down by a sniper, but he stopped the Japanese breakthrough and restored the battalion's position. His posthumous Victoria Cross was the first won on Australian territory.

Despite this heroism, after four days of non-stop hand-to-hand fighting in which more than 500 Japanese were killed, the Australians were forced to withdraw from Isurava to avoid being outflanked. The withdrawal took place in nightmarish conditions of mud, rain and total darkness, with soldiers dressed in rags, ill with malaria and dysentery and very short of food and ammunition. They dared not leave the wounded behind, as Japanese patrols routinely mutilated and executed any wounded, sometimes using them to draw Australian soldiers into ambushes. Returning later, the Australians found many Japanese corpses with no wounds—the men having died from malnutrition, typhoid and dysentery—and several corpses of Australian soldiers with flesh removed, a result of the starving Japanese resorting to cannibalism. The Japanese commander, Major General Horii, disappeared while withdrawing across the Kumusi River, when the fierce current swept his canoe out to sea.

Despite their temporary retreat the Australians had done well: with only a total of 1000 men against 6000 Japanese they had held up the enemy long enough to stop them invading down the Track; but the 39th Battalion was no longer a fighting force. Huge numbers had been killed or wounded, though Kevin Surtees and Dick Secker had both survived, returning safely to Australia.

'Worn out by strenuous fighting and exhausting movement and weakened by lack of food, sleep and shelter, many had literally come to a standstill.'

The hard-pressed Australian diggers were always pleased to supplement their limited arms and ammunition by capturing Japanese weapons in New Guinea, which they could then turn against the enemy.

Finally, more regular soldiers of the 7th Division arrived from the Middle East and by September 1942 the Japanese had been turned back. This 7th Division, with a few remaining 39th Battalion soldiers in tow, reoccupied Kokoda village on 2 November 1942 and drove the retreating Japanese to Gona and then out of New Guinea.

As their commanding officer, Lieutenant Colonel Ralph Honner said of his battalion's achievement at Isurava:

Physically the pathetically young warriors of the 39th were in poor shape. Worn out by strenuous fighting and exhausting movement and weakened by lack of food, sleep and shelter, many had literally come to a standstill. Practically every day torrential rain fell all through the afternoon and night, cascading into their cheerless weapon-pits and soaking the clothes they wore—the only ones they had.

He called the Kokoda Track Australia's Thermopylae, comparing his men to the three hundred Spartans who in 480 BC led a valiant but doomed stand against the 10,000-strong Persian army.

Postscript

The 39th Battalion may have done a great job, but back in Australia they got little thanks. The US Commander-in-Chief, General Douglas MacArthur, displayed his ignorance of the terrain when he criticised their temporary retreat, claiming: 'Australians have proven themselves unable to match the enemy in jungle fighting. Aggressive leadership is lacking.' He and Prime Minister John Curtin ordered General Thomas Blamey to go to Papua New Guinea and 'energise' the situation, and when Blamey arrived he criticised the 39th and the regulars of 2/14th for their fighting retreat.

Speaking at Koitaki camp, near Port Moresby, to a parade of the surviving soldiers, Blamey said the Prime Minister had told him to say that retreats like the one at Kokoda would not be tolerated. The Australians had been 'beaten' by inferior forces and 'no soldier should be afraid to die'. 'Remember,' Blamey was reported as saying, 'it's the rabbit who runs who gets shot, not the man holding the gun'. Rage and disbelief swept the ranks and, although officers and sergeants managed to quieten the angry soldiers, many said later that Blamey had been lucky to escape with his life.

1943

ENID LYONS BECOMES FIRST WOMAN ELECTED TO FEDERAL PARLIAMENT

'**H**ow does it feel, Dame Enid, to be the first woman to win a seat in the House of Reps?' a newspaper reporter, notebook in hand, asked as Enid Lyons stepped from her taxi outside Parliament House in Canberra.

'I am very honoured and of course humbled by the trust voters have placed in me at this time, when so many men are away fighting,' Lyons said. 'But please, just let me pay the driver.'

The reporter stood back until Lyons was headed towards the steps of Parliament.

'Your late husband Joseph was Prime Minister,' he said. 'Now that you're the Member for the seat of Darwin, in north-west Tasmania, do you feel you are following his lead?'

'Of course. Joe founded our United Australia Party and led it to government, but the poor dear worked too hard as Prime Minister,' Lyons said. 'The strain of trying to lead Australia out of the Depression killed him . . . despite having been ill for months, he was working over the Easter holidays when he died four years ago. Of course I want to continue his work, and the humane politics he espoused.'

'But as a woman, do you think you can succeed?' the reporter dared to ask.

'With my experience as a very active political wife and the mother of twelve children, I don't expect to have any trouble holding my own on the floor of Parliament,' she said briskly. 'During the seven years Joe was PM, I was averaging three speeches a week. I've been known to make more than half a dozen in a

Enid Lyons, who had gained much experience of politics from her marriage to former Prime Minister Joe Lyons, was elected as the first female member of the House of Representatives in 1943.

single day. Once I gave ten speeches in twelve hours! I travelled more than 200 miles that day—and without Joe.'

'What are the main issues you will focus on in the House of Representatives?' the reporter asked as they reached the top of the steps.

'First of all we must win this wretched war, of course, although the tide seems to have turned in our favour in Russia and North Africa,' Lyons said. 'But I intend to fight for the rights of women, and for a better deal for families, mothers and housewives. I want to improve maternity care and increase the widow's pension, and put an end to discrimination in employment.'

'That sounds like Edith Cowan's platform all over again,' the reporter teased.

'Indeed—and why not?' Lyons said. 'She was a great pioneer. We women have a great deal of lost time to make up.'

'Do you feel that you too are a trail-blazer?' the reporter asked.

'Not at all. I am just one in a long line of Australian women engaged in politics,' she said. 'Never forget Catherine Spence in South Australia, who won women the rights to vote and stand for election in 1902, or Vida Goldstein from Victoria, who became the first female candidate to receive 50,000 votes way back in 1903.'

Lyons paused so the reporter could finish jotting down her words. 'And you mentioned Edith Cowan—she first won a seat in Western Australia in 1921. I am merely the first woman to be elected to Federal Parliament.'

'Are you pleased that the West Australian Dorothy Tangney also won a Senate seat—which means there will now be a woman in each House?'

'Yes, Dorothy did very well. With so many men away fighting, Australia needs as many women as possible to take their places in all fields, including Parliament.'

'Do you think this could be the shape of things to come?' the reporter asked.

As a capable mother who reared eleven children, Enid Lyons was well equipped to pioneer women's issues in Federal Parliament once elected.

After the voting was counted for the Senate, in the 1943 election, Enid Lyons, left, was joined by Dorothy Tangney, right, one of nine children from an impoverished family, who became the first female elected to the Senate.

'Undoubtedly. Prime Minister John Curtin is a happily married family man, and I dare say he will make us both welcome.'

'More so than Robert Menzies?' challenged the reporter.

'Hmm . . . I think people are familiar with my view of Mr Menzies. He resigned from my husband's Cabinet before the war, and his public withdrawal of confidence undermined poor Joe's government. No, I won't be fraternising with "Pig-Iron Bob",' she said with some bitterness.

'But what can a couple of women do among all the men here in Canberra?'

'Just watch the way things change. Besides, one day there will be many women in Parliament—and at the highest levels,' Lyons said, going through the door.

'What do mean? Surely you don't think a woman could become prime minister?'

'Just you wait,' she called back. 'But I must go. It's time to make my maiden speech.'

IT WAS A GREAT MOMENT because for women, it was indeed a new beginning. In August 1943, Dame Enid Lyons became the first woman elected to the House of Representatives, and Dorothy Tangney was the first elected to the Senate. Lyons's achievement was the greater because candidates for the

Lower House compete directly against the candidates of rival parties; senators are elected as part of a party ticket and on the basis of a state-wide count.

Lyons's maiden speech would serve as a guiding light for women in the years to come. She said:

> I believe, very sincerely, that any woman entering the public arena must be prepared to work as men work; she must justify herself not as a woman, but as a citizen; she must attack the same problems, and be prepared to shoulder the same burdens.
>
> But because I am a woman, and cannot divest myself of those qualities that are inherent in my sex, and because every one of us speaks broadly in the terms of one's own experience, honourable members will have to become accustomed to the application of the homely metaphors of the kitchen rather than those of the operating theatre, the workshop or the farm. They must also become accustomed to the application to all kinds of measures of the touchstone of their effect upon the home and the family life.

'Any woman entering the public arena must be prepared to work as men work; she must justify herself not as a woman, but as a citizen.'

Historical background

Enid Muriel Lyons was born in the far north-west of Tasmania at Duck River, now Smithton. She started her working life as a teacher, but soon became involved in politics. In 1915, at the age of seventeen, she married thirty-five-year-old Joseph Lyons, Tasmania's Treasurer and Minister for Education and Railways (he later became Premier, then served as Australian Prime Minister from 1932 to 1939). They formed a strong political partnership and had twelve children, one of whom died in infancy. Enid was also a talented orator, who made her first political speech in 1920. A devout Catholic—she converted from Methodism to her husband's faith—she dedicated herself to improving the lot of women and defending family life. She persuaded the government to pay child endowment, and opposed divorce and abortion. In 1949, Liberal Prime Minister Robert Menzies appointed her to Cabinet, though in a role she described as 'toothless'—vice-president of the Executive Council. (Joe Lyons's United Australia Party had become the Liberal Party in 1945.) Enid Lyons was initially made a Dame Grand Cross of the Order of the British Empire and received this title when she visited England for the coronation of King George VI in 1937. She was also made a Dame of the Order of Australia, receiving this title in 1980. When she died the following year, she received a state funeral.

Postscript

Enid Lyons's achievements were all the more remarkable because they were accomplished in the face of chronic and often severe physical distress. The birth of her first child had fractured her pelvis, an injury that would not be identified for forty years. Under the strains of political life and constant travel her health collapsed, and she was forced to resign from Parliament in 1951, in the middle of her second term.

Remarkably, however, in retirement Dame Enid took up the cudgels again, writing a newspaper column (1951–54), becoming a commissioner of the then Australian Broadcasting Commission (1951–62), and continuing to campaign for family and women's issues.

1945

DR FLOREY WINS NOBEL PRIZE FOR SAVING SOLDIERS' LIVES

'Great news, Ethel,' Dr Howard Florey said to his wife as he walked through the doorway of their Oxford home.

'You're late as usual,' she said, 'but if you're ready to eat I'll take your dinner out of the oven—if it isn't ruined.'

'Don't you want to hear my news?' the biologist asked, hanging up his coat and hat.

'All right, Howard, tell me, but please eat,' she said.

'I just heard that Ernst Chain and I are to be awarded the Nobel Prize in Physiology or Medicine this year, along with Alexander Fleming,' Florey said as he tucked into his bangers and mash. 'The Nobel Prize!'

'Sausages still edible?'

'Did you hear what I just said? I know your hearing is getting pretty bad. That's *the* Nobel Prize,' Florey said.

'Yes, I heard. After all, I helped you with those trials of penicillin early on.'

'Fleming's being recognised for discovering that the mould he found growing on dishes in his lab in 1928 was lethal to bacteria. And Chain and I are getting the prize for working out how to isolate the active element from the *Penicillium* mould and mass-produce it,' Florey said excitedly. 'Remember how Fleming called the bacteria-killing agent "mould juice" at first? Then he came up with "penicillin".'

'Well, antibiotics are such remarkable medicines that it's no wonder they're giving you the Nobel,' Ethel said.

'Ernst and I are sharing it for developing it into a form that could be used to help all those wounded soldiers,' Florey said through a mouthful of sausage. 'It saved hundreds of thousands of lives in this war.'

'Well, if the number of nights you've been late for dinner is any measure of your effort, you certainly deserve it.'

'Thank you, Ethel. So many wounded men died unnecessarily in the First World War from dreadful infections,' Florey said, lifting another forkful of mashed potato. 'It is nice to have helped save so many people.'

'The prize might do a bit more to help pay the bills than the knighthoods you and Alec got last year, dear,' Ethel said. 'How much is it worth?'

'Well, it hasn't been confirmed, so I wouldn't do any sums just yet. But the honour means far more than the money,' Florey said, wiping his mouth with a napkin. 'I've devoted so much of my life to this research. The prize, if we get it, and all the lives penicillin has saved are proof that all those years weren't wasted.'

The timely invention of penicillin by Dr Howard Florey and Ernst Chain saved the lives of thousands of soldiers in the Second World War who would otherwise have died from infected wounds—as had so many of their counterparts in the First World War.

IT WAS A GREAT MOMENT because for his work on penicillin, in 1945 Howard Florey did share the Nobel Prize for Physiology or Medicine, the first Australian to receive it. Fleming abandoned his efforts to develop useful medicines from the germ-killing *Penicillium* mould, but Florey and Chain, a Jewish refugee from Nazi Germany, carried on Fleming's research. They purified penicillin and in 1941 took their findings from wartorn Britain to the United States, whose War Department soon made penicillin production a top priority. It became the first in a long line of antibiotics and saved countless lives, but during the war it was largely reserved for the military. In 1944, with advice from Florey, Australia became the first nation to manufacture the drug for civilian use.

Historical background

The son of a bootmaker, Howard Florey was born in Adelaide in 1898, the youngest of five children. Nicknamed 'Floss' at school, a name that stayed with him for life, he was an outstanding student. After graduating in medicine from the University of Adelaide, he won a Rhodes Scholarship to Oxford in 1921 and thereafter lived in England. Fellow medical researchers were struck by his ability and his boundless ambition, saying: 'A fire seemed to burn within him, and . . . we could all see the power in him and wondered whether he would ever find the right outlet for his greatness.'

At Oxford, Florey became fascinated by naturally occurring antibacterial agents, which he hoped could be used to treat infections. He started working on lysozyme, an enzyme found in saliva, tears and egg white which acts as a mild antibacterial agent. In 1938 Florey and Chain, decided to focus on the mould *Penicillium notatum,* whose antibacterial properties had been observed and explained by Alexander Fleming. The Nobel Prize recognised their successful effort to harvest a safe and effective antibacterial agent from the mould and to design mass-production methods. Florey spent most of his life at Oxford University, becoming Provost of Queen's College in 1962. Apart from

Although celebrated as an Australian, Dr Howard Florey—the son of an Adelaide boot-maker who co-invented penicillin—spent most of his life in England after winning a Rhodes Scholarship to Oxford University and later joining the staff.

his 1944 knighthood, he was made a baron, becoming Lord Florey of Adelaide in 1965, in recognition of his scientific achievements. He was also the first Australian president of the Royal Society in 1960, nicknamed 'the Bushranger President'. He was Chancellor of the Australian National University from 1965 to 1968, although he remained in England, and was one of the founders of the university's John Curtin School of Medical Research.

Postscript

Ethel, whom Florey had courted at university in Adelaide, became a doctor herself. She was involved in managing early clinical trials of penicillin and later wrote a four-volume book on antibiotics. But the couple's marriage, unhappy from the start, grew more and more strained as Ethel's health and hearing deteriorated. She died in 1966, and a year later Florey married his long-time colleague and friend Dr Margaret Jennings. He died the following year, aged sixty-nine.

'A fire seemed to burn within him, and . . . we could all see the power in him and wondered whether he would ever find the right outlet for his greatness.'

1945

DANCING MAN CELEBRATES SECOND WORLD WAR VICTORY

'Come on, Frankie, you fancy showman—don't stop now, do it again,' teased law student Chester Porter as his friend cavorted down the street.

'Do what again?' Frank McAlary asked, pausing to catch his breath on tickertape-strewn Elizabeth Street, in downtown Sydney, where trams and traffic had given way to joyous crowds.

'You bloody know, Frank,' their fellow law student, Barry Egan, called out. 'That dance you just did so elegantly.'

'No, I'm buggered,' McAlary called back. 'I'm studying to be a lawyer, not a bloomin' ballet dancer. I've done my dash—why don't you wallflowers give it a go? It is the end of the bloody war, after all.'

'Come on, Frank! That cameraman has been filming you, so put your best foot forward,' Porter said, pointing across the street.

'Yes, McAlary, show 'em what we budding lawyers are made of,' Egan laughed.

'Where's the cameraman?' McAlary asked, spinning around in surprise. Spotting the man handling a big movie camera on a tripod, he called, 'Hey, Mr Cameraman—do you want me to keep dancing, mate?'

'You bet,' the man called out. 'The more the merrier. I want as many shots of people celebrating as I can get—and your happy dance looked pretty good, son . . . would you mind doing it again?'

'Who are you filming for?' McAlary asked cautiously.

'Movietone News,' the cameraman called out. 'It's to remind cinema audiences how happy we all were the day the war ended.'

'Go on, Frankie,' Porter urged. 'It's a good cause . . . just pretend you're at the uni commencement ball trying to impress that beautiful girlfriend of yours.'

'Or the recovery ball, more like it, after this bloody war,' Egan added.

'Oh, all right, all right! There's certainly plenty to celebrate, so here goes,' McAlary said. And with a loud 'Whoopee!', he leaped off down the street and into history as Sydney's Dancing Man, celebrating victory in the Pacific.

IT WAS A GREAT MOMENT because the Allies had just won the Second World War and Australians were filled with euphoria. It was 15 August 1945, and after six years of struggle and hardship and millions of deaths worldwide, the war was over.

Historical background

Germany had begun the war by invading first Czechoslovakia and then—despite an ultimatum from Britain—Poland. Australia became involved when Britain declared war on Germany in 1939. After Italy sided with Germany, Australia declared war on her as well. After Japan attacked Pearl Harbor in 1941, Australia also declared war on Japan.

The Allied defeat of Germany and her Axis partners came on 8 May 1945 (Victory in Europe or VE Day), and against Japan on 15 August (Victory in the Pacific Day or VP Day, although the Americans call it Victory over Japan—VJ Day).

Australians had fought long and hard in many theatres: Europe, North Africa, the Middle East, Malaya and Singapore, Papua New Guinea—and on their own shores. Japanese planes had bombed Darwin, Broome, Wyndham and Townsville, and mini submarines had entered Sydney Harbour. More than 39,000 Australians were killed or died as prisoners during the war and some 170,000 were wounded or injured. The conflict had cost the nation millions of pounds and left the economy exhausted. It was the longest war fought by Australia and its Allies, and came only twenty years after the end of the First World War, which had left the nation badly scarred.

Little wonder people thanked God it was over—or that a conventional young lawyer spontaneously danced down the street. His exuberance, captured on film, epitomised the joy and relief the whole nation felt.

Postscript

Over the ensuing decades, as the newsreel and stills from it became increasingly famous, eleven men came forward claiming to be the Dancing Man. The Royal Australian Mint upset the applecart. When it put out a 'Dancing Man' $1 coin in 2005 to mark the sixtieth anniversary of the war's end, it portrayed him as Ern Hill, a former electrical fitter from Sydney's Westmead, who had said: 'When the camera came along I did a bit of a jump-around.' Another contender, Patrick Blackall, signed a statutory declaration to back up his public claim that he was the man in the film.

The man most commonly accepted as the Dancing Man is the modest lawyer Frank McAlary, a retired barrister who has repeatedly insisted he was the man photographed pirouetting in Elizabeth Street. He also has two of the most high-powered witnesses: Chester Porter, who became a Queen's Counsel, and Barry Egan, who became a Compensation Court Judge. Both have stated that they saw McAlary dancing for the camera on 15 August 1945. McAlary's claim was also confirmed by a forensic scientist who studied the film footage.

'I want as many shots of people celebrating as I can get—and your happy dance looked pretty good, son . . . would you mind doing it again?'

1954

QUEEN ELIZABETH II CONQUERS AUSTRALIAN HEARTS

'**I**s everything ready for Her Majesty's arrival, Prime Minister?' asked the white-uniformed Governor-General, Sir William Slim, standing on the red carpet at the Fleet Steps and looking out across Sydney's Farm Cove to where the SS *Gothic* stood at anchor.

'Yes, Sir William, all correct,' Prime Minister Sir Robert Menzies assured him.

'We must get it right—this is, after all, the first time a ruling British monarch has visited Australia,' Slim said.

'We've checked and rechecked all the locations Her Majesty will be visiting,' replied Menzies, leaning forward to see if *Gothic*'s royal launch was approaching. 'I have asked the police to double the number of security officers just to be sure.'

'I doubt that there will be any difficulty. We who know her all love her, and surely all Australians will too,' said the British Field Marshal. 'No one could ever do this heart-warming young Queen any harm.'

'Let's hope not, but there are communist ratbags in Australia who serve as a fifth column for the international revolution desired by Moscow and Peking,' Menzies said, looking at the spectator boats moored at a safe distance and scanning the crowd on the far side of the cove. 'As you know, the communists assassinated Tsar Nicholas and his family after the revolution in Russia.'

'Well, in all my time with the British and Indian armies, I have never seen cause to worry about unpleasantness towards members of the Royal Family,' Slim said, pulling back his white glove to check his watch. 'Her Majesty should be

'I have always looked forward to my first visit to this country, but now there is added satisfaction for me that I am able to meet my Australian people as their Queen.'

231

After she stepped ashore in Sydney's Farm Cove in 1954, millions of Australians turned out to see Queen Elizabeth II as she toured the nation, visiting all capital cities except Darwin; an estimated 75 per cent of Australians saw the first reigning monarch to visit Australia.

here any moment . . . perhaps the large flotilla of spectator craft has held things up.'

'Are you aware of what happened in this very harbour, not far from here, the first time we had a royal visitor, Sir William?' Menzies asked.

'Remind me, please,' Slim said, tapping on the hilt of his ceremonial sword.

'The Fenians tried to assassinate Queen Victoria's son, Prince Alfred,' Menzies said, pointing north-east across the harbour. 'They shot him with a pistol in 1868 at Clontarf Beach, just over there. The prince recovered from his wounds, but it is a disturbing precedent.'

'I see what you mean,' Slim said, tightening his grip on the sword. 'I suppose if there is going to be a politically motivated attack, this could be the moment—there must be a million people surrounding us on land and water.'

'I am not saying there are reds under every bed in Sydney,' Menzies said, turning to look behind him at the packed crowd lining the hill above the shore, 'but it is not impossible that my referendum attempting to ban the Communist Party a couple of years ago may incite some communists to try to emulate those Fenians.'

'Well, perhaps it is a good thing that you did increase security,' Slim said. 'It is a great honour to be Her Majesty's representative for this grand occasion, and I would not want anything to go wrong.'

'It won't, Sir William, we have left no stone unturned . . . I can't afford any trouble, with a Federal election due in May,' Menzies said. 'And this historic visit may help me win that election.' He pointed across to Sydney Cove. 'Right near these Fleet Steps, just over 150 years ago, the First Fleet landed its first passengers, and Governor Arthur Phillip, a loyal subject of the Queen's ancestor George III.'

'I am sorry to cut short your musings, Prime Minister, but I can see Her Majesty's launch heading toward us,' Slim said. 'What a great moment!'

IT WAS A GREAT MOMENT because within seconds the launch tied up and Her Majesty Queen Elizabeth II stepped onto Australian soil. It was 3 February 1954, and she was the first reigning monarch to visit any of the Australian colonies established under King George III.

Well aware of the significance of the occasion, the Queen said on arrival: 'I have always looked forward to my first visit to this country, but now there is added satisfaction for me that I am able to meet my Australian people as their Queen. Standing at last on this spot that is the birthplace of the nation, I want to tell you all how happy I am to be amongst you and how much I look forward to my journey through Australia.'

It was also a great moment for the people of Australia, as millions saw the Queen, at least in passing. Many Australians would have felt like their doting Prime Minister, who recalled the occasion a decade later with a quote from an Elizabethan poet: 'I did but see her passing by, and yet I love her till I die.' The two-month tour was an unqualified success, with not a whiff of unpleasantness. As Menzies wrote at the conclusion of her visit:

It is a basic truth that for our Queen we have within us, sometimes unrealised until the moment of expression, the most profound and passionate feelings of loyalty and devotion. It does not require much imagination to realise that when eight million people spontaneously pour out this feeling they are engaging in a great act of common allegiance and common joy, which brings them closer together and is one of the most powerful elements converting them from a mass of individuals to a great, cohesive nation. In brief, the common devotion to the Throne is a part of the very cement of the whole social structure.

Historical background

Born in 1926, Princess Elizabeth had been crowned Queen Elizabeth II in 1953, after her father, King George VI, died. Her coronation aroused great interest around the Commonwealth of Nations, especially Australia, where she became popular overnight. The euphoria grew when, on the eve of the coronation, one of her New Zealand subjects, Edmund Hillary, with his Nepalese companion, Tenzing Norgay, became the first man to climb Mount Everest. The Queen had begun a tour of the Commonwealth, including Australia and New Zealand, in

1952, but her father's death had forced her to call off the trip. Now she resumed it as Queen.

Although Australia was enjoying increasing economic prosperity, the conservative Prime Minister, Robert Menzies, was highly alert to the menace of communism, particularly after Mao Zedong and his followers seized control in China in 1949. In a referendum two years later, however, Australians refused to ban the Communist Party. Seemingly unconcerned by such debates, the Queen toured Australia with her husband Prince Philip, Duke of Edinburgh, visiting all capitals except Darwin before sailing for England. The Queen travelled more than 3000 kilometres by road and 16,000 kilometres by air. She opened Parliament and greeted 70,000 ex-servicemen and -women at the Melbourne Cricket Ground. This extensive program enabled about 75 per cent of the population to see the Queen at least once during the tour, by the end of which she had become a very popular monarch indeed.

Aware that an alleged Fenian or Irish nationalist had shot Prince Alfred in a failed assassination attempt when he was visiting Sydney in 1868, Australian security forces took no chances during the Queen's 1954 visit, especially as Prime Minister Robert Menzies had just outraged communists by trying to outlaw their party.

Postscript

The Australian Government had cause to be on alert not only because of the 1868 shooting of Prince Alfred by an alleged Fenian, or Irish nationalist (the Prince survived), but also because there was still plenty of republican sentiment alive in the community. In 2009, a former police detective claimed that on a 1970 royal visit to Australia, a group of suspected republicans attempted to derail the Queen's train by placing a log on the tracks near the New South Wales town of Lithgow. When the train struck the log, it was brought to a halt.

Retired detective Cliff McHardy, who was in charge of Lithgow police at the time, recalled: 'It was an act of deliberate sabotage . . . and catastrophe was only averted because the train driver was travelling unusually slowly. If the train had reached its normal speed it would have plunged off the tracks and into an embankment.' He said his investigations had established that the culprits had knowledge of the official train's schedule. Some of the suspects he interviewed included Irish Republican Army supporters who harboured republican sentiments. He claimed that the incident had been kept secret for almost forty years by a Federal Government suppression order. However, Buckingham Palace officials said their archives made no mention of a train stoppage. The rest of the 1970 trip unfolded as smoothly as the 1954 one had done.

1956

GOLDEN GIRL STARS IN FIRST OLYMPICS 'DOWN UNDER'

'The press are now calling me the "Golden Girl", Betty Cuthbert said, dropping into her blocks at the Melbourne Cricket Ground for a training run. The coach had organised a special race so the 4 × 100 metres relay team members could run against each other.

'I'm not surprised, Betty. "Golden Girl" suits you because you have such lovely blonde hair,' Shirley Strickland said as she took her place beside Cuthbert.

'It's not just the hair—they reckon I'm going to win more gold medals at these first Australian Olympic Games than any other track-and-field athlete before me. It puts a bit of pressure on me, especially with these new television cameras following us everywhere,' Cuthbert laughed nervously, bouncing up and down as she settled into the blocks.

'You deserve every bit of praise you get, Betty,' Strickland said.

'But don't you see, it means we have to win our relay race,' Cuthbert said. 'Let's push each other really hard over this 100 metres test now to see if we can bring our times down.'

'Do you really think we can win gold in this relay?' Fleur Mellor asked with a squeal, glancing up in awe at the rows of empty seats in the vast stadium as she adjusted her blocks.

'Well, our very own "Golden Girl" may be only eighteen, but she has already won the hearts of the press by winning gold in the 100 and 200 metres—beating even the Americans and the Soviets,' Norma Croker said, tapping down the pins to secure her blocks to the track. 'And Betty—what else did one of the reporters call you?'

The 'Golden Girl' of the 1956 Melbourne Olympics, Betty Cuthbert won the hearts of Australians as she sprinted down the track—mouth always wide open—to win three gold medals in the 100 metres, 200 metres and 100-metres relay.

'[Cuthbert] didn't think she would win a place on the Australian team, so she bought tickets to attend the Olympics as a spectator.'

'Oh, the Blonde Bombshell, I believe,' Cuthbert said, staring down the track. 'That really embarrasses my family back in Merrylands. So does reporters saying I look stupid always running with my mouth wide open.'

'Who cares? You gulp in more air like that. But what about Shirley? She's done all right too,' Mellor said. 'Fancy taking gold in the jolly 80-metre hurdles against the world's best.'

'So we Australians are way in front!' Cuthbert said with a shout, bursting out of the blocks in a practice start. She called back over her shoulder: 'Come on, girls, all we gotta do is beat the Yanks and Russkies and we'll all become Golden Girls.'

'That'd be nice, except we don't all have blonde hair,' Strickland said. 'But did you see that the *Herald* predicted Australia would come third overall after the two superpowers, even beating the old Mother Country, not to mention Germany and France?'

'I think that's quite likely, because it's not just us track-and-field athletes,' Mellor chipped in. 'We've got plenty of stars in the pool with the dashing Dawn Fraser in the 100-metre freestyle and Lorraine Crapp in the 400-metre freestyle. So we're not alone, we've just gotta do our bit to help with the tally.'

'And the blokes are going great too, especially Murray Rose and Jon Henricks,' Cuthbert said, back in the blocks and tensing every muscle as she prepared to take off. 'But if little old Aussie came third overall that would be fantastic.'

With the four sprinters all lined up waiting for the gun, their coach put down his notebook, pulled out his stopwatch and stepped forward: 'All right, girls, now I want you to push yourselves beyond your limits . . . drive each other hard and go for a personal best. On your marks . . . set . . . BANG!'

And off raced the runners of the 4 × 100 metres, determined to shave their times to the bare minimum in their last preparation for the relay the following day.

IT WAS A GREAT MOMENT because, inspired by Golden Girl Cuthbert, the four did run around that 4 × 100-metre relay track faster than any other female team to claim the gold medal and a place in the history books. They also set a new world record of 44.5 seconds.

And Betty Cuthbert herself—anchor of the relay—did better than any Australian track-and-field athlete before her. By the end of the Games she had also won the 100-metre sprint, having set a new Olympic record in her heat, and the 200 metres, with a time that equalled the Olympic record.

1956

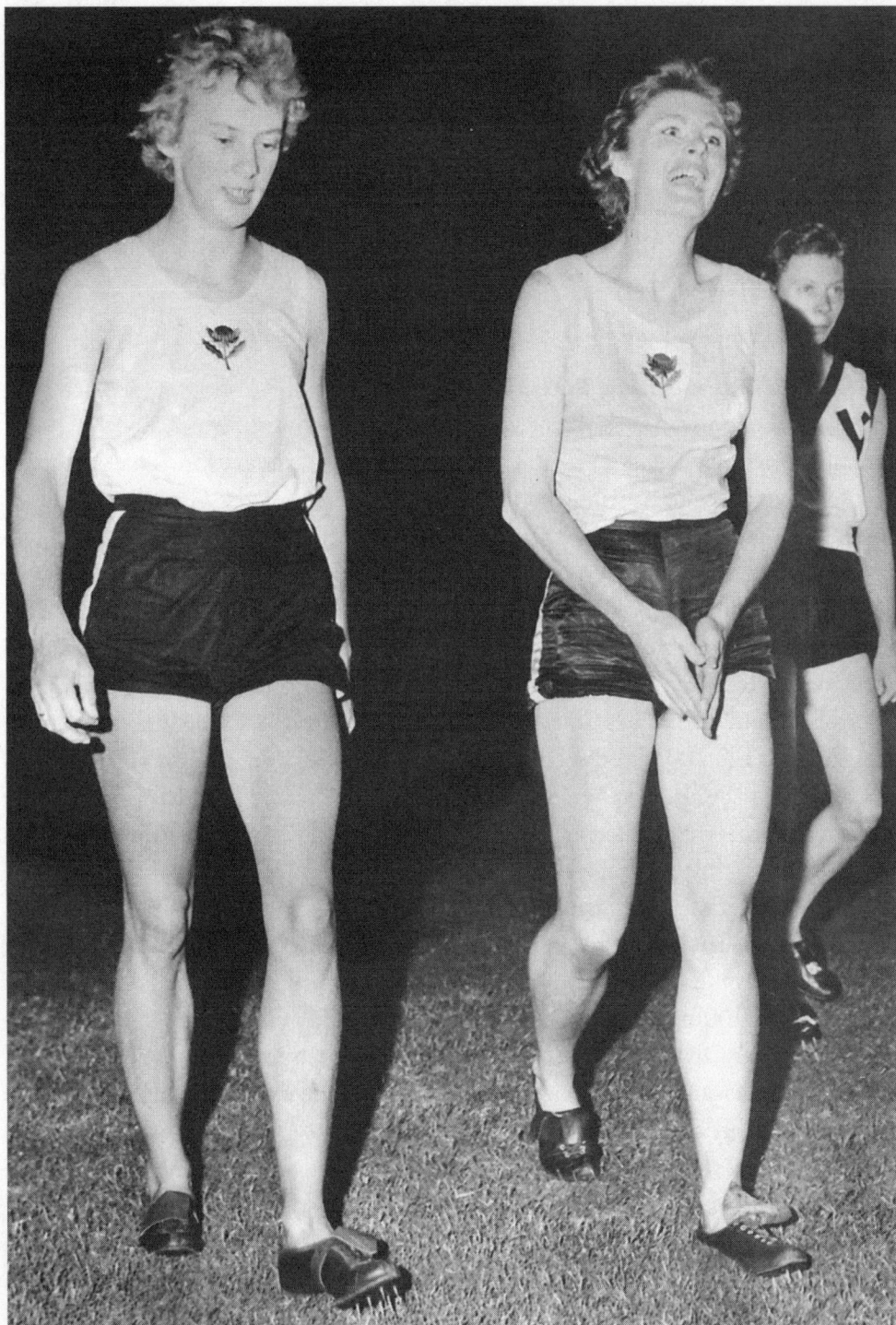

Although the other members of the relay team, including Marleen Matthews, right, helped her win the 4 x 100-metre relay at the 1956 Melbourne Olympics, the deeply religious 'Golden Girl' said God also helped her win all her races.

It was also a great moment because at these 1956 Olympic Games in Melbourne—the first held in the Southern Hemisphere—Australia burst onto the world stage as an athletic nation, winning more track-and-field events per capita than any other country. Thanks to these girls Australia did, as the *Herald* predicted, come third behind the United States and the Soviet Union. Those nations had populations in the hundreds of millions; Australia's was less than ten. Australia won thirteen gold medals, more than doubling its tally of six at the previous Olympics in Helsinki, Finland.

Historical background

Betty Cuthbert, who was born near Newcastle, New South Wales, in 1938, won four Olympic sprinting gold medals—and the heart of the nation. Thanks to the new television service, introduced in Australia in time for the Games, thousands of people could see her performances in their own homes.

Not long before, however, this eighteen-year-old had been virtually unknown. In fact, she didn't think she would win a place on the Australian team, so she bought tickets to attend the Olympics as a spectator. A devout Christian, she prayed hard and started peaking just before the Games. Soon she was beating her world record-breaking teammates Shirley Strickland and Marlene Mathews. In just nine days she won the 100 and the 200 metres and anchored the team that won the 4 x 100-metre relay. She also became the first Australian, male or female, ever to win three gold medals at a single Games. The Golden Girl certainly held the hearts of sports-mad Australians in her hands at that 1956 Olympics. Nearly half a century later, at the second Australian Olympics, held in Sydney, Cathy Freeman would also capture the nation's heart, winning gold in the 400 metres after Cuthbert had helped carry in the Olympic Torch and Freeman herself had lit the flame.

It was the 400-metre event that had sealed Cuthbert's greatness: eight years after the 1956 Olympics, she came out of retirement to run that race at the Tokyo Olympics and, after a brilliant sprint, finished with her fourth gold medal. But she did not do it on her own. 'Sure, I ran the race,' she said, 'but God took over. He picked them [her feet] up, and I put them down.' Until the end of that century only two others, Dawn Fraser and Murray Rose, had won four gold medals, but in 2004 Ian Thorpe took the record to five.

There were many other stars from Australia competing in the 1956 Olympics and many wonderful performances. The great distance runner Ron Clarke created a sensation when he ran into the venue at the Melbourne Cricket Ground and lit the torch—and scorched his arm while lighting the flame. Swimmers also made a big splash: Dawn Fraser won the 100-metre freestyle, Lorraine Crapp the 400-metre freestyle, Murray Rose the 400- and 1500-metre men's freestyle, John Hendricks the 100-metre freestyle and David Theile the 100-metre backstroke. Lorraine Crapp broke eighteen world records just training for the Games. People's appetite for the Games had been whetted with some great lead-up events, including the great battle between Australia's John Landy and England's Roger Bannister to be first to break the four-minute mile. Bannister won that contest, but in 1954 John Landy had cut the record down to 3 minutes 58 seconds in a meet in Helsinki, Finland.

Postscript

Despite her fitness, stamina, and apparent invincibility, in 1969 Betty Cuthbert developed multiple sclerosis and was eventually confined to a wheelchair. Her faith and high spirits helped her cope with this cruel twist of fate. Despite her disability, she still managed to carry that torch into the Sydney stadium for the opening ceremony of the 2000 Olympics—to tumultuous applause from the spectators, many of whom remembered the Golden Girl sprinting around the Melbourne track forty-four years earlier.

While the 1956 Olympic Games appeared a picture-perfect event, behind the scenes there were some nasty moments. Soviet forces had recently invaded Hungary with tanks, crushing a peaceful uprising. The Hungarian water polo players resolved to get their own back in their match against the Soviet team. The game turned nasty, with scratching, hitting and kicking, leaving players bruised and bleeding. Bent on revenge, the Hungarians thrashed the Soviets 4–0. Despite the best intentions of the organisers—and the promotion of the Golden Girl as the face of the Games—the peaceful image of the international competition had been shattered.

1965
CHARLIE PERKINS' FREEDOM RIDE CONFRONTS RACISM

'You can't come in here, mate,' the Moree swimming pool manager warned Charlie Perkins, blocking the entrance to the gate. 'Especially with all them black kids.'

'Why not?' asked Charlie Perkins, stepping forward. 'It's a hot day. There's lots of other adults and kids in the pool. What's wrong with us?'

'The local council makes the rules, and right now this is a whites-only pool,' the manager said, crossing his arms.

'But this is our country, mate—we got here thousands of years before you whitefellas!' Perkins said. 'We have more of a right to swim here than you do!'

'I know all about you troublemakers in your so-called Freedom Ride bus,' the manager said angrily. 'You're the ones who stirred up all those decent folks in Walgett by trying to get Abos into the Returned Services League, eh?'

'Were they the same "decent folks" who drove their truck into our bus three times as we travelled out of town, forcing us into a ditch?' Perkins asked. 'They might have killed some of those students in the bus who were badly bruised—and there are men and women on this Student Action for Aborigines tour as white as you are, mate.'

'You bloody commos from the big smoke are just getting what you deserve— you "social reformers" are trying to destroy our way of life,' the manager said. 'You have no business out here!'

'No business out west . . . in Aboriginal country?' Perkins scoffed. 'That's exactly why us uni blackfellas, Gary Williams and me, started this campaign, to remind you white Australians there are more blacks out here than whites.'

242

Aboriginal activist Charlie Perkins was angry about racial discrimination laws in Australia, and inspired white university students to help him. They formed 'Student Action for Aborigines' and embarked on outback anti-racist bus tours.

'Now come on, mate, this is a disgrace,' a stranger interjected, appearing beside Perkins and confronting the pool manager. 'You know me, I'm a local store owner, Bob Brown—I used to be on the council. Just let these people in.'

'Yeah, I know you, Mr Brown—a "white blackfella", that's who you are,' the manager retorted. 'You tried to get them blacks permission to swim here before. You know they're barred unless it's the kids learning to swim.'

'But we have entrance tickets,' Brown said. 'Look, I've got tokens for six adults and eight Aboriginal children who we brought here in the Freedom Bus—and I've got the parents' permission.'

'Doesn't matter. They're still black, aren't they?' the manager challenged.

'So? What's wrong with that?' Perkins asked.

'It's a matter of cleanliness,' the manager said, running out of excuses. 'And now you are blocking a whole lot of people trying to get in.'

'We're not moving till you let us in,' Perkins said. 'We don't care how long this standoff lasts, and it's your fault that all these people have come to gawk!

Charlie Perkins started breaking down segregation laws by persuading the manager of the whites-only Moree municipal swimming pool to allow him to enter the pool for a swim in 1965, accompanied by a group of black children.

If it really is a matter of cleanliness, why don't you inspect the kids to see if they are clean enough?'

'Just wait a minute,' the pool manager said. 'I'll go and phone the mayor.'

So they waited: Perkins, the other five adults and eight Aboriginal children, all fidgeting about and looking longingly at the swimming pool.

'All right, youse can go in,' the manager said, returning to the gate. 'The mayor said he doesn't want any bad newspaper stories. He said to inspect the kids, and if they're clean youse can go all go in for a swim.'

Giving the children a cursory inspection, he opened the gate. Running to the water's edge with whoops of joy, they all jumped in and swam among the whites to their hearts' content.

IT WAS A GREAT MOMENT

because black Australians had successfully overturned an unwritten colour bar and established their right to swim in a public pool whenever they chose. Charlie Perkins and his Sydney University mate Gary Williams—the first Aboriginal people to attend a university—and their white supporters in Student Action for Aborigines—had made a breakthrough. Within two years a referendum would be held that would bring black Australians into the census and, more crucially, allow federal law to apply to them to override any discriminatory state law.

Historical background

Charles Perkins was born in 1936 on an Alice Springs Aboriginal reserve. He started his working life as a fitter and turner but soon became a professional soccer player, and distinguished himself on the soccer field in Australia and

Britain, where he saw black people mixing freely with whites. He went on to obtain an Arts degree at the University of Sydney, becoming Australia's first indigenous tertiary graduate. In 1965 he decided to put his education, sporting status and skills to use by improving life for his fellow Aborigines, as black activists had been doing in the US since 1961.

Australia, riding on the sheep's back and with copious mineral resources, was enjoying prosperous times under long-serving Liberal Prime Minister Sir Robert Menzies. Little had changed for many years, but the early 1960s saw the start of great social upheavals in Australia as in the rest of the Western world.

Perkins's initial desegregation breakthrough was not straightforward, however. No sooner had he and his fellow Freedom Riders left Moree for the next town in outback New South Wales than the pool ban was reinstated. Outraged, Perkins and his campaigners returned, only to find that white opposition to their campaign had grown. ABC journalist Darce Cassidy, who was travelling with Perkins, said:

> It seemed the word had spread quickly, and the whole town had gathered outside of the swimming pool. For more than three hours we tried to get the Aboriginal children admitted to the pool, but to no avail. One of our students from the bus would take a swimmer to the front entrance of the pool only to have their arms pinned behind their backs and led away, including Charlie Perkins. The police and town officials handled the students and Aboriginal children from the bus pretty roughly, but that was nothing compared to the actions of the townspeople. The local residents threw handfuls of gravel at Perkins as well as tomatoes and rotten eggs, as well as shouting and spitting at him. At one stage he thought he was going to be killed by the white mob.

As it was, a screaming white woman attacked a black woman in Perkins's group, slapping her, scratching her and pulling her hair. Another angry white protester stopped Cassidy from recording the fight by cutting his microphone cable and throttling him from behind. The Freedom Riders were forced to leave Moree without restoring their right to enter the pool.

But the Moree residents could not stop progress. Front-page stories in city newspapers reported on the Freedom Ride and on protests in Aboriginal centres at Lismore, Coonamble and Bowraville. Aboriginal people were soon admitted to previously segregated swimming pools, cinemas and even hotels. Perkins also

'The local residents threw handfuls of gravel at Perkins as well as tomatoes and rotten eggs, as well as shouting and spitting at him.'

As the first Aboriginal to graduate from university, the passionate racial reformer Charlie Perkins believed he had a moral responsibility to help achieve equal status for fellow Aborigines around Australia, and committed the rest of his life to this cause.

received support from white community leaders such as Sydney's Reverend Ted Noffs. Noffs founded and was first president of the Aboriginal Affairs Foundation, the forerunner of the Department of Aboriginal Affairs in the New South Wales Government. Sydney University economics lecturer Bill Ford, who had participated in the US Freedom Rides a few years earlier, was also a supporter.

Perkins said he based his protest tour on the American Freedom Rides against entrenched racism in southern states like Alabama and Mississippi. One of those buses had been forced off the road and firebombed, and two white students and a black student had been murdered. Perkins dedicated his Freedom Rides to them.

Within two years of the Freedom Rides at least 90.8 per cent of Australians voted 'yes' in a referendum giving the Federal Government power to count Aboriginal people in the census. It was the largest majority recorded in an Australian referendum, although the voting pattern revealed lingering resentment and discrimination against Aborigines where most of them lived—in Queensland and Western Australia. The referendum also gave the Federal Government power to legislate on Aboriginal affairs; Prime Minister Harold Holt claimed this would allow it to protect Aborigines against any discrimination embedded in State laws.

The 'yes' campaign was directed by poet Faith Bandler for the Federal Council for the Advancement of Aborigines and Torres Strait Islanders. She said the results of the referendum showed that voters finally wanted to help Aboriginal people, and urged the Federal Government to introduce a law banning racial discrimination and set about improving their living and working conditions.

Although the Federal Government had announced in September 1948 that the first 'full-blooded aborigines' would be allowed to vote 'with certain reservations' (as promised before), many had been discouraged from voting. The referendum nineteen years later made voting mandatory.

After the 1967 vote, clauses in the constitution that discriminated against Aborigines were removed, a Minister for Aboriginal Affairs was appointed and an Office of Aboriginal Affairs was set up to develop state policies. These reforms also inspired authorities to remove the remains of Tasmania's 'last Aborigine', Trugannini, from a museum where they had been on display and have them properly buried. In 1984 Perkins, who had been chairman of the Aboriginal Development Commission, was appointed head of the Department of Aboriginal Affairs—the first Aboriginal person to hold the post.

Postscript

Despite improving conditions for thousands of indigenous people, Charles Perkins died prematurely from renal failure—a complication of Type 2 diabetes, a consequence of poor diet that affects many Aborigines as they get older. Perkins became yet another statistic confirming the poor health and low life expectancy of Aborigines compared with those of white Australians. In 2008, newly elected Prime Minister Kevin Rudd officially said 'Sorry' to all indigenous people on behalf of the nation. Many Aborigines remain in poor health because of a bad diet, alcoholism, drug abuse or petrol sniffing.

1971
JACK MUNDEY INTRODUCES WORLD'S FIRST GREEN BANS

'So you want me and my Builders Labourers Federation mates to chain ourselves to these trees to stop developers cutting them down—is that right, ladies?' Jack Mundey said, half-joking as he walked among the trees at Hunters Hill, in northern Sydney.

'No, of course not, Mr Mundey,' said housewife Betty James. 'Please don't make fun of us. I know we're just a group of suburban housewives, but we're trying to save this bit of bush for our kids to play in. That's why we formed the Battlers of Kellys Bush—and we want your advice.'

'No relation to Ned Kelly, I suppose?' Mundey joked. 'Mind you, that would be an advantage. He certainly knew how to stop the authorities in their tracks, eh? And by the way, it's Jack.'

'All right, Jack,' Mrs Kathy Lehany chipped in. 'But this forest here is original scrub, the last of the bush from pre-colonial times: it's beautiful, it's God's bush and belongs to the people. We don't want greedy developers destroying it for profit—we want our children to be able to play among the trees and enjoy the clean air.'

'How big is it and what do the developers want to do with it?' Mundey asked, looking down at the water through the trees. 'Sure is beautiful, isn't it?'

'Kellys Bush is five hectares. The developers have cut back the original plans but they still want to squeeze in twenty-five luxury homes—unless we can stop them,' said Mrs James.

'Couldn't be a better cause. The city needs to hang on to bushland and preserve as much open space as possible,' Mundey said, walking around a tall gum tree. 'We don't need to destroy every bit of bushland for profit.'

'So you'll help our little band of housewives, Jack?' Mrs. Lehany asked.

'Of course. Housewives are the salt of the earth, and I'm sure I can persuade the BLF to get behind it, but we gotta work out a strategy,' Mundey said. 'Writing letters to the top people would be a good start.'

'OK. Which top people?' Mrs. Lehany asked, pulling a notebook out of her handbag.

'Should we write to our local Member of Parliament?' asked Mrs. James.

'Go to the top. Write to influential people with a social conscience: Prince Philip—he's the patron of the Australian Conservation Foundation—the Governor-General, the Prime Minister, Premier, the leaders of the Federal and

Jack Mundey, who pioneered the green bans in Australia with the help of the Builders Labourer's Federation, was often arrested by police for blocking so-called 'progress' but managed to save many environmental and historic treasures in and around Sydney.

State Oppositions.' Mundey looked up at another huge old tree. 'Magnificent, aren't they?'

'But if those people supported us, would the BLF actually come out here and help?' Mrs. James asked.

'Too right. The way we see it, this is now part of the unions' role in society. It's no use campaigning for higher wages and better working conditions if our members then live in cities devoid of parks and trees and cloaked in pollution. I reckon we can blockade the building site.'

'You are wonderful, Jack—a real visionary, like St Francis,' said Mrs. Lehany, scribbling more notes. 'But what next?'

'We need to organise a big community meeting in the area to see if you housewives really have local support,' Mundey said, running his fingers over the rough surface of a large banksia flower.

'We can help organise that meeting,' Mrs. Lehany said, scribbling down Mundey's plan. 'And what if all the locals vote to support our campaign to save the bush?'

'Then the BLF will impose bans on construction work for the development. Usually when we ban a work site we call it a black ban. I suppose we could call this one a green ban.'

At that meeting, the local community voted overwhelmingly to support the Battlers of Kellys Bush. Jack Mundey and the BLF imposed a green ban on the development, preventing any work on the site. When the developer, A.V. Jennings, tried to use non-union labour, the BLF stopped work on all other A.V. Jennings building projects and said that if 'a single blade of grass' was removed from Kellys Bush those projects would never be completed. This forced the company to abandon its plans. In 1977, the new Premier of New South Wales, Neville Wran, decided to buy the land and proclaim it a state recreation area.

IT WAS A GREAT MOMENT because ordinary people had fought to save a piece of bushland from being destroyed—and they had won. The Kellys Bush green ban of 1971 was the first of its kind in Australia. Its success led the BLF, with considerable popular support, to launch a campaign of bans against developments seen as detrimental to the environment or local communities. It went from strength to strength and was influential worldwide. In Germany, Petra Kelly, a leader of the world's most politically successful Green Party, cited the

Kellys Bush victory and the green bans as an example of the effective use of people power.

Historical background

Jack Mundey was born in Queensland in 1929. His political outlook was influenced by Marxism, which inspired him to join the Communist Party of Australia in 1957. He became a crusading unionist and, in 1968, secretary of the NSW Builders Labourers Federation. In that role he instigated the union's campaign of green bans. Unlike the black bans used to win better pay and conditions for union members, these were industrial actions waged on behalf of the local community with the aim of preserving the environment (including old parts of Sydney) from excessive development.

The environmentalist movement began to develop in the 1960s with the publication of books such as the American writer Rachel Carson's *Silent Spring* (1962), which alerted the world to the dangers of the indiscriminate use of pesticides. Mundey and his BLF colleagues were among the first 'green' activists, and their campaign inspired others around the world.

As the price of space in the central business district climbed higher and higher, Mundey complained that government and developers were destroying the history and livability of inner-city communities, evicting residents, demolishing their houses and dispersing them to suburbs—or, in some cases, leaving them homeless. He later recalled:

> I think the green bans were probably the most exciting innovation that the Builders Labourers became involved in. There was so much development taking place and at the outset there was this feeling that 'all development was good'—it was progress . . . But as historical buildings and buildings worthy of preservation were knocked down, and whole neighbourhoods were disrupted—for example, when all the working class people in The Rocks were going to be thrown out for high-rise development—a segment of the population said 'well, we should be concerned about our vanishing heritage'.

But it was the Hunters Hill housewives who provided the foundation for the campaign. Learning of the proposal to develop local bushland, three residents, Kath Lehany, Betty James and Chris Dawson, formed a well-organised group of thirteen

'The city needs to hang on to bushland and preserve as much open space as possible. We don't need to destroy every bit of bushland for profit.'

women called the Battlers of Kellys Bush to try to stop the project. The developer's idea was to construct luxury townhouses on one of Sydney's few remaining untouched waterfront sites. The Battlers protested to Hunters Hill Council, the State Planning Authority and Premier Robert Askin, but to no avail.

When they took matters into their own hands and joined forces with the BLF, their opponents raised an outcry. Lehany said:

We made enemies. Other Hunters Hill residents thought we were all communists. Most of us lived in Prince Edward Parade, which John Merrington, of Hunters Hill Council, called Red Square. Dr Joan Croll, who had been raised on Methodism and Menzies, actually thought working with a 'communist' was too much and withdrew from the Battlers; but when her husband, Frank, was disgusted by her lack of resolve she rejoined.

The union movement, which had since 1856 won better employment conditions for workers—like the eight-hour day—began to campaign for better living conditions in the early 1970s, saving green spaces like Kellys Bush.

The preservation of Kellys Bush set a precedent for further green-ban action around Sydney. The largest ban was imposed on The Rocks in Sydney in 1972 after the New South Wales Government unveiled a plan for the redevelopment of the area that meant demolishing old terrace houses and a large amount of public housing to make way for a $2 billion commercial skyscraper development. This would have destroyed a precinct and community with a cultural memory going back more than 160 years.

Encouraged by the success of the Kellys Bush action, a residents' protest group turned to the BLF, whose members marched, picketed against non-union labour and occupied buildings marked for demolition. Many were arrested, but the green ban was ultimately successful.

Between 1971 and 1975 the BLF placed green bans on forty-three projects with a value of about $3 billion. In the wake of this campaign, the State Government enacted heritage protection legislation that led, among other things, to the establishment of the Historic Houses Trust, of which Jack Mundey later became chairman.

Sydney had already lost much of its historical identity to development. Without the Battlers of Kellys Bush and the green bans, the city would be a much bleaker place. The bans prompted residents and local councils to recognise the importance of urban heritage and environment.

Postscript

In 1975 Mundey, along with other members who were putting their environmental and social consciences first, were expelled from the New South Wales branch of the BLF by Norm Gallagher, the union's federal secretary. Gallagher was later jailed for corrupt dealings with developers, but was freed after a retrial overturned his conviction. Mundey maintained his vision outside the union and dedicated the rest of his life to protecting the environment.

1971

BOOMERANG THROWER BECOMES FIRST ABORIGINAL PARLIAMENTARIAN

'**A**s the first Aboriginal elected to Parliament, I want to tell you politicians how we Aborigines think,' Neville Bonner said, 'and also show you that we haven't lost our traditional skills with things like boomerangs.'

'Boomerangs!' a Labor senator called from the other side of the chamber. 'What's that got to do with politics?'

'It's got a lot to do with politics,' the newly elected Senator Bonner said, unfazed by the interjection, 'because a lot of fake boomerangs are made by white people for tourists these days, which don't work as well as the boomerangs we Aborigines make ourselves.'

'How would you know?' another Labor senator challenged.

'Well, I came fourth a few years ago in the 1966 Boomerang Throwing Titles in Melbourne, so I'm pretty good at throwing them,' Bonner replied.

'Even so, Senator Bonner, how do you know the home-made Aboriginal boomerangs are better than the professionally made tourist copies?' another Opposition senator asked.

'Because I've been making them for years in Queensland,' Bonner said, 'with my company Bonnerang in Ipswich.'

'But how can you prove they actually work better than the tourist versions manufactured by the bigger companies down south?' the Labor man scoffed. 'What proof can you give us that Aboriginal-made boomerangs return to the thrower better than the mass-market boomerangs made more cheaply and efficiently?'

Australia's first Aboriginal Member of Parliament, Neville Bonner astounded fellow senators in 1971 when he took them out onto the parliamentary lawns to demonstrate boomerang-throwing techniques to gain support for local boomerang manufacturing.

'Come outside and I'll show you,' Senator Bonner challenged. 'I brought some boomerangs that I made myself with local wood and I'll show you how well they come back to you.'

So saying, the new senator wound up his maiden speech, collected his boomerangs and led his disbelieving colleagues out of the Senate chamber to the lawn in front of Parliament House. Then, as the astounded senators gathered in a group, he selected his favourite boomerang, lowered the tip over his shoulder, then threw it high into the air. The boomerang swooped around in a big half circle and flew straight back to Senator Bonner, who caught it effortlessly in his outstretched right hand—to the applause of the senators.

'There you are,' he said proudly. 'Now, I am an Aboriginal, I made that boomerang and it works perfectly. I reckon the Parliament should support local Aboriginal people in rural areas making these traditional boomerangs and stop white entrepreneurs down south from taking the business away just to make fake boomerangs that don't even come back!'

IT WAS A GREAT MOMENT because Federal Parliament had just admitted its first Aboriginal representative. As Bonner recalled: 'For the first time in the history of this country there was an Aboriginal voice in the Parliament, and that gave me an enormous feeling of overwhelming responsibility. I made people aware, the lawmakers in this country; I made them aware of indigenous people. I think that was an achievement.' It was August 1971 when Neville Thomas Bonner, a member of the Liberal Party, was sworn in as Australia's first Aboriginal Senator. He was almost certainly the only politician in the world who listed among his activities 'boomerang throwing'.

Historical background

Bonner's path to Parliament was not easy. His mother was an Aborigine but he never knew his father, an Englishman who went back to Britain before Bonner was born. 'I was born on Ukerebagh Island, in the mouth of the Tweed River, because there was nowhere else for my mother to go,' he said.

In those days—people won't know too much about it, but in those days Aboriginal people had to be out of the towns before sunset. And they couldn't

'For the first time in the history of this country there was an Aboriginal voice in the Parliament, and that gave me an enormous feeling of overwhelming responsibility.'

get back into town again until sunrise the next day; my mother was not allowed to go to hospital to give birth to me. She gave birth to me in a little gunya under the palm tree that still lives down there, on a government-issued blanket. Those are the kind of things that we had to cope with when I was born and when I was a small child, right up into my teenage years and into my manhood.

After his mother died, Bonner lived with his grandparents in a camp on the banks of the Richmond River, near Lismore in northern New South Wales. Life was tough, but his grandmother spoke beautiful English and insisted he learn to speak properly and read and write.

With little formal education, Bonner worked as a farm labourer and stockman in Queensland. He became well known as a rough-rider and competed in rodeos, buck-jumping and bullock riding. After working on stations in north-western Queensland he eventually became head stockman at Mount Emu Plains Station. There he met his first wife, Mona Banfield, with whom he started a family. When the first of their five sons became ill in 1946 Bonner decided to move the family to join his wife's people on the Palm Island Aboriginal settlement in northern Queensland. They lived on the island for seventeen years. It was during this time he took an interest in changing the way his people lived. He formed several committees and rose to the position of Assistant Settlement Overseer. In 1960 the family moved to Ipswich, where he joined the board of the One People of Australia League, a moderate indigenous rights organisation; he later became its Queensland president.

In 1967, a referendum allowed Aborigines to be included in the national census and affirmed that the Commonwealth, not just the States, could make laws affecting Aboriginal people. It was a time of growing indigenous self-confidence, and Bonner decided it was time to enter politics. He joined the Liberal Party, and in 1970, after his wife died, became the first Aboriginal person to contest a Senate election. He was No. 3 on the joint Liberal–Country Party ticket, a spot that effectively guaranteed he would not be elected. In June 1971,

Despite his cheerful demeanour, the nation's first Aboriginal member of Federal Parliament, Neville Bonner, was caught in a political no-man's land; Labor voters claimed he had sold out by representing Liberals, and Liberal voters said he was betraying their cause by advocating radical racial reforms.

the Queensland Government chose him to fill a casual Senate vacancy created by Dame Annabelle Rankin's resignation; he took his place in the Senate two months later. He married Heather Ryan in 1972, and was elected a senator in his own right in 1972, 1974, 1975 and 1980. In 1979 he was named Australian of the Year with conservationist Harry Butler.

In the Senate, Bonner served on committees but was never a serious candidate for the ministry, voting with Labor on some Aboriginal issues. After a dispute with the Queensland branch, he was dropped from Liberals' Senate ticket at the 1983 election; he fell just short of winning as an independent. As an indigenous activist and a political conservative, Bonner was the subject of savage personal criticism from left-wing indigenous activists, who accused him of serving as the Liberals' token Aborigine—a charge he vehemently rejected.

Bonner was appointed an Officer of the Order of Australia in 1984 and attended the Constitutional Convention of 1998 as a representative of Australians for a Constitutional Monarchy. After he died of lung cancer in 1999, the new Queensland federal electorate of Bonner was named in his honour. One of his boomerangs is on display at Old Parliament House in Canberra.

Postscript

Despite his best intentions, Neville Bonner fell between political stools. Attacked by the left as too conservative, he was eventually marginalised by his own Liberal Party for criticising its policies towards Aborigines. The first Aboriginal parliamentarian was caught in the uncomfortable overlap between the white world and the black.

1972
ABORIGINES ACHIEVE SEPARATE REPRESENTATION WITH TENT EMBASSY

'The government has decided that it is in the national interest, as well as largely in the interests of the Aboriginals themselves,' Prime Minister William McMahon announced on ABC Radio, 'for mineral exploration and development on Aboriginal reserves to continue.'

'What a load of rubbish!' Aboriginal activist Michael Anderson said. He and a group of mates were drinking coffee as they listened to the broadcast in his Redfern home. 'How is whitefellas mining on our reserves largely in our interests? It's not going to do us any good at all.'

'Mr McMahon understands the deep affinity between Aboriginal people and the land,' the ABC presenter said, commenting on the Prime Minister's speech, 'and has announced new policies on landholdings on Aboriginal reserves and elsewhere.'

'I bet they didn't consult any of us blackfellas about these new policies,' Billy Craigie said.

'McMahon accepts the desire of Aboriginal people to have their affinity with the land recognised by law,' the presenter went on, 'but wishes to outline that there will be constraints applied to Aboriginal access to the land.'

'Constraints! So now they're gunna try and keep us off the land the bloody whites have already said is ours,' Bert Williams said.

'Any significant handover could lead to uncertainties and possible challenges in relation to land titles in Australia that are presently unquestioned and secure,' the presenter explained.

'Unquestioned? Well it's about bloody time we blackfellas asked some questions about the title to our land, eh?' Tony Coorie butted in.

'While the Prime Minister acknowledges that assimilation is now a matter of choice,' the presenter continued, 'the idea of the separate development of indigenous Australians as a long-term aim is utterly alien to the Government's objectives in creating one Australian society.'

'Assimilation is bullshit,' Craigie protested. 'Separate development is not alien, it's our only hope—we've never got anything from assimilation and trying to be part of the white culture.'

'Hey, we've gotta show those whitefellas in Canberra we are separate,' Michael Anderson said, slamming his coffee mug down on the table. 'How can we show 'em how separate we really are?'

For the activists in the Redfern living room, the announcement had amounted to a rejection of land rights for Aboriginal people. Switching the radio off, Anderson looked around at the others.

'Let's get down to Canberra and make a point about this. The Communists support us—we'll get some cash from them for the bus ticket and head down there. Someone's gotta protest this for real!'

'You're right! Let's do it tonight,' his mate Craigie agreed, jumping up in anger. 'Someone's got to. We'll go down to Canberra!'

'How 'bout this?' Bert Williams said, taking the cups to the sink and laughing to himself. 'We set up shop in front of Parliament House and call it the "Aboriginal Embassy"—so they know that we're treated like strangers in our own land!'

The others all laughed, picturing an embassy for the 'Aboriginal nation' flying the distinctive Aboriginal flag in the middle of a capital already full of embassies.

'That's actually not a bad idea,' Craigie said. 'We'll bring the plight of our mob into the full view of the world by setting it down right at the nation's front door.'

It was 25 January 1972—the day before Australia Day—when Prime Minister William McMahon delivered his state-of-the-nation address. This group of Aboriginal activists in Sydney's crowded inner city were incensed by what they saw as an insulting, backward-looking policy. The next day the four visionaries travelled to Canberra to set up the Tent Embassy.

'Separate development is . . . our only hope—we've never got anything from assimilation and trying to be part of the white culture.'

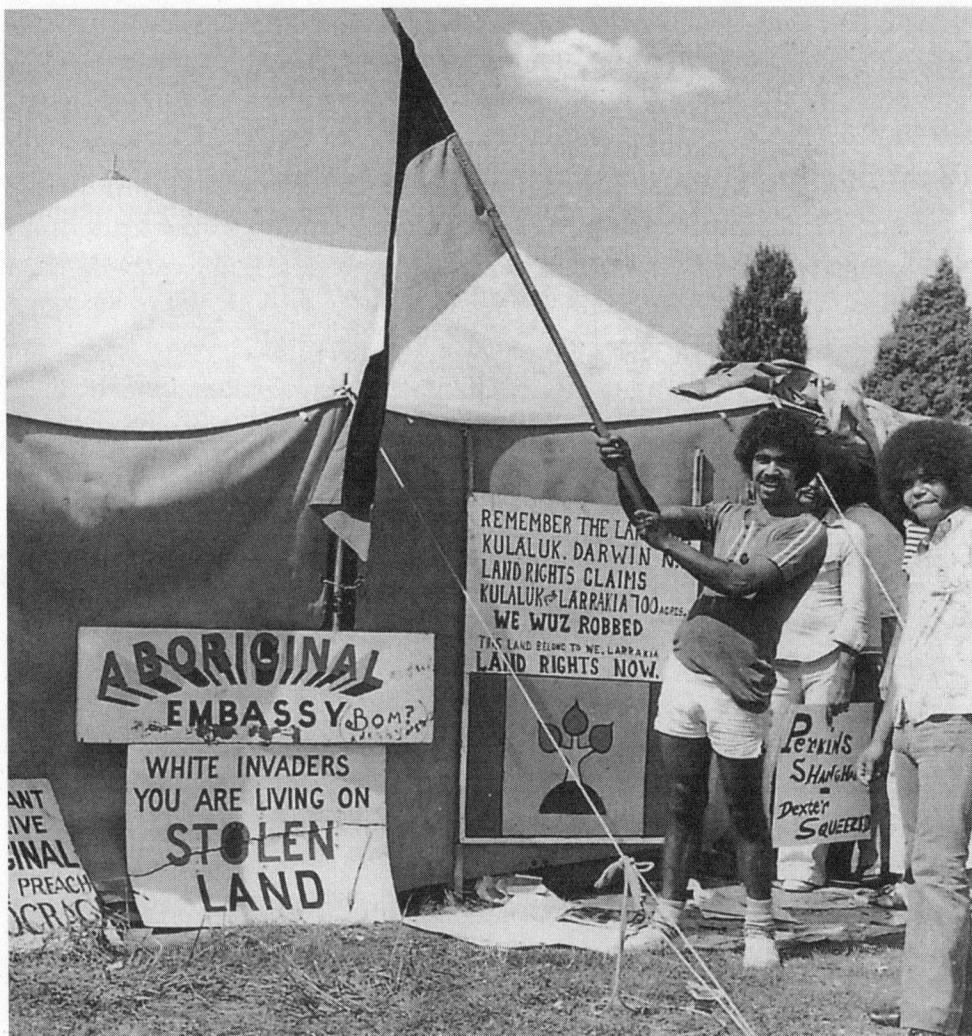

By establishing their controversial Aboriginal Tent Embassy right in front of Federal Parliament in 1972, indigenous Australians embarrassed white politicians into framing legislation that began to improve their living conditions.

IT WAS A GREAT MOMENT because the Tent Embassy made an immediate statement—that Australian Aborigines saw themselves as a separate nation that had nothing to do with the white invaders who had taken over their land. The Embassy became one of the most successful press and parliamentary lobbies in Australian political history—as well as the most enduring protest site in Australia. Adapting notions of the civil-rights and Black Power movements in the US, the founders of the Tent Embassy expressed Aboriginal people's anger over the dispossession of their land, and their determination to fight till they won it back.

The Tent Embassy became a symbol of successful Aboriginal activism and inspired other activists in the years to come. It was a permanent statement of resistance and the demand for sovereignty and justice, a rallying point and a focus of dissent. It was also a declaration that Aboriginal people wanted to control their own lives and futures, and that to do so they needed to control their land and have an economic base. The Embassy drew global attention and placed land rights high on the agenda of Australian politics. Trade unions declared their support. Labor Opposition Leader Gough Whitlam, soon to be Prime Minister, held a conference with the activists soon after the Embassy was set up, saying that if he won the coming election his government would enact a 'complete reversal of the present government's land rights policy, where it denies corporate title to reserve lands'. The Embassy also provided the impetus for the Whitlam Government's *Racial Discrimination Act*, which was passed in 1975.

Historical background

In 1972 Australia was experiencing the last of twenty-three consecutive years of government by the conservative Liberal–Country Party (today National Party) coalition. The Aboriginal Tent Embassy sprang up on 26 January, Australia Day, which commemorates the original claim made on the Australian continent by the British Crown. For the young Aboriginal activists descending on Canberra, this was a day for protest, not celebration. They saw the coming of the British as the cause of Aboriginal dispossession and appalling health, education and housing conditions.

Since the 1930s, in each State and Territory 'Aboriginal protection' legislation had denied Aborigines living on government reserves the right to move freely around the country without a permit or to 'consort' with non-Aborigines; Aboriginal children were often placed under departmental control. A conference of Native Welfare Ministers in 1961 began the transformation from a policy of assimilation to one of integration. Aboriginal activists responded by promoting a sense of separate nationhood, of which the Tent Embassy and the Aboriginal flag were the most striking symbols.

The four young men from Sydney started their Embassy by planting a beach umbrella in front of Parliament House, but within hours their protest had evolved into an encampment of tents, canvas tarpaulins and plastic sheets. The protesters declared that their intentions were peaceful. Michael Anderson told the media:

'The land was taken from us by force . . . We shouldn't have to lease it . . . Our spiritual beliefs are connected with the land.'

The Embassy activists told the media they wanted Aborigines to be given control of the Northern Territory, with full title and mining rights to all Territory land. They also sought title and mining rights to all other reserves and settlements in Australia, including areas in and around capital cities; the preservation of all sacred sites; and monetary compensation for lands that could not be returned to Aboriginal control, starting with a payment of $6 billion, plus an annual percentage of the gross national income.

Australians by that time were aware of the American civil-rights movement, and the 1967 referendum had shown a strong popular desire to include Aboriginal people in Australian society and civil life. A January 26 editorial in the national

Although the British settlers in 1788 were trespassing on Aboriginal land, their descendants had the hide to remove the Aboriginal Tent Embassy in 1972 for trespassing on government property. Cartoon by Ron Cobb.

newspaper *The Australian* acknowledged that in the Aboriginal calendar Australia Day was 'the day of defeat' and argued that 'these people in their difficulties deserve to be treated as an integral part of the nation'.

Postscript

The authorities regarded the Aboriginal Tent Embassy protest as a major disturbance. It was a highly visible and embarrassing reminder of the conditions found in many fringe-dweller camps in rural towns. But while the building of permanent structures on the site was prohibited, camping there was technically legal. This loophole allowed the Embassy to gain six months of publicity. In July 1972, however, the encampment was demolished by police in the face of protests from staff and supporters. The violence of the closure provoked widespread anger. Soon afterwards, the Embassy was resurrected. When police again tried to remove it, they were stopped by 1500 people. Over the next few years the Embassy came and went, but it eventually became so well established on the lawns of Parliament that it was entered on the National Heritage Register in 1995, where it remains to this day.

Late in July 2000, indigenous activists erected another, larger, Aboriginal Tent Embassy at Victoria Park in South Sydney to highlight indigenous issues during the Sydney Olympic Games. Despite some disagreements with authorities, that Embassy also survived. Isabelle Coe, an activist who was instrumental in establishing the original Embassy, said: 'They reckon we are an eyesore. But we say we are concerned about the eyesore that our country is turning into.'

An estimated three million spectators greeted the tall ships of the First Fleet Re-enactment Expedition when they sailed into Sydney Harbour to start the bicentennial celebrations on Australia Day 1988; you could almost have walked across the harbour from boat to boat.

Despite a brief mechanical hitch, Cathy Freeman took the nation's breath away the night she lit the torch at the beautiful ceremony that opened the Sydney 2000 Olympic Games. Fairfax Photos /Australian Olympic Committee

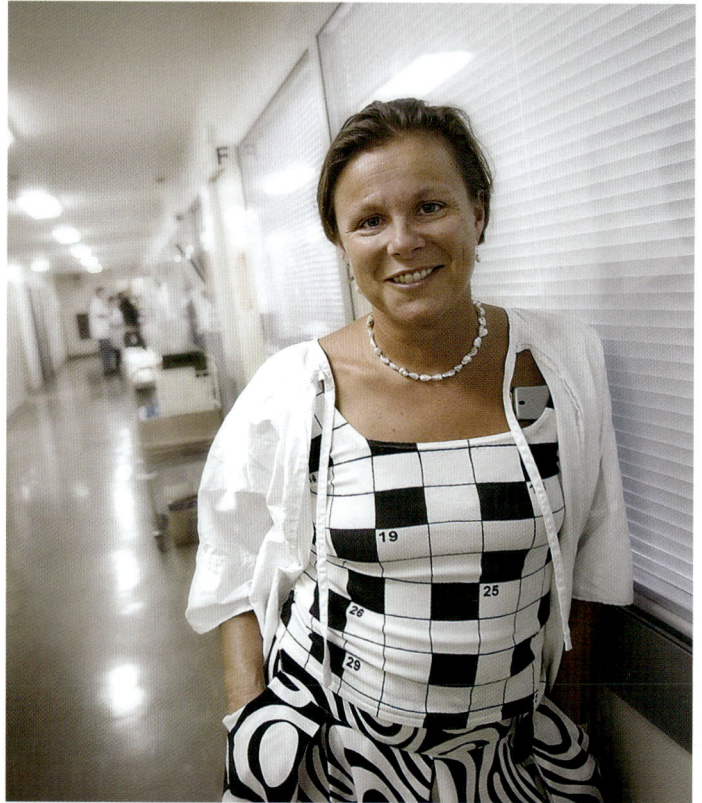

The angel of the Bali bombings, Dr Fiona Wood, from the Royal Perth Hospital, saved many lives with her revolutionary 'spray-on skin' technique, and went on to become Australian of the Year in 2005. Fairfax Photos

Julia Gillard has climbed higher up the political ladder than any woman in Australian history, becoming Deputy Prime Minister in 2007 when the Labor Party won the election under the leadership of Kevin Rudd. Fairfax Photos

The indigenous leader Pat Dodson was one of the most prominent Aborigines to attend Federal Parliament for the Sorry Day in 2008 when Prime Minister Kevin Rudd apologised for the 220 years of mistreatment of original occupants by Europeans since 1788. Fairfax Photos

The guns had certainly fallen silent by the time searchers found HMAS *Sydney* at the bottom of the Indian Ocean in 2008, where she had lain since November 1941. Finding Sydney Foundation

The unprecedented 'Black Saturday' bushfires in February 2009, which killed 173 people in Victoria, heralded a new post-global warming regime of bushfires— a deadly warning of the need to reduce greenhouse gases.

News Limited

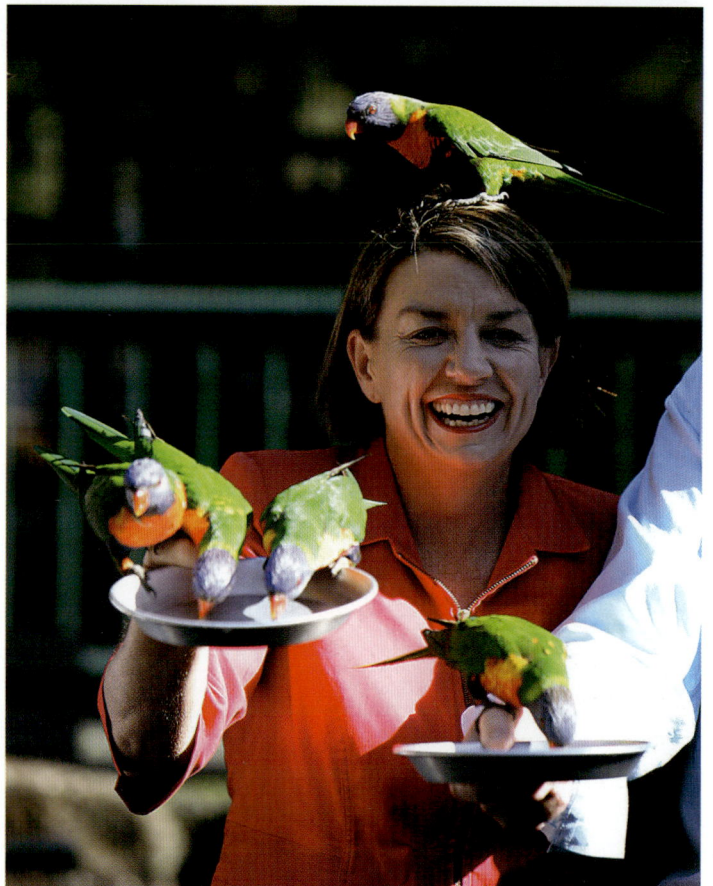

When she won the 2009 Queensland election the colourful Anna Bligh made history, becoming the first female elected by the people to serve as a state Premier.

Fairfax Photos

1972

WHITLAM LEADS LABOR TO POWER, BREAKING 23-YEAR DROUGHT

'**D**o you think we've got much of a chance, Jim?' Federal Opposition Leader Gough Whitlam asked his longtime Labor colleague, Dr Jim Cairns, as they walked briskly towards Canberra's main polling booth on election day. 'Can we dare to dream that tonight we will finally win government, or am I having myself on?'

'You're not dreaming, Gough,' Cairns said, striding with a real bounce in his step. 'As our campaign slogan says, It's Time. We've got the best chance we have had since Ben Chifley last won for Labor at the end of the Second World War.'

'Yes, I really think it is time—our time,' Whitlam said, waving at voters returning from the booth, 'but you don't think your recent statements in support of Ho Chi Minh might have alienated swinging voters?'

'Gough, if we win tonight it will be because of my passionate opposition to that unwinnable Vietnam War,' Cairns said, lightly punching Whitlam's arm. 'That's our winning card, mate. You know how many people I got to that Vietnam Moratorium in Melbourne?'

'Yes, I know, Jim—100,000, one of the largest demonstrations in Australia's history . . . you've told me a million times,' Whitlam said, reaching for an ALP how-to-vote card from a party volunteer. 'Thanks, comrade.'

'So stop worrying about ideology, Gough. Sure, Menzies defeated our last Labor Prime Minister, Ben Chifley, in 1949 by telling the voters there were reds under all the Labor Party beds,' Cairns said, 'but that was a long time ago. Now Australians are starved for social reform.'

'Look, Jim, I'm committed to big social reforms too, and I don't think we've portrayed ourselves as being too far left,' Whitlam said, refusing the offer of a Coalition how-to-vote card. 'It's just that Australia is so conservative I have eleventh-hour nerves.'

'And if a big bloke like you can't beat this little squeaky-voiced clown,' Cairns said, pointing to a poster of Prime Minister William McMahon, 'then I'll go back to working as a cop! I know the only poll that counts is today's, but we've won all the latest opinion polls.'

'So you reckon it will be a case of the government losing an election as much as us winning it,' Whitlam said.

'There's a lot of people desperate for change, Gough. It's not just opposition to the Vietnam War. Women want more rights, and Aborigines too, with that Tent Embassy they put up in January,' Cairns said, summing up the ALP platform. 'And what about the greenies desperate to save the environment, and the poor crying out for changes to the welfare system? You name it, the policies me and my so-called communist mates have been advocating are right on the money— you'll see when the returns come in tonight, Mr Prime Minister-elect.'

'I hope you're right, Mr Deputy Prime Minister-elect. And your doctorate in economic history will come in handy, Jim—I'm going to need a Treasurer.'

'I'll give it a go,' Cairns said.

'Between us we will rekindle Labor's traditional "light on the hill", Jim,' Whitlam said, bounding up the stairs into the polling booth.

'And lead the nation into that golden age Curtin and Chifley used to promise . . . that's always been my dream too, Gough,' Cairns called. 'Be careful with your vote, comrade.'

'Make yours count too, Jim,' Whitlam said with a laugh as he headed for a cubicle. 'We need as many as we can get.'

IT WAS A GREAT MOMENT because when the votes were counted that night, Labor had won government after twenty-three years in the wilderness. It was a great moment for democracy as well, because every democratic system needs a strong Opposition, and if the Coalition had ruled for much longer, the political system might have been seriously damaged. The Coalition, which went to the election under the ageing McMahon, had been trying to block change for too long. Campaigning with the apposite slogan 'It's Time', the tall young

Queen's Counsel Gough Whitlam swept Labor into power with a 3.5 per cent swing that gave it 49.6 per cent of the vote and a nine-seat majority in the House of Representatives.

Historical background

Born in Melbourne in 1916, the barrister Edward Gough Whitlam was a different breed of Labor leader from those who had followed the traditional path of rising through union ranks. Having won the election on 2 December 1972, he immediately broke with tradition by dispensing with 'ladies and gentlemen' and opening his first address to the nation with: 'Men and women of Australia . . .'

Labor then made history as Whitlam introduced, at breakneck speed, the largest raft of economic, social and political reforms of any Prime Minister in Australia's history. He reshaped Australia, cancelling the commitment to fighting the war in Vietnam, withdrawing the troops, releasing anti-conscription protesters from prison, recognising and setting up new trade links with China and North Vietnam, recognising the East German regime and banning tours of Australia by South Africa's apartheid rugby team.

Having campaigned so hard together, Labor allies Gough Whitlam, second from left, and Jim Cairns, right, were pleased to win the 1972 election but as they prepared to be sworn in by Governor-General Sir John Kerr they had no idea that Kerr would dismiss their government within three years.

At home he appointed Elizabeth Reid as Adviser to the Prime Minister on Women's Affairs. He also appointed Elizabeth Evatt as the first woman on the bench of the Commonwealth Conciliation and Arbitration Commission; gave permission for women to serve in combat roles in the army; relaxed divorce laws; increased welfare benefits; and lowered the voting age from twenty-one to eighteen.

Whitlam also gave Aborigines more equality, set up the National Aboriginal Consultative Committee and returned the first parcel of land to Aboriginal ownership when he handed over a lease to a representative of the Gurindji tribe at Wattle Creek in Australia's north.

He also funded many new artistic endeavours, spent large sums on modernist paintings such as Jackson Pollock's *Blue Poles* and inspired hippies and other alternative communities to hold festivals that celebrated cultural freedom. Change spread across the country like wildfire.

Labor leader Gough Whitlam and his wife Margaret (left) were elated with the 3.5 per cent swing to Labor in the 1972 election, which gave Labor a comfortable nine-seat majority in the House of Representatives and the chance to introduce wide-ranging political and social reforms.

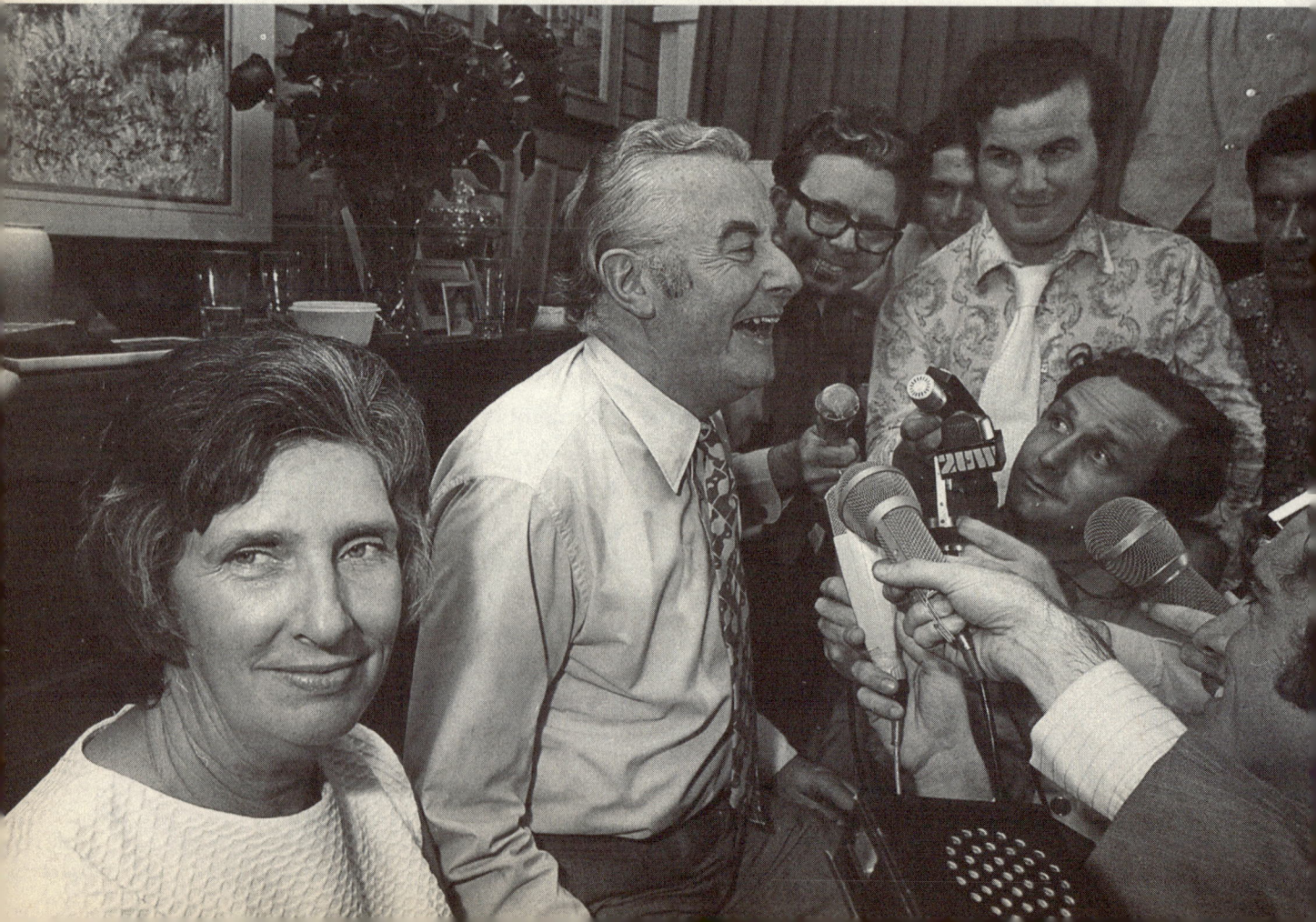

Postscript

Whitlam's reforms were at first very popular with the electorate and the media, but they were expensive and his government found it difficult to raise enough money to pay for them. Many people found the pace of the changes unsettling, and the media began to criticise his style of government and its program. Despite winning a second election in 1974, Whitlam failed to secure control of the Senate, a situation worsened when the arch-conservative Queensland Premier Joh Bjelke-Petersen refused to adhere to protocol in replacing a dead Labor senator. This allowed the conservative Coalition, led by Malcolm Fraser, to block the Supply bills, starving the Whitlam Government of operating funds. The Governor-General, Sir John Kerr—once an ALP member—dismissed Whitlam, dissolved Parliament and called an election, which Fraser's Coalition won. The great social experiment was over.

Yet Whitlam's reform program was not in fact all that radical: it followed standard social-democratic lines and was achievable without violating the Constitution. Such reforms were commonplace in countries where social democrats were in power, such as the United Kingdom, Canada, New Zealand, West Germany, the Scandinavian nations and Austria. Even the United States had accepted liberal reformism from Kennedy and Johnson. Whitlam's program was also timely, because reforms based on social-democratic ideals had not been tried in Australia for so long. Supporters of Whitlam have claimed that while his government was certainly an experiment, he failed because he was before his time. For intellectuals, Whitlam has been vindicated by his legacy and the passage of years. But populists will also remember that this 'big fella', Gough Whitlam, was—like the original 'Big Fella', Jack Lang—dismissed by a representative of the Crown in league with conservative forces, as predicted by Tocsin, the Melbourne anti-Federation group of the late nineteenth century.

'It's not just opposition to the Vietnam War. Women want more rights, and Aborigines too.'

1973
QUEEN OPENS SYDNEY'S OPERA HOUSE WITHOUT UTZON

'**S**ydney is really putting on a great show for you, Your Majesty,' Prime Minister Gough Whitlam said, walking with Queen Elizabeth past the cordoned-off crowd towards the stage on the forecourt of the Opera House. They were accompanied by his wife, Margaret Whitlam; the New South Wales Governor, Sir Roden Cutler; and the State Premier, Robert Askin.

'And I dare say for the Opera House itself,' the Queen replied. 'It must be a long-awaited day.'

'Of course, Your Majesty,' Whitlam said. 'I understand there are 15,000 guests here in front of the Opera House, but police estimate there are at least 750,000 more spectators around the foreshores and out on the Harbour in yachts and craft of all description.'

'I must say, I do like the way the curved white roofs look like the sails of some of those yachts,' the Queen said, turning to survey the crowded Harbour waters.

'Especially the spinnakers, Your Majesty,' he said.

'It is certainly different from our beloved Covent Garden,' the Queen said. 'But I think this modern building will breathe new life into opera, attracting patrons who might not ordinarily attend such performances.'

She approached the special stage set up for the opening: 'That would be a fine outcome, don't you think?'

'You're right,' Whitlam said. 'It has taken more than fourteen years and $100 million to build this place, and I'm sure opera lovers can't wait to reap the benefits.'

'I'm told it is not just an opera house, Prime Minister,' the Queen said.

'That's right, Your Majesty,' Margaret Whitlam chipped in. 'Apart from the opera theatre there are a concert hall, a drama theatre, a playhouse and other performance spaces.'

'I understand its construction has not been entirely without problems—although I believe any great imaginative venture must be tempered in the fire of controversy.'

'There were certainly a few problems along the way, Your Majesty,' the Prime Minister replied, motioning the Queen towards the steps to the stage. 'But every imaginative venture does provoke controversy—even imaginative social programs undertaken by reformist governments,' he added cheekily.

'I am not surprised the building of this creative masterpiece was so controversial, because there has never been anything like it,' she said, ignoring his remark as she was shown to her seat. 'It puts one in mind of the gleaming white Taj Mahal.'

'In this case the argument was between the creative genius Joern Utzon, who conceived and designed the Opera House, and state bureaucrats, who did not like Utzon changing his mind or exceeding the budget,' Whitlam said. 'So there was indeed a controversial parting of the ways.'

'Which is why Utzon is not here today,' Margaret Whitlam added, leaning over from her seat. 'He retreated to Denmark and never returned to Australia.'

'Well, be that as it may,' the Queen said, 'it is now my duty to open his beautiful creation.'

When the moment arrived, she stepped forward and said: 'I have much pleasure in declaring the Opera House open!'

Hundreds of white pigeons flew skywards, dispersing above Sydney in all directions. They were followed by the release of 30,000 'champagne-bubble' helium balloons and a fly-past of F-111 fighter jets, after which the orchestra played *God Save the Queen*. Atop the Opera House, on one of those curved white roofs the Queen had admired, Aboriginal actor Ben Blakeney called out: 'I am Bennelong. Two hundred years ago on this point, the fires of my people burnt and into the flames from shadows all about our warriors danced . . .'

That night different kinds of fires burned when the city of Sydney put on a spectacular fireworks display above the Opera House.

Not long after Joern Utzon won the international competition to design the Opera House and began implementing his beautiful vision, government bureaucrats began accusing him of changing his plans and exceeding the budget; they eventually dismissed the architectural poet and sent him back to Denmark.

When Queen Elizabeth opened the controversial Opera House at the invitation of New South Wales Premier Robert Askin, right, she knew the government had dismissed Utzon but said she believed, 'Any great imaginative venture must be tempered in the fire of controversy.'

IT WAS A GREAT MOMENT because Sydney, and Australia, now had a beautifully designed and distinctly original world-class Opera House—a building that from its beginning seemed destined to become one of the modern Seven Wonders of the World. Although Utzon's daring concept was very difficult to build, Australians had succeeded in constructing a magnificent architectural monument.

Historical background

It was 20 October 1973, and after years of controversy Sydney's gleaming white icon was finally operational. It was far more than an Opera House: with those white sails rising optimistically into the sky, it was also a symbol of the soaring confidence of Sydney and of the young Australian nation.

The Danish architect Joern Utzon won the international competition for a design for the new Opera House in 1957 and signed the contract for the building of the first stage in 1961. He once said he saw the Opera House as a large hollow rock perched on the end of the headland named after the colonial-era Aboriginal leader Bennelong; when the people of Sydney entered that rock they would be in a realm of enchantment, cut off from ordinary life. For the form of the curved roofs, he said he was inspired by the images of sails on the harbour and orange peels unravelling. Utzon said he had presented such a radical design because he believed that if anybody could build it, it would be Australia. And its successful completion indeed showed that Australians could achieve great things. With spaces for so many types of performance, the Opera House confirmed that sports-mad Australia also had time for the arts. By Australia's bicentennial year in 1988, the Opera House was voted one of the Wonders of the Twentieth Century and had become the most recognised symbol of Sydney, ahead of the Harbour Bridge and Bondi Beach.

'With those white sails rising optimistically into the sky, it was also a symbol of the soaring confidence of Sydney and of the young Australian nation.'

Postscript

Queen Elizabeth was right when she noted that the Opera House's construction was not without problems. Architectural genius though he was, Utzon was prevented from personally bringing his dream to fruition by a change of government. Bureaucrats and politicians who had opposed the whole plan while in Opposition lacked the flexibility to respond to Utzon's evolving ideas, which

When visiting to open the long-awaited Opera House Queen Elizabeth II with the Duke of Edinburgh received a warm reception from the people of Sydney where she was welcomed by Lord Mayor Nicholas Shehadie and his wife, the popular Professor Marie Bashir who went on to become Governor of New South Wales.

demanded more time and money than at first planned. They held back funds he needed, and in early 1966, when he could not pay his staff, he resigned and returned to Denmark, leaving the Australians to finish his masterpiece. He died in November 2008, never having been back to see it.

Although Utzon's creation became an internationally recognised icon, he was so bruised by the fight over its construction that he never again attempted anything so ambitious. His son Jan, however, did carry on his father's work, coming to Australia when refurbishments were needed and suggesting changes to the interior and exterior that were accepted by the authorities.

1975
GOVERNOR-GENERAL SACKS PRIME MINISTER WHITLAM

'**W**ell may we say "God save the Queen", the recently dismissed Prime Minister, Gough Whitlam, said to the reporters and shocked Labor supporters gathered on the front steps of Parliament House, 'because nothing will save the Governor-General.'

Then, staring straight into the lens of the nearest television camera, he rammed home the point: 'The proclamation you have just heard read by the Governor-General's official secretary,' he intoned, straightening to his full height and shifting his rhetoric into top gear, 'was countersigned "Malcolm Fraser"—who will undoubtedly go down in Australian history from Remembrance Day 1975 as Kerr's Cur.'

Whitlam was incandescent with fury because he had just been to Government House to advise the Queen's representative, Sir John Kerr, that he wanted to call a half-Senate election. Instead, Kerr had dismissed him from office.

'Kerr's Cur', as Whitlam now called Opposition Leader Malcolm Fraser, had beaten him to the punch. Fraser had met with Kerr five days earlier, urging him to dismiss the Prime Minister—and warning that if the Governor-General did not act he would leave himself open to dismissal by Whitlam. Fraser's Opposition had succeeded in blocking passage of the Supply bills that released funds to the government for the day-to-day running of the country. Fraser had now told the Governor-General that only a general election could resolve the crisis. While Whitlam was with the Governor-General, his political rival—having been summoned by Kerr—was waiting in another room.

When Whitlam arrived at Yarralumla, Kerr asked him, 'So are you prepared to recommend a general election?'

Sir John Kerr may have had a working class background, but this did not stop the Queens Councillor from dismissing the Labor Prime Minister, using values he had acquired while rising through the conservative legal profession.

'No,' Whitlam said, taken aback. His intention was to hold a half-Senate election on December 13; he had come to see the Governor-General simply to give him a formal copy of the written advice for that election.

'In that case, I am afraid I have no alternative but to dismiss you,' Kerr said, handing Whitlam a document terminating his commission.

'What!' the startled Prime Minister retorted, wondering if he had misheard. 'What do you mean? You can't do that. You don't have the constitutional power to dismiss a Prime Minister.'

'Yes, I am afraid I do,' Kerr replied. 'Section 64 of the Constitution states that you hold office only "during the pleasure of the Governor-General".'

'That's preposterous!' Whitlam spluttered, seething at the betrayal by Kerr, a protégé of Labor icon H.V. Evatt who had been put forward for the post by Whitlam himself. 'What's got into you? You can't try that on. As Prime Minister I'll appeal and advise the Queen to remove you immediately.'

'It is too late,' Kerr said coldly, pointing to the document in Whitlam's hand. 'I have already withdrawn your commission—you are no longer Prime Minister of Australia.'

'We'll see about that,' Whitlam retorted, storming out.

Kerr called Fraser in and, having asked for and received guarantees from the Opposition Leader that he would pass Supply and call a general election, commissioned him on the spot as caretaker Prime Minister.

IT WAS A GREAT MOMENT because it was the first time an Australian Governor-General had dismissed a Prime Minister, and it sent a shockwave around the nation. Kerr had chosen to exercise the reserve powers for resolving just such a deadlock that were given to the Governor-General by the 1901 Constitution. Aside from inspiring one of the most passionate political speeches in Australian history, the dismissal was a watershed for the nation, inspiring many people to pay attention to the Constitution for the first time. (The reserve powers of the Governor-General have never been removed.) It also launched the modern movement to make Australia a republic (a proposal rejected by a narrow majority at a referendum in 1999). Pro-republican sentiments had been simmering since the 1890s, when the Melbourne-based Tocsin group warned that a non-elected governor-general might one day dismiss elected Labor leaders.

Overleaf: After hearing the proclamation read by the Governor-General's official secretary confirming his dismissal, the irate Gough Whitlam grabbed the microphone and uttered his most famous words, 'Well may we say, "God save the Queen", because nothing will save the Governor-General!'

Historical background

After serving with the RAAF in the Second World War, Gough Whitlam joined the Labor Party and was admitted to the New South Wales bar. He won the seat of Werriwa in 1952 and within fifteen years was party leader. Harnessing the support of the anti-war movement and promising no fewer than 140 reforms, Whitlam and Labor swept to power in 1972 on the slogan 'It's Time'.

Wasting little time himself, he rapidly pushed through his promised changes, winning the hearts of many voters but alienating many others. The conservative Liberal–Country (later National) Party Coalition, which claimed Whitlam was bankrupting the nation with Labor's 'crash-through or crash' style, used its numbers in the Senate to cut off funds to the government. Conservative Premiers Tom Lewis of New South Wales and Joh Bjelke-Petersen of Queensland worsened the situation by refusing to follow convention and appoint Labor senators to fill vacancies left by the death and departure of other Labor senators. (In 1977 this procedure was made mandatory.)

Whitlam's credibility was eroded by a series of scandals. In the 'Loans Affair', Minerals and Energy Minister Rex Connor was forced to resign after he tried to circumvent the Senate's obstruction by borrowing money through unorthodox channels and continued doing so even after his authority was revoked. Treasurer Jim Cairns, who had been married for years, also raised eyebrows with his liaison with an aide, Junie Morosi, and was also dismissed from Cabinet for misleading Parliament over the loans issue.

Malcolm Fraser decided on the unprecedented tactic of blocking in the Senate the money Supply bills that had traditionally been passed as a matter of routine. Since this would stop Whitlam from governing, Fraser believed it would force him to call a general election, which the Coalition had a good chance of winning.

To resolve the impasse, Whitlam wanted to hold a half-Senate election on December 13 in the hope of getting more Labor senators elected. When he went to advise the Governor-General of this, he did not know that Kerr had secretly sought advice from the Chief Justice of the High Court, Sir Garfield Barwick— once Attorney-General in the conservative Menzies Government—and decided to resolve the deadlock another way: by dismissing Whitlam.

The reason he gave for doing this was that Whitlam had failed to muster enough parliamentary support to pass the Supply bills. He could have negotiated and given Whitlam more time, but under pressure from Fraser he did

'Well may we say "God save the Queen", because nothing will save the Governor-General.'

not do so. Kerr later offered this rationale: 'Here the confidence of both Houses on supply is necessary to ensure its provision. In the United Kingdom the confidence of the House of Commons alone is necessary.' In Kerr's view, the previous sole criterion for which party formed government—a majority in the House of Representatives—no longer applied.

When Fraser advised his members to vote in favour of the Supply bills, Labor senators were still unaware of the events at Yarralumla. Supply was passed, Fraser called a general election, and Kerr dissolved Parliament.

What made Whitlam so angry was that Fraser had conspired with Kerr and counter-signed the proclamation of his dismissal. After fewer than three years in government, all the while battling Opposition attempts to obstruct its reform platform, Labor had been sacked by the Governor-General with support from a conservative Opposition leader.

Despite being dismissed out of hand by the Governor-General, Gough Whitlam remained supremely confident that voters would be outraged and would vote him back into government.

Postscript

Despite his apparent popularity, Whitlam was thoroughly defeated in the December election. However, like Ned Kelly, who seemed to have pointed the bone at Justice Redmond Barry for sentencing him to be hanged on an earlier November 11, Whitlam consigned Kerr to the perdition of hounding by the media and placard-waving protesters. After standing down on grounds of ill-health, he lived in Europe for many years and died in 1991.

Malcolm Fraser did not go down in history as 'Kerr's Cur'—in fact, somewhat to his surprise, he was re-elected in 1977. The results confirmed that the electorate had had enough of Whitlam-style reforms. Whitlam eventually forgave Fraser, who began sounding more like a Labor man than a conservative. In their twilight years the two men were the best of friends. In 1999 both 'Kerr's Cur' and his victim supported the proposal to make Australia a republic.

1983
GREEN PIONEER BOB BROWN HELPS SAVE FRANKLIN RIVER

'Look out, Bob, the cops are coming—there must be about fifty of them, and they look like they mean business!' Paul Smith warned as police moved through the Tasmanian forest towards the protesters and their 'NO DAMS' signs.

'Well, they can't hurt us . . . the worst thing they can do is lock us up,' Bob Brown said as the officers drew closer. It was just before Christmas in 1982, and he and the rest of the group were blocking bulldozers from making a road to the site of a proposed dam in south-western Tasmania. 'It will be good publicity in the fight to save the river and this beautiful wilderness.'

'Look, they're kicking over our signs,' Smith said. 'Pity the media aren't filming that.'

'Just stand firm, Paul,' Brown said calmly, arm in arm with the protesters who were standing across the path. 'Remember Lake Pedder! Just remember what happened ten years ago.'

'That was a tragedy,' Smith said, taking photos of the police tearing up posters and throwing placards into the bush either side of the road. 'I'd die before allowing that to happen to the Franklin River. It's the most beautiful river on earth.'

'I'll never forget you introducing me to the Franklin, Paul. After all, that and losing Pedder were the main reasons we founded the Tasmanian Wilderness Society in 1976,' Brown said, watching the police close in.

'It's a pity you had to give up practising medicine to save the wilderness,' Smith said.

'When you took me rafting down the Franklin,' Brown said, bracing himself for the first of the police, who were now just metres away, 'that really opened my eyes. But we'll win this one, Paul—we won't lose it like Pedder.'

Brown got ready to confront the police, who were arresting protesters in front of them and putting them into paddy wagons.

'How can you be so sure, Bob?' Smith asked, packing his camera away carefully to protect the evidence it now contained.

'Franklin is different from Pedder because the Federal Government got the World Heritage listing through,' Brown said, watching his fellow protesters being taken away one by one. 'So Canberra can't let the State Government destroy a listed World Heritage area, can they, Paul?'

'I suppose not,' Smith said, zipping up his backpack, in which the camera was now well hidden.

'The Australian Democrats' Heritage Protection Bill has been passed by the Senate, too—that was a big turning point,' Brown added, adjusting the tie he always wore to convey respectability.

'And it was a great help finding all those Aboriginal relics going back more than 20,000 years in caves that will be flooded if the dam goes ahead,' Smith said.

'We've also got Bob Hawke the Opposition leader on side, now that Labor has promised to save the Franklin,' said Brown, packing his backpack ready to be arrested. 'And there are hundreds more supporters here today because of that mainland tour I did last year calling for nonviolent action.'

'Bit like Mahatma Gandhi, eh?' Smith teased.

'Steady on—anyway, I know some of those 14,000 people who came to the Melbourne rally are here today,' Brown said.

'Yeah, and we need 'em. More than fifty were arrested on our first day, and the tally's now 1400 arrested and jailed—just like *we* are about to be any second. Let's hope the boys in blue will be gentle this time,' Smith half-joked, 'because it looks like you're next, Bob.'

'Dr Brown?' a police officer asked as he walked up to the pair.

'Yes, I am Dr Brown.'

'I am placing you under arrest for being in this area without specific authority, trespassing on public property, causing a public nuisance and disturbing the peace,' the policeman said. 'Any thing you say will be taken down and may be used in evidence in court—will you come quietly or will I have to use force?'

'Of course I will come quietly, officer,' Brown said.

Brown spent nearly three weeks in jail, during which time a Democrat, Dr Norm Sanders, resigned as a Member of Tasmania's House of Assembly in protest over the dam and treatment of protesters like Brown. On an electoral countback, Sanders's seat went to Brown, who had stood on a 'No Dams' platform at the same election. This was a real turning point for Brown and the Franklin campaign. He went from prison to Parliament in less than twenty-four hours, and used his newfound authority to help save the Franklin River.

Then the big guns started firing. When he became Prime Minister in March 1983, Labor's Bob Hawke fought the Tasmanian Government's High Court challenge to Federal laws blocking the destruction of the wilderness area. In July, the High Court declared the area a national heritage park. The proposed dam was forbidden and the Franklin saved.

IT WAS A GREAT MOMENT because Bob Brown and his 'No Dams' supporters saved the Franklin—one of the world's most remote and pristine rivers—by persuading the Federal Government to overrule a State and put the environment ahead of jobs or profits. Labor had used external-affairs powers in the Constitution to declare the Franklin-below-Gordon region a national park immune from development.

Brown and his fellow protesters also established the environment as a national and international issue. (The previous year, New South Wales Premier Neville Wran had also protected state forests such as Hastings Valley, Washpool and Forbes River by creating national parks—the first victory of an Environment Department, along with the National Parks and Wildlife Service, over the pro-development Forestry Commission.) Bob Hawke had even used the Franklin controversy to win votes in the election. The environment had irrevocably arrived on the Australian political agenda.

Having led the successful Tasmanian Wilderness Society campaign to save the Franklin River, committed conservationist Bob Brown entered state then federal politics, creating the Greens political party to fight for environmental causes.

Historical background

Born in Oberon, New South Wales, in 1944, Bob Brown graduated in medicine from the University of Sydney before becoming interested in the environment. After moving to Liffey, near Launceston, in Tasmania, he quit his medical practice to become the full-time voluntary director of the Tasmanian Wilderness Society

(later The Wilderness Society). At around the same time, plans firmed up to dam the Franklin River for hydroelectricity.

In June 1980, the Tasmanian Labor Government of Doug Lowe decided to place the Franklin into a Wild Rivers National Park. But this compromise involved building another dam upstream—the Gordon-above-Olga scheme. Since this would still destroy important wilderness, it was opposed by conservationists; they were joined by unions, business interests and the state's Hydro Electric Commission, which still wanted to flood the Franklin. As a result, Tasmania's Legislative Council amended the government's dam legislation by replacing the words 'Gordon above Olga' with 'Gordon below Franklin'. This led to a deadlock between the Upper and Lower Houses and precipitated a constitutional crisis.

In late 1981 the State Government tried to resolve the deadlock by holding a referendum. The Tasmanian Wilderness Society ran a strong 'No Dams' campaign. In the referendum, the Gordon-above-Olga scheme received 8 per cent of the vote, 47 per cent voted for the Franklin option, and 45 per cent voted informally. But during this crisis the pro-dam Labor politician Harry Holgate ousted Doug Lowe as Premier and the government lost its majority in the House of Assembly. In March 1982 an election had to be called.

Despite a vigorous campaign by the Tasmanian Wilderness Society in favour of Bob Brown, the strongly pro-dam Liberal Party of Robin Gray won nineteen of the thirty-five seats. Legislation to dam the Franklin passed Parliament in 1982 and the bulldozers started rolling.

Before leaving office, Lowe had asked the Federal Government to nominate the area for World Heritage listing, and the Australian Democrats' World Heritage Protection Bill passed in the Senate soon after. So Brown toured Australia to gather support for the 'No Dams' campaign. By August 1982, the Federal Labor Party adopted a policy of saving the Franklin, strongly supported by Bob Hawke. The Tasmanian Wilderness Society soon had seventy branches around Australia, many in marginal electorates, all urging a vote for the ALP in the House of Representatives and the Democrats in the Senate. Hawke easily won the 1983 election and announced that the dam would not proceed.

But Gray defied the Federal Government's order and continued work on the dam, prompting Brown to lead the protest on site. The conflict was then placed before the High Court, which ruled in July 1983 that the Commonwealth had the power to stop the dam. The Franklin was saved. Later that year, a $270 million compensation package for Tasmania was agreed between Hawke and Gray.

'I'd die before allowing [what happened to Lake Pedder] to happen to the Franklin. It's the most beautiful river on earth.'

It may have resembled the biblical David versus Goliath story but members of the campaign to stop the damming of the Franklin River nevertheless managed to stall construction workers by blockading the river with their rafts until the Federal Government declared the area a national park.

The Commonwealth power was subsequently used to protect other natural assets. Bob Brown went on to form the Tasmanian Greens and later formed the Australian Greens, then was elected to Federal Parliament. He continued to serve as a senator and a world leader on environmental issues.

Postscript

Despite Brown's open-hearted commitment to peaceful action to protect the environment, he was often roughly handled by police, sent to jail three times, and vilified by detractors including members of the media. Nevertheless, by the early twenty-first century the Greens was the fastest-growing party in Australia, sometimes doubling its vote between elections.

1983

JOHN BERTRAND WINS AMERICA'S CUP IN *AUSTRALIA II*

'She sails beautifully, Alan,' skipper John Bertrand shouted as he steered *Australia II* across the blue waters off Newport, Rhode Island, during a pre-race run around the America's Cup course. 'She's as slippery as a snake, smooth as silk and dances over the water like a ballerina.'

'So she bloody well should, given the price tag,' Bond said, laughing back at Bertrand from just forward of the helm. 'So you reckon our boys in the boat from Down Under can beat *Liberty*?' he added, shouting into the wind.

'You bet,' the deeply tanned Bertrand said with a grin. He adjusted his cap so he could see the green flag, with its boxing kangaroo, fluttering on the forestay. 'If she flies like this on the big day!'

'That winged keel of Ben Lexcen's, do you like it?' Bond asked.

'I'll say. I can really feel it. Together with these fantastic sails, it's pure magic,' Bertrand said, wiping some spray off his face. 'It's our secret weapon, eh?'

'That and our Vegemite sandwiches,' Bond said, playing on the words of the Men at Work song *Down Under*, which had become *Australia II*'s theme song. 'But let's keep our fingers crossed that these neurotic Yanks don't protest, claiming the keel gives us an unfair advantage. Keeping it covered at the docks is driving them absolutely nuts!'

'But it's not just the keel,' Bertrand said. 'She's a beautiful boat, with an efficient deck and perfectly rigged.' He looked up at the Kevlar/Mylar sails. 'And not a bad crew either—I think we've got a bloody good chance.'

'Just don't be too cocky, Captain Bertrand. The Americans won't give their America's Cup away,' Bond warned, watching *Liberty* sailing in the distance.

Although champion yachtsman John Bertrand was 3–1 down against American yacht *Liberty*, he came from behind in the final race as the yachts turned into the last leg for the finish, becoming the first non-American to win the coveted America's Cup.

288

'There's a reason nobody has beaten them in 132 years. We'll have to fight tooth and nail for the trophy, on every inch of the course.'

'Well let's get a good night's sleep tonight,' Bertrand said. 'I'm satisfied with her now. Everything is shipshape, and I'm confident she's ready for the big day. Shall we head in?'

'Yes. We've done all the preparation we could possibly do,' Bond said. 'It's all in the lap of the gods now.'

As it was, the gods smiled down on the Australians in September 1983 as they raced around the America's Cup course in their mysterious winged-keel superyacht. *Australia II* defied the odds and defeated *Liberty* over the final leg of the last race of the series—to the delight of millions of Australians watching the race live on television in the small hours of the morning.

IT WAS A GREAT MOMENT because skipper John Bertrand had won the holy grail of yachting, the America's Cup, with financier Alan Bond's yacht *Australia II*. The unprecedented win by a non-American boat gave Australians a huge morale boost. The national daily *The Australian* proclaimed right across Page 1: 'We Can Do Anything!' Prime Minister Bob Hawke said it was such an historic moment that all bosses should give their workers a day off to celebrate, saying 'Any boss who sacks anyone for missing work today is a bum.'

Historical background

John Bertrand was born in Melbourne in 1946. His great-grandfather was chief engineer on two British yachts that challenged in vain for the America's Cup. Growing up near the beach, Bertrand started sailing as a teenager. He represented Australia in yachting at the 1972 Olympic Games, and won a bronze medal in 1976 in Montreal. He also took part in several America's Cup challenges.

His *Australia II* victory ended the 132-year US monopoly on the America's Cup—the longest winning run in the history of sport. After some gear failures, the yacht was 3-1 down, and the final-race victory, where Bertrand came from behind as the boats turned into the last leg for the finish, was one of the greatest upsets in sports history. The Confederation of Australian Sport voted *Australia II*'s win the greatest team performance in 200 years.

Prime Minister Bob Hawke was so excited by the *Australia II* victory in the America's Cup, which he—and millions of Australians—stayed up late to watch on television, that he announced, 'Any boss who sacks anyone for missing work today is a bum.'

The British-born entrepreneur Alan Bond, from Western Australia, was the chairman of the *Australia II* syndicate. After decades of failed Australian challenges, it had *Australia II* especially designed and built for the race. The designer, Ben Lexcen, had experimented with winged keels before, but never on a yacht of *Australia II*'s size.

Australia II's prospects looked good because in the sea trials leading up to the main races she appeared to be the fastest yacht competing. After gear failures cost her at least two early races, she had to win three in a row to take the Cup. In the event, Race 7 would decide the issue. *Australia II* surged to an early lead, but failed to cover *Liberty*, which then dominated for most of the race. Then a good wind shift, Bertrand's skill—and, without doubt on the long reach home, that winged keel—helped *Australia II* overhaul *Liberty* on the final leg to finish just 41 seconds ahead. It was the shortest winning margin in the entire seven-race series.

Bertrand said: 'Alan Bond told me many times the Americans would never give us the America's Cup and we would have to fight for it tooth and nail. It was the fightback of a lifetime.' Bond added: 'They say something good comes along once a lifetime, and certainly something good has come along for Australia. I have never seen a country so united under one flag.'

When Bertrand, Bond and the team visited the White House, US President Ronald Reagan said: 'You did an outstanding job. You captured the imagination of the people the world over. You have shown the stuff you Australians are made of . . . we salute you in your moment of triumph.'

'The winged keel's our secret weapon, eh? That and our Vegemite sandwiches.'

Postscript

Even though *Australia II* indisputably won the Cup, the Americans—who had been thoroughly psyched out by the Bond team's refusal to let anyone see the winged keel until after the last race—protested on several grounds, including the keel issue, in a desperate attempt to keep the trophy in New York. Some even said it was not possible to remove the Cup from its base. Others claimed it was too valuable to be transported all the way to Australia, but the protests were overruled and the trophy was transferred to the Royal Perth Yacht Club. The losing skipper of *Liberty*, Cup veteran Dennis Conner, would win it back for San Diego Yacht Club at the next challenge in 1987.

Bertrand was subsequently awarded the Order of Australia, the Australian Sports Medal and later the Centenary Medal for services to society. He was also appointed chairman of the Sport Australia Hall of Fame and made a member of the America's Cup Hall of Fame. He told his story in the bestselling book *Born to Win*. Although he said he had climbed the Mount Everest of yachting and could never improve on his 1983 victory, he did return to the America's

Cup fray when he was hired to skipper *One Australia* in 1995—but the boat snapped in two during rough weather.

Although he was good at raising funds and organising successful yachting syndicates, Alan Bond's sense of history left a little to be desired. He claimed that *Australia II*'s triumph at Newport was the greatest victory since Gallipoli—which had, of course, been a defeat for the Allies. The high-flying Bond later fell foul of the law: in 1997 he was sentenced to seven years' jail for unlawfully fiddling $1.2 billion into Bond Corporation's coffers from another company. He served nearly four years.

Once the victorious *Australia II* was back in Australia, Australians could inspect the yacht and its innovative winged keel, which had helped the beautifully designed vessel win the race of the century.

1988

'FIRST FLEET' TALL-SHIPS THRILL AUSTRALIA

'What should we do with that police warning about Aboriginal marksmen lying in wait for us when we sail into Sydney Harbour tomorrow, Wally?' Commodore Mike Kichenside asked, standing at the window of the Botany Bay Yacht Club and surveying his First Fleet as it rode safely at anchor.

'Nothing, Mike,' said Wally Franklin, executive director of the First Fleet Re-enactment Expedition, studying a chart of Sydney Harbour spread out on the boardroom table. 'Nothing at all. Don't give any of your energy to negative thoughts like that.'

'But do you think we should just sail right into Sydney Harbour with thousands of spectators crowding around us on their boats?' the commodore asked, turning to study his characteristically calm executive director. 'Even though police informers say both the project founder, Jonathan King, and I have been targeted by Aboriginal marksmen?'

'Mike! This little underdog fleet has got all the way from London to Sydney on pure faith. We've never had enough money, sponsors or paying passengers, yet we've made it,' Franklin said, leaping up from the table to join the commodore at the window. 'Have more faith. Look at your little fleet. It's the people's fleet—don't you think Sydney will give our ships the best welcome? There's nothing to worry about. We've won the people over—their donations have helped us get this far.'

'But look at this story,' the commodore said, picking up a tabloid newspaper. '"Aborigines Threaten to Board Ships and Toss Sailors into Harbour". What do you think of that?'

'Rubbish . . . tabloid sensationalism,' Franklin said, picking up an Aboriginal flag on the table. 'Look, we're flying their flag, we're publishing our own *makarrata* in the *Herald*, we've called for the Federal Government to sign a treaty, and our own sailors are casting a memorial wreath with flowers in Aboriginal colours into the harbour in memory of those killed by white settlers, and some of the crew are wearing black armbands.'

'All that should make the Aborigines happy,' the commodore replied.

'This can be a new beginning for Aborigines. Governments might gloss over the brutal truth, but we're actually showing people how the British invaded the Aborigines' country 200 years ago. Aboriginal Australians will be on our side—it's the start of our future together.'

'So you've won over the original inhabitants of your country—you've neutralised any opposition?' the English commodore asked.

'Absolutely. Aboriginal activist Charlie Perkins told Jonathan he believed us whitefellas have gotta have our own Dreamtime or we'll get lost and won't know

The three million spectators who turned out to greet the eleven square-rigged tall-ships of the First Fleet Re-enactment Expedition that sailed across the high seas from England had no idea of dramas that threatened to sink the fleet from start to finish.

where we've come from, nor where we are going—so he's endorsed it. Have some faith, Mike.'

'I've always respected your faith, Wally. It's certainly got the First Fleet this far. But as commodore I just want to get us across the finishing line safely,' Kichenside, said surveying his fleet again. 'And I know Jonathan's wife has hired an SAS bulletproof vest to protect him from would-be assassins.'

'That's understandable,' Franklin said. 'He dreamed up the First Fleet re-enactment, and he's particularly vulnerable because his ancestor, Governor Philip Gidley King, sailed with the 1788 fleet. Besides, after ten years working on the project and sailing the whole way from England, he's at the end of his tether. I'm not surprised he's taking precautions. Jane probably insisted.'

'So for the rest of us it's full steam ahead, Wally,' Kichenside said, with a laugh of relief. 'Or should I say plain sailing?'

'That's right, Mike. Anyway, we've got enough on our plate just trying to get the fleet there. We're still short of funds, and we don't even have the eleventh tall-ship confirmed. Jonathan's working on that right now, trying to get the *Leeuwin* to join us. I'm waiting for his call.'

'Well, he'd better hurry,' Kichenside said. 'If all goes well we'll be weighing anchor and setting sail at four in the morning. We hope to sail all eleven ships of the First Fleet Re-enactment Expedition through the Heads into Sydney Harbour by 9 a.m.'

IT WAS A GREAT MOMENT because all went well, and the second First Fleet sailed triumphantly through the Heads on time and with the full complement of eleven square-riggers. On television or in person, millions of Australians watched the flotilla entering the Harbour under near-full canvas and in near-perfect weather. With a local crowd estimated by police at three million, it remains Australia's largest ever live spectator event. The Fleet sailed (rather than motored) on the north-east wind all the way into Farm Cove, carefully negotiating the thousands of spectator craft that covered the harbour so completely that it seemed possible to walk across it from boat to boat. The reception was overwhelming. As soon as the Fleet dropped anchor, Prince Charles officially opened the Bicentennial Celebrations on the forecourt of the nearby Opera House.

After a ten-year 'touch and go' struggle to organise the First Fleet Re-enactment Expedition, prime movers Wally Franklin, right, and Jonathan King, left—also the author—celebrated the fleet's long-awaited arrival in Sydney Harbour.

The success of this unofficial, private project also showed that ordinary people can—if they have a popular and worthy cause—overcome the strongest government opposition. Spectators warmed to the Fleet because of its unofficial underdog status, with many saying that watching it sail into the Harbour was one of the best days of their lives.

Historical background

Jonathan King, the author, is a descendant of Governor Philip Gidley King, the naval officer who had helped organise the 1788 First Fleet, then sailed on it and was later appointed Governor of the new colony. He had conceived the idea of the First Fleet Re-enactment Expedition in 1976 while he and his wife, Jane, watched the tall-ships sail into New York to commemorate the United States' Bicentenary. As an historian lecturing at Melbourne University, he believed the reenactment would remind fellow Australians of the daring and successful voyage of the first European settlers. He planned to collect eleven square-rigged tall-ships to play the part of the original 1788 vessels and sail this fleet from London to Sydney along the same route—via Portsmouth, Rio de Janeiro, Cape Town and Botany Bay—and according to the same timetable, to arrive in Sydney Harbour on Australia Day 1988. After initial research into feasibility and talks with indigenous people, who agreed to support the expedition, the pair launched the project on Australia Day 1978, giving themselves ten years to organise it.

They formed the First Fleet Re-enactment Company, chaired by Allen Allen & Hemsley lawyer Philip King (another descendant of Governor King's), with airline executive and tourism manager Wally Franklin as executive director and the author, Jonathan King, as creative director. Board members included Bill Macartney and Brian Rosen from Hoyts Edgley International, Richard Harper as financial controller and Alan Brown as secretary. As the Australian Bicentennial Authority (ABA) banned any RAN personnel from participating, the board appointed British Commodore Mike Kichenside to lead the Fleet, supported by legendary square-rig master Captain Adrian Small, who had sailed on the last commercial wind-powered vessel, *Passat*, in 1948. Despite their credentials, status and experience, this board of directors was still hard-pressed to raise the projected $11 million cost of the Fleet.

Although they imagined the Federal Government would support the venture, the hastily created Australian Bicentennial Authority (ABA) opposed the expedition because it wanted to stage its own parade of tall-ships on Sydney Harbour. To discredit the Fleet, the ABA produced a bogus 'feasibility study' in 1982 to justify axing the project. The study claimed it would be a politically unacceptable, racist event reminding modern Australians of the British invasion of 1788; that it would support South Africa's apartheid regime because the Fleet would, like the original, call into Cape Town for supplies; that it was too risky for modern Australians to sail tall-ships on the high seas; that it would be too difficult to recruit a commodore to take the place of the 1788 Commodore Arthur Phillip, let alone eleven captains and crews; that it would remind Australians of their unsavoury origins as convicts; and that it would place too much emphasis on the British origins of Australia at a time when the government wanted to engage more closely with Asia.

To contest these claims, the organisers appointed a team of influential supporters who included the first European to climb Mount Everest, Sir Edmund Hillary, as honorary chairman; the '*Kon-Tiki* man', Thor Heyerdahl, as honorary president, and the captain of the *Joseph Conrad*, Alan Villiers, as patron. They also sought commercial advice from one of Australia's top impresarios, Michael

'This little underdog fleet has got all the way from London to Sydney on pure faith. We've never had enough money, sponsors or paying passengers, yet we've made it.'

Edgley, who had already defied conservative governments by importing the Moscow Circus from the Soviet Union, and from the world's most successful historical reenactment leader, Tim Severin. They also persuaded the Queen and the Duke of Edinburgh to farewell the Fleet.

As the Federal Government refused to endorse, let alone support, the Fleet until the last minute (writing to leading companies in Australia warning them against sponsoring it), the organisers spent the next five years travelling overseas to raise funds, managing to get companies like Coca-Cola in London and Mobil in New York on board. Aware of the potential audience, Channel 7 and Radio 2GB also defied Canberra by buying media rights, and Qantas provided travel support. Entrepreneurs such as Alan Bond also helped. The organisers also raised funds by selling berths to passengers for different legs of the journey. They managed to collect eleven ships from around the world and even buy the *Bounty* replica. Once it became clear that the Fleet would indeed sail, the ABA lent the project $500,000 the day before the departure and promised a further $1 million once the Fleet reached Rio de Janeiro.

The Queen farewelled the Fleet on 13 May 1987, two hundred years to the day after the original First Fleet departed, and it sailed without incident to Tenerife and then Rio de Janeiro, when the money ran out. Rather than honour its promise, the ABA conducted another bogus survey that claimed the public did not want the Fleet to finish its journey, and reneged on its $1 million commitment. By then, however the Fleet had become extremely popular thanks to the extensive media coverage. When 2GB announcers John Laws and Mike Carlton got wind of the cash crisis, they raised the $900,000 shortfall from enthusiastic listeners in three days—which Jane King took to Rio de Janeiro concealed in her bra.

The Fleet was thus able to continue via Cape Town to Australia. With Radio 2GB advertising the arrival and Channel 7 airing the documentary *First Fleet: Rite of Passage* on January 25, hundreds of thousands of people flocked to the harbour on Australia Day 1988 to watch the fleet sail through the Heads to a spectacular welcome.

Postscript

The First Fleet Re-enactment Expedition was the single most popular event of the 1988 Australian Bicentennial Celebrations. It had successfully sailed from one end of the world to the other according to the original timetable and more or less along the original route. Of the thousands who sailed with the fleet, one sailor died: *Anna Kristina* first mate Henrik Neilsen.

But despite the public acclaim, this unofficial private expedition remained cash-strapped to the last and unpopular with a resentful Federal Government, which only reluctantly converted its last-minute loan into a grant. The ABA refused to allow the Commodore, captains or crew to come ashore for the first twenty-four hours after they dropped anchor in Farm Cove, for 'fear of sparking a racial riot'. The bureaucracy also withheld standard certificates of appreciation and continued to criticise the First Fleet, even after the National Australia Day Council named it the Best Event of the Bicentenary (a title shared with the government's Brisbane Expo 88) and the author Australian Achiever of the Year in 1989. This inspired the author, and the Fleet's communications officer, David Iggulden, to produce a tell-all book, *The Battle for the Bicentenary*.

1993
EDDIE MABO WINS LAND RIGHTS VICTORY

'This Land Rights bill will be the greatest turning point in Australian history,' Prime Minister Paul Keating advised the House of Representatives, leaping to his feet and waving his right arm towards Coalition members sitting on the other side of the chamber. 'It'll be the biggest breakthrough since the First Fleet of British settlers invaded this country in 1788—it will kill that great British lie of *terra nullius* and become a great tribute to the late Eddie Mabo.' (Mabo was a Torres Strait Islander who had led a High Court case claiming that indigenous Australians had legitimate title to traditional lands.)

'Well, I think it would be a disgrace,' Opposition Leader John Hewson protested, leaping to his feet and eyeballing Keating across the table. 'If we pass this bill it will be a day of shame for the Australian Parliament.'

'A day of shame—that's rich, that is, coming from silvertails like you whose ancestors probably stole the land from indigenous Australians to begin with,' Keating retorted. 'You should be ashamed of what your lot did in the past.'

'We can't be held responsible for the past, and I think it would be a disaster for Australia,' Hewson said, standing his ground and looking around as his fellow Coalition MPs nodded their support.

'This bill breaks with the past. It is the beginning of a whole new deal—the basis for social justice and reconciliation,' Keating said. 'You old conservatives had better get used to it.'

'But giving Aborigines the right to claim native title would be the thin edge of the wedge, opening the way for them to take away land badly needed by the mining and pastoral industries that are the backbone of this country,' Hewson persisted.

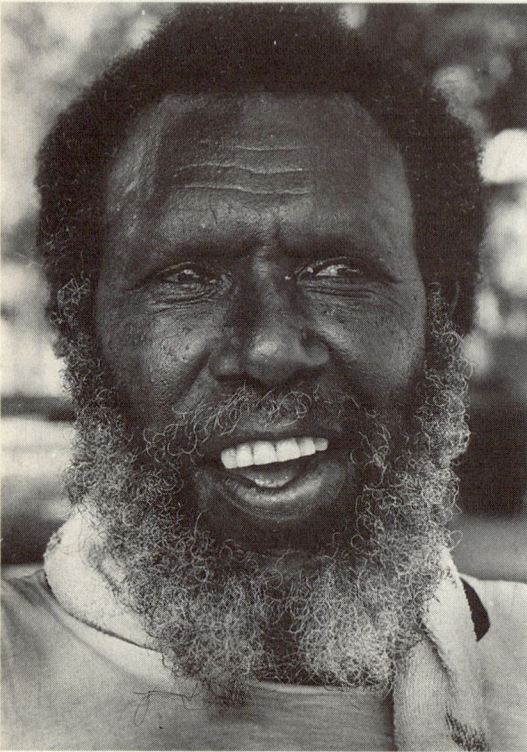

Although Eddie Mabo died before his historic land rights claim over Murray Island succeeded, his victory had established such a historic precedent that his legacy should live on forever.

'That's right, bring out the tired old scaremongering rhetoric . . . go on, tell us how we're all going to lose our backyards next,' Keating spat back at Hewson. 'You scaremongers are just trying to frighten the voters, aren't you?'

'Well it's true—we would all stand to lose land if this bill was passed,' Hewson argued.

'Rubbish, tired old rubbish. The Mabo bill won't be taking away anybody's rights—miners, pastoralists, let alone people's backyards—and it will be a fair deal for all.'

'Tell that to the pastoralists and mining companies who have told us this will ruin the future of their industries,' Hewson said, waving a sheaf of documents.

'It sounds like you just want to protect the vested interest of the companies that help fund the Coalition,' Keating accused Hewson, 'but you just don't have the conscience or the guts to right the wrongs on your side of the house, do you?'

'I can promise you the Coalition will not vote for an end to the mining or pastoral industries that have fuelled this economy for so long,' Hewson said.

'We have the numbers anyway, and the passage of this visionary legislation will demonstrate that this generation of Australians will not buy that sort of bigotry or your brand of politics,' Keating said, sweeping an arm to cover the Coalition side of the House.

At the conclusion of an exhaustive debate on the deeply controversial Mabo bill, the vote was taken. Keating's Labor Government, with the assistance of the Greens and Democrats, had the numbers and the *Native Title Act* was passed.

IT WAS A GREAT MOMENT because Eddie Mabo and his supporters had achieved a land-rights breakthrough. Aboriginals could now claim title to traditional lands even after their original title had apparently been extinguished. It was 19 December 1993, and the Federal Parliament had just passed legislation confirming the High Court's decision to give back land to Eddie Mabo's people on Murray Island, off northern Queensland, many years after that title had been assumed by the Crown. Starting in the nineteenth century—and as recently as

1993

1971—judges had ruled that Aborigines had never owned the land, so the British had settled a *terra nullius*, or 'land belonging to no one'.

Aboriginal leaders welcomed the bill as 'a vital step towards reconciliation' and Prime Minister Paul Keating called it a turning point for Australia, which marked the end of 'the great lie of *terra nullius* and the beginning, we all hope, of a new deal on the basis of social justice and reconciliation'. The High Court and then Parliament had set an important precedent by ruling in favour of the Mabo claim and passing the legislation. Fittingly, in the same year Mandawuy Yunupingu—lead singer of Yothu Yindi, which had produced the best-selling song *Treaty*—was named Australian of the Year.

Aboriginal land rights activists had won significant land rights in the deserts of South Australia and also at Uluru (Ayers Rock) but had never had a breakthrough as successful as the Eddie Mabo case; this victory inspired them to renew their efforts.

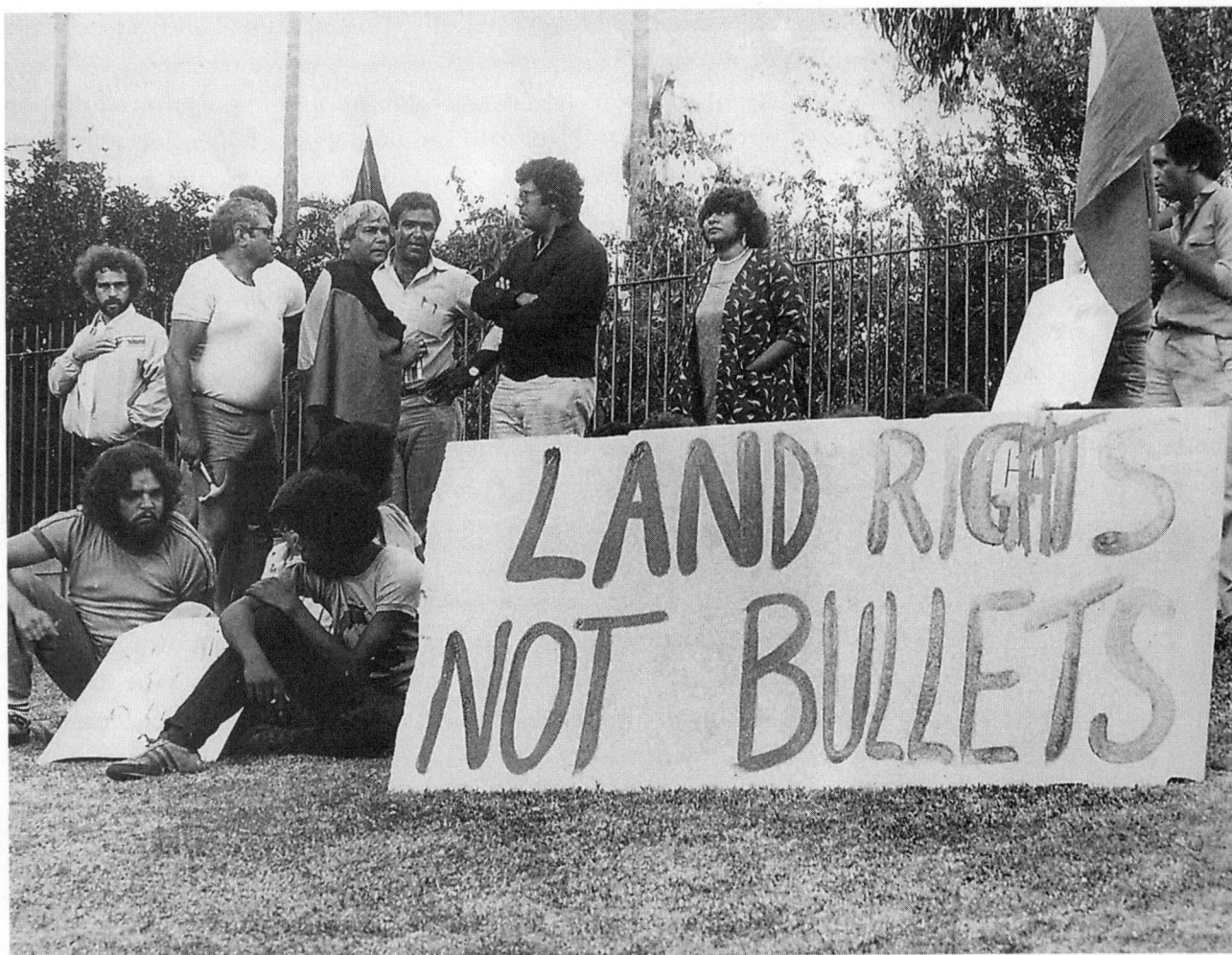

Historical background

Eddie Koiki Mabo, from Murray Island (Mer), in Torres Strait, worked as a gardener at James Cook University, Townsville. While there, he began attending lectures and talking to the academic staff. He learned to his dismay that, legally, he had no rights to the island he regarded as his land. In 1981 he spoke at a land rights conference, and on 20 May 1982, he, Dave Passi and James Rice brought an action against the Queensland and Federal governments claiming 'native title' to their lands.

In December 1988 the High Court confirmed their right to bring the case. Mabo said Murray Island had been the ancestral home of his Meriam people for more than thirty generations. The High Court ruled in June 1992 that they did indeed have native title, quashing the notion that Australia was unoccupied when the British settled it in 1788.

On 19 December 1993, the *Native Title Bill 1993* was enacted despite opposition from the Liberal–National Coalition, whose leader, John Hewson, described it as 'a day of shame for the Australian Parliament and a disaster for Australia'. The Coalition also spoke for mining and pastoral interests, which claimed the legislation would become a precedent allowing Aborigines to take away miners' and pastoralists' property rights. Having passed in the House of Representatives, the Bill was debated for a record seventy hours in the Senate before it was passed.

This successful land rights claim followed earlier landmarks, such as the Gurindji tribe's walk-off at Wave Hill Station in protest over appalling pay and conditions, described in Frank Hardy's book *The Unlucky Australians*. In 1984 tribal elders Tommy Queama and Jack Baker and their people had also won land rights over desert areas around the nuclear test site of Maralinga, which gave them 8 per cent of South Australia. In 1985 Governor-General Sir Ninian Stephen handed back Ayers Rock, Uluru, to traditional owners Nipper Winmarti and his Mutitjulu people, despite protests from the Northern Territory Government. After the Mabo decision, the Wik people also gained rights to their lands in 1996.

'This bill . . . is the beginning of a whole new deal—the basis for social justice and reconciliation.'

Postscript

The ten-year legal case was two years too long for Eddie Mabo, who died of cancer on 21 January 1992. Despite the importance of the Mabo victory, it was

Prime Minister Paul Keating, a strong supporter of Aboriginal rights, who described the Native Title Bill passed for the Eddie Mabo case as a vital step towards reconciliation, said it also marked 'the end of the great lie of *terra nullius* and the beginning, we hope, of a new deal on the basis of social justice and reconciliation'.

not long before conservative forces, buoyed by John Howard's election victory in 1996, began trying to put restrictions in place to stop further land rights claims succeeding. Land rights for indigenous Australians remains very much a work in progress, although many gains have been made as a result of Mabo's breakthrough.

2000
CATHY FREEMAN WINS OLYMPIC GOLD IN SYDNEY

'On your marks . . . set . . .' BANG! Shooting out of their blocks, the eight female sprinters in the final of the 400 metres at the Sydney 2000 Olympic Games took off to the deafening roar of a nearly hysterical crowd. The spectators rose like a wave from their seats to cheer the thin, dark-skinned athlete in her green, yellow and white 'swift suit'.

'Go Cathy, go Cathy, go Cathy, go Cathy!' the crowd of more than 112,000 screamed over and over: 'Go Cathy, go Cathy, go Cathy, go Cathy!' With their collective will, they were pushing one runner, Cathy Freeman, to victory.

Then, 49.11 seconds later—49.11 seconds of that deafening 'Go Cathy' roar—she had done it. The slim Aboriginal woman, who had made the entire nation catch its breath when she lit the Olympic Flame in the opening ceremony, had lived up to all expectations.

Freeman did not seem fazed by the 112,524 people jam-packed into the stadium, or the fact that most of her fellow Australians and hundreds of millions of people around the world were watching on television. Nor did she react much when, moments before the race, the announcement of her name over the public address system provoked the most deafening roar yet heard in the new stadium. She gave a quick wave, then stared down her lane, showing no emotion. It was as if she were alone on the track.

When the starter's pistol went off, Jamaica's Lorraine Graham took an early lead, but Freeman turned up the heat after 200 metres and her finishing burst kicked in to give her the biggest win of her life. The stadium exploded with joy; hard-bitten members of the Australian media had tears in their eyes.

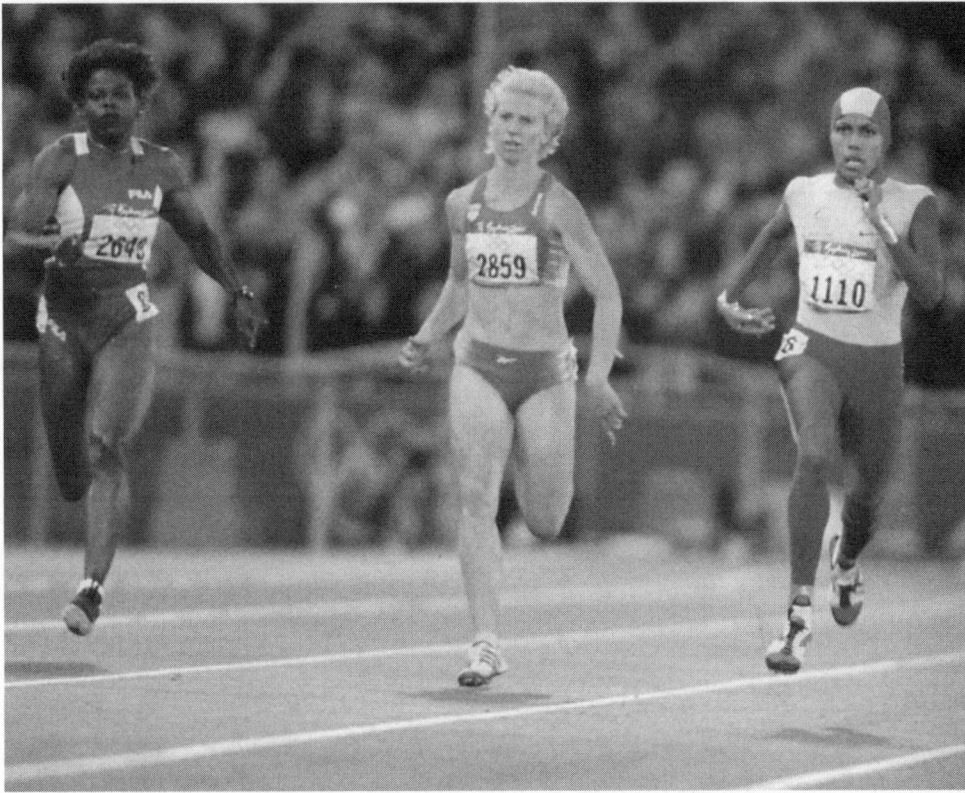

Empowered by her distinctive new running suit, Cathy Freeman defeated all opponents in the 400 metres at the Sydney 2000 Olympics, crossing the line in 49.11 seconds to win both the gold medal and the hearts of the spectators watching the epic event.

After crossing the finish line Freeman fell to the ground exhausted, her strained face showing she had put everything she had into the race. As she told the media later: 'It was more relief than anything. When you have dreamt something for so long and it finally happens, it really spins you out. It turns your world around and upside down. I had to sit down. I think I felt everyone's emotions inside of me all of a sudden. It blew me away.' She added: 'I could feel the crowd all over me . . . I felt the emotion being absorbed into every pore of my body.'

Freeman then sat down on the track, unlaced her shoes—in the yellow, black and red of the Aboriginal flag—and ran her victory lap barefoot, carrying both the Aboriginal flag and the Australian flag together. Although she had been criticised for carrying the Aboriginal flag on victory laps before, now she was praised for it. Those who were watching believed she had done it for all Australians.

IT WAS A GREAT MOMENT because Freeman had won gold for Australia in the most traditional of Olympic events—running around the track. It was the first track-and-field gold medal an Australian had won since Debbie Flintoff-King's victory in the 400-metre hurdles in 1988. It was also Australia's hundredth gold medal, which had an especially nice ring coming as it did in the year 2000. Although weighed down by the expectations of nearly 20 million Australians, Freeman delivered one of the greatest gifts in Australian history. Not since Betty Cuthbert—the Golden Girl—had any female athlete held the hearts of the Australian crowd so firmly in the palm of her hand.

Freeman was also Aboriginal, and in that moment she became a symbol of self-respecting indigenous power—and did more for reconciliation than decades of meetings around negotiating tables. Never before had the nation supported an Aboriginal person so passionately. Aborigines had come a long way since Bennelong was kidnapped and 'transported' back to England to have tea with King George III.

Because she had been criticised in the past for running victory laps with just the Aboriginal flag, Cathy Freeman got around this by celebrating her wins by running around the track with both the Aboriginal flag and Australian flag.

Historical background

Catherine Astrid Salome Freeman was born in 1973 in Mackay, Queensland. The local athletics track at Slade Point was later named after her. She began competing as a child along with her brothers Garth and Norman, coached by their stepfather, Bruce. In her early teens she started winning regional titles, competing in 100- and 200-metre events. In 1990 Freeman was chosen as a member of Australia's 4 x 100-metre relay team for the 1990 Commonwealth Games in New Zealand, where they won gold, making sixteen-year-old Freeman the first Aboriginal Commonwealth Games gold medallist as well as one of the youngest.

She represented Australia well at the 1990 World Junior Championships in Plovdiv, Bulgaria, and in Seoul, South Korea, where she won the silver medal in the 200 metres. In 1992, at her first Olympic Games, she made it to the second round of her new specialty, the 400 metres. She also did well at the 1994 Commonwealth Games in Canada, winning gold in both the 200 metres and 400 metres. In 1996 she set many personal and Australian records, emerging as the biggest challenger to France's Marie-José Pérec at the 1996 Olympics. She finished just behind Pérec, whose winning time of 48.25 seconds was an Olympic record and the third-fastest ever. Freeman then won the 400 metres at the World Championships in Athens in 1997.

She successfully defended her world title in 1999 and seemed well positioned for the 2000 Olympics. Her popularity soared when she was revealed as the torchbearer for the climactic moment of the Opening Ceremony, stepping forward in her white suit to climb a waterfall stairway and light the Olympic Flame.

At these Games she was the home favourite for the 400-metre title. Although she was expected to run head-to-head with Pérec, her rival abruptly quit the Games after an encounter with an Australian photographer. Freeman won the Olympic title in 49.11 seconds, becoming only the second Australian Aboriginal Olympic champion (the first was Nova Peris-Kneebone for field hockey in Atlanta) and the first individual champion. She retired in 2004.

'I could feel the crowd all over me . . . I felt the emotion being absorbed into every pore of my body.'

Postscript

Despite her great fame, achievements and popularity, like many indigenous people Freeman has had more than her share of personal challenges to overcome. Her parents separated when she was very young; she had to put up with racism

After she won gold at the Sydney 2000 Olympic Games Cathy Freeman said, 'When you have dreamt about something for so long and it finally happens, it really spins you out. It turns your world around and upside down.' She also said, 'I felt everyone's emotions inside of me all of a sudden. It blew me away.'

during her childhood; a sister, Anne-Marie, born in 1966, suffered from cerebral palsy and spent much of her life in a home for the disabled before she died in 1990; and her brother Norman, with whom she had trained, died after a motor vehicle accident in 2008.

After she separated from her first husband, Nike executive Sandy Bodecker, Freeman married Melbourne stockbroker James Murch. Through her public and private challenges Freeman seems to have been sustained by her faith. She was raised a Baha'i, and has said of her faith: 'I'm not a devout Baha'i, but I like the prayers and I appreciate their values about the equality of all human kind.'

2002
DOCTOR SAVES LIVES AFTER BALI BOMBINGS

'Terrible news about those bombings in Bali,' West Australian surgeon Tony Kierath said, turning off the radio news and looking at his wife, Dr Fiona Wood. 'Sounds like a lot of Australians might have been in or near the nightclubs where the bombs went off.'

'Absolutely sickening,' she said, shaking her head. 'I heard about it earlier. There have been some terrible burns.'

'They're saying well over a hundred people could be dead, and hundreds more injured. The hospitals in Bali won't be able to cope with so many,' Kierath said, making two cups of coffee.

'No, they can't. The authorities are flying some of the victims down for treatment at Royal Perth Hospital,' Wood said. 'We're going to save as many lives as we can here—we may get as many as twenty-eight patients.'

'Will you be able to pull together a big enough team to treat them all?' he asked, handing her a coffee.

'I'll just have to,' she said, 'using all my contacts in plastic surgery.'

'Think you'll use your new spray-on skin treatment?' Kierath asked, stirring his coffee.

'Absolutely—it will cover the burned areas faster than sheets of cultured skin, and with less scarring.'

'And you are confident you can treat so many all at once?'

'I'm sure it will work,' she said. 'Remember when we first used spray-on skin cells to save the life of that teacher who had petrol burns to 90 per cent of his body?' she said. 'That's ten years ago now, Tony. We've come a long way since then thanks to some brilliant lab work by Marie Stoner.'

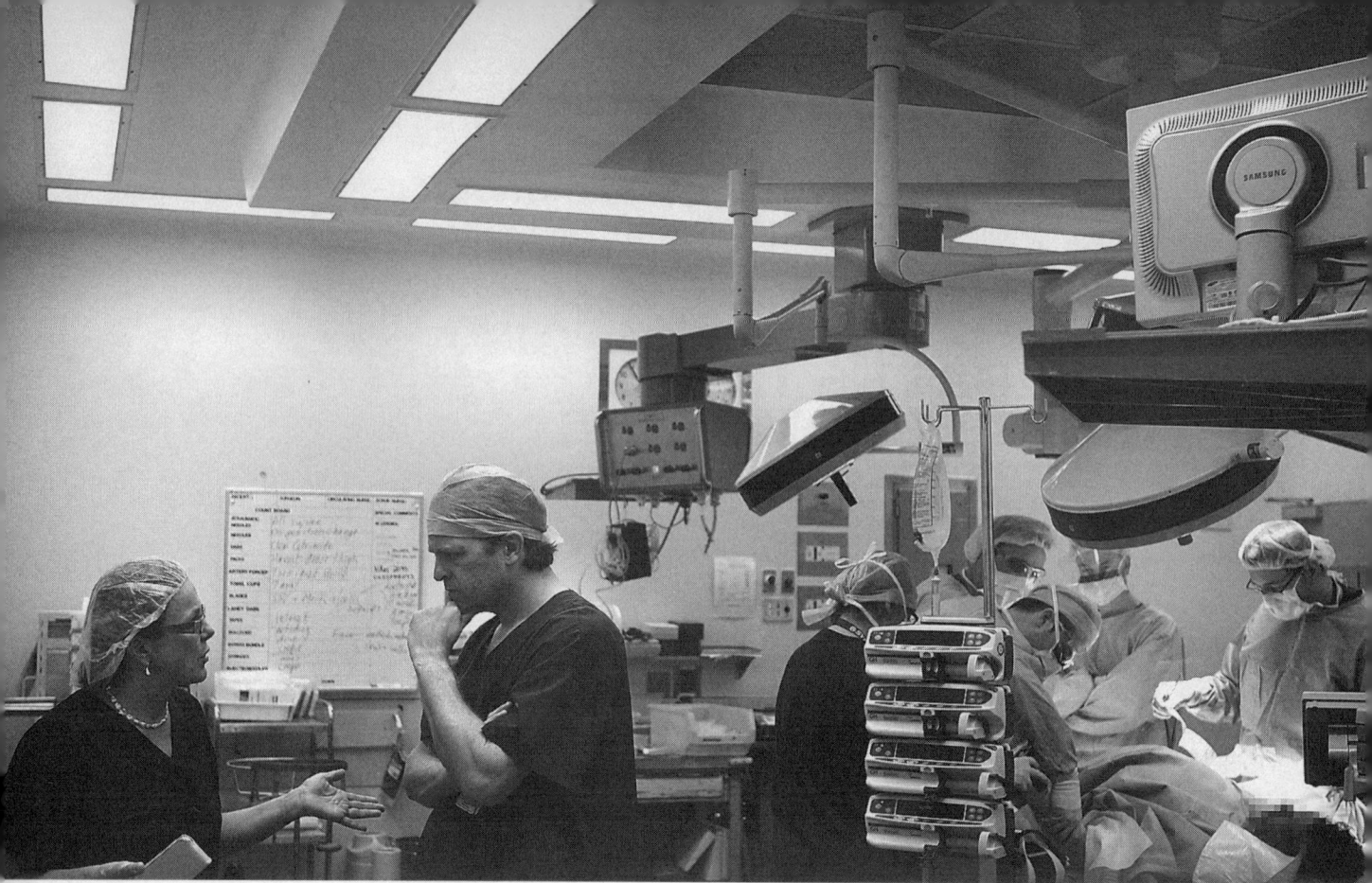

Having perfected her 'spray-on skin' techniques at the Royal Perth Hospital, the visionary Dr Fiona Wood was well qualified to help treat the victims of the Bali bombings.

'You've done some real pioneering work, Fiona,' Kierath said proudly.

'It's our only hope of helping these burns victims from Bali. Now we can culture small amounts of tissue from the patient into big volumes of skin-cell suspensions in as little as five days,' Wood said. 'It's hard to believe it once took us three weeks to produce enough cells to cover major burns.'

'And that's important, isn't it, because the risk of scarring is so much less when you can apply the new skin cells within ten days. A lot of people are going to be very, very happy that this is available to help them and their loved ones,' he said.

'Yes, my dream was always scarless, woundless healing.'

'Well, good luck, Dr Wood,' he said. 'It will be your biggest challenge yet—but I know you will achieve miracles once the survivors arrive.'

In all, twenty-eight badly burned victims of the Bali bombings were flown to Royal Perth Hospital, the nearest major specialist burns unit to Bali. It was the largest group of people injured in the attacks, and, using spray-on skin as well as more conventional skin grafts, Wood and her team did achieve miracles.

Some of the injured had burns covering 90 per cent of their bodies. Three of them died. Wood's CellSpray technique has since revolutionised burns treatment around the world.

IT WAS A GREAT MOMENT because the visionary Wood not only saved lives with her spray-on skin but also repaired the bodies of the Bali victims with fewer scars than they would have had with conventional treatment. It was another instance of Australian medical innovation, ranking with Dr Howard Florey's successful production of penicillin.

Historical background

On 12 October 2002, terrorists belonging to the militant Islamist group Jemaah Islamiah detonated two bombs in the Kuta tourist area of Bali. A suicide bomber wearing an explosive vest walked into Paddy's Bar and several seconds later a van packed with explosives was detonated outside the nearby Sari Club. A small bomb outside the American consulate in Denpasar injured one person.

The nightclub bombings killed more Australians than any previous terrorist attack, and struck uncomfortably close to home. They also evoked memories of 11 September 2001, when almost 3000 people, including ten Australians, were killed in New York City in the worst ever attack by Islamist terrorists.

Fiona Wood, born in Yorkshire, England, in 1958, planned a career as a sprinter before becoming a doctor. After marrying Australian surgeon Tony Kierath, she moved with him to Perth. While bringing up six children, Wood continued her training in plastic surgery and became director of the Royal Perth Hospital burns unit and the Western Australia Burns Service.

Wood developed and patented a technique in which skin is taken from burns patients and cultured in a laboratory. The new cells are then harvested while they are proliferating rapidly and sprayed onto the body. They spread over the wound surface much faster than sheets of cultured skin. The sooner denuded areas can be recovered, the faster and more cleanly burns heal. Only postage-stamp-sized pieces of skin need to be taken from patients who may have very little skin left. Wood and Stoner started a company called Clinical Cell Culture (C3) in 1993 to commercialise the CellSpray procedure. Royalties from the venture are invested in a research fund, the McComb Research Foundation.

'A lot of people are going to be very, very happy that this is available to help them and their loved ones.'

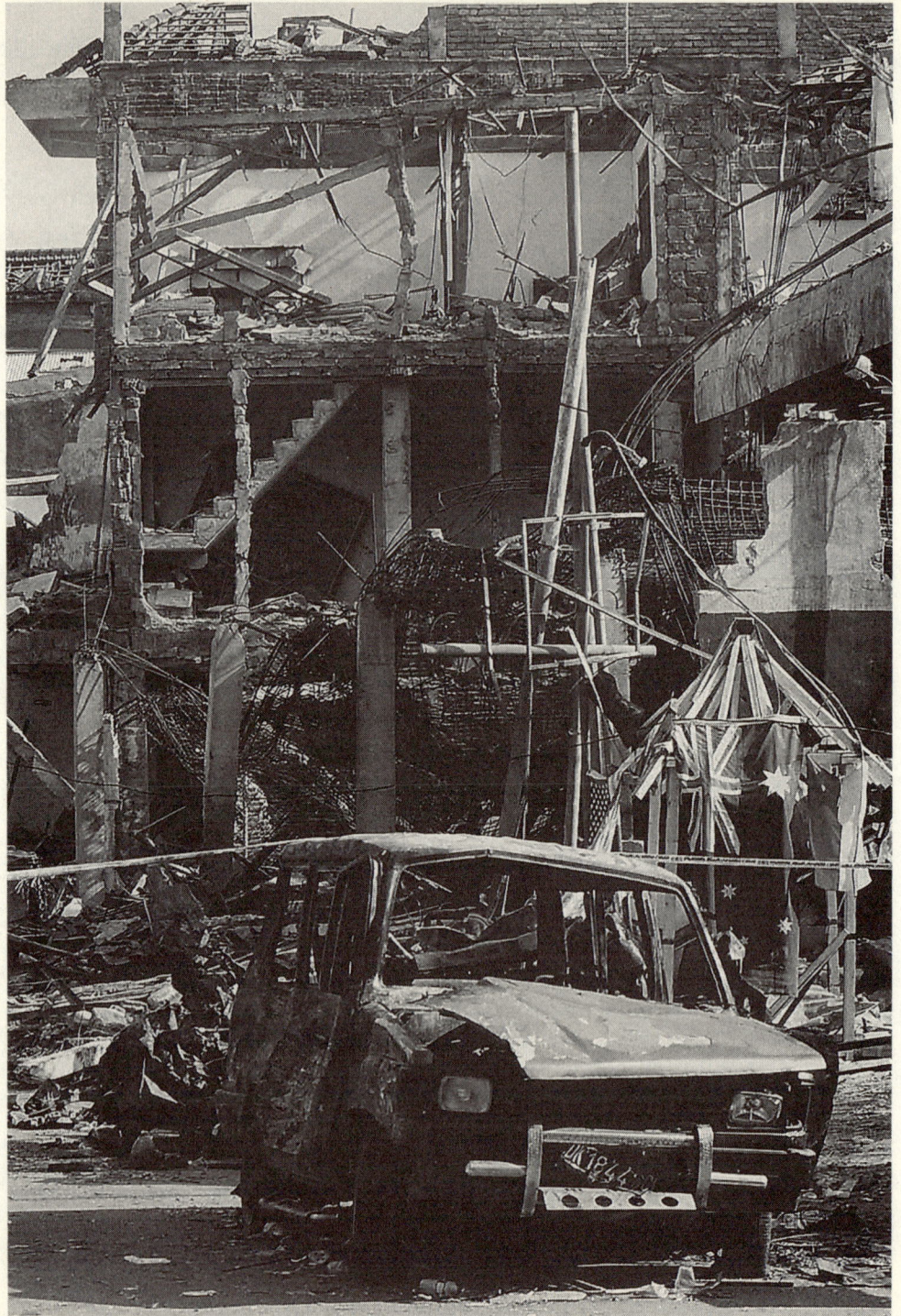

The Bali bombings—which killed more Australians than any previous terrorist attack—were the work of militant Islamist group Jemaah Islamiah which detonated two bombs in the Kuta tourist area of Bali; one was carried by a suicide bomber wearing an explosive vest who walked into Paddy's Bar, and the second detonated in a van packed with explosives parked outside the Sari Club.

Postscript

Wood has said she hates seeing people suffering, and noted that relatively small burns can be psychologically devastating as well as physically damaging, but she has been criticised by other physicians for promoting her spray-on skin before putting it through clinical trials, and for using what was still an experimental procedure on the Bali victims. Anthony Svilicich, of Perth, was burned over two-thirds of his body in Bali. Just over two years later, he said he'd almost completely recovered, thanks to Wood: 'She reconstructed my entire back in one operation when things weren't looking too good . . . and I came through with flying colours.' No doubt all of the patients Wood treated would describe her as the 'angel of the Bali bombings'.

2007
JULIA GILLARD BECOMES HIGHEST-PLACED WOMAN IN POLITICS

'So, you're telling me that if the ALP wins government,' Tim Mathieson said, turning to look at Julia Gillard as they walked along Altona beach, southwest of Melbourne, 'you could actually be Deputy Prime Minister?'

'That's right, Tim,' said Gillard, striding briskly alongside her partner. 'That's been on the cards since I became Labor's deputy leader last December.'

'Not that long after I came back from living in America—where of course politics is quite different,' Tim said, pausing to pat a dog. 'Not that we hairdressers are all that up to speed on politics.'

'Well, you know I don't particularly want a partner who's full bottle on politics,' Gillard said.

'Deputy PM has to be the highest post any woman's ever had in Australian politics,' Mathieson said.

'You're right,' Gillard said. 'There's never even been a female state premier—not an elected one, anyway.'

'But would you want the job?' he asked.

'It would give me a better chance to improve all those things in Australian life that I've cared about for so long,' Gillard said. 'Industrial relations for a start, which the Howard Government has made such a mess of with WorkChoices. My experience as an industrial lawyer will help with that.'

'That'd be good. Most of my customers hate Howard's so-called WorkChoices,' Mathieson said. 'And education? You're keen on that, too.'

'Of course we need to reform education. I want to make sure young working-class people have access to the educational opportunities that I enjoyed in Adelaide in the 1970s,' she said.

Just over a century after Catherine Spence first won the vote for women at the federal level, Julia Gillard was elected as the first female Deputy Prime Minister much to the delight of her partner Tim Mathieson.

'So you would have a real mission,' he said, pausing to watch some wind-surfers hurtling through the water just off the beach. 'There's an open-air restaurant down this way.'

'I've told you how hard my parents worked, Dad with two jobs—and he was a union rep, too. But it takes hard work to change things,' she said, 'and politicians are in the business of change. I also want to try to do something about the pressures on women juggling work and family duties, like those migrant women I helped in the clothing industry,' she said, as they arrived at the restaurant and found a table.

'Fingers crossed then, Julia, that Labor wins,' Mathieson said slipping into his seat opposite her and picking up the menu. 'Now, what would you like?'

Labor did win the election on 24 November 2007, and having campaigned as deputy to Opposition leader Kevin Rudd, Julia Gillard did become the nation's first Deputy Prime Minister—just over 100 years after women were first given the vote in Federal elections. Not long after the election Gillard was sworn in not only as Deputy Prime Minister but also as Minister for Education, Minister for Employment and Workplace Relations, and Minister for Social Inclusion.

IT WAS A GREAT MOMENT because it proved that having a woman at the top did not hurt—and could even help—a party's electoral chances. And it broke through women's last political glass ceiling: Federal Government leadership. Before long, in the absence of Kevin Rudd, Gillard became Acting Prime Minister—another great first. Yet until 1921, when Edith Cowan won a seat in Western Australia, no woman had even been a member of an Australian Parliament.

Gillard had picked up the social-conscience baton from a line of female relay runners who had started the race in the second half of the nineteenth century—women such as Catherine Spence, Vida Goldstein, Cowan and, later, Dorothy Tangney, who became a Senator in 1943. They would have been proud of her, especially Spence, whose campaigning helped win the vote for women in South Australia.

Not long after being elected Australia's first female Deputy Prime Minister, Julia Gillard chalked up another first for women when Prime Minister Kevin Rudd travelled overseas, becoming Acting Prime Minister—confirming her ability to handle increased media scrutiny.

Historical background

Julia Gillard was born in Wales in September 1961 and migrated to Australia with her family five years later. Her parents chose Australia because Julia had suffered from bronchial pneumonia and needed a warmer climate. Gillard's father grew up in a Welsh mining village, but although highly intelligent he wasn't able to take up a scholarship because his family needed him to work. Her far-sighted mother, who worked in aged-care homes while raising her children, taught Julia and her sister to read before they started school.

While studying arts and law at university in Adelaide, Gillard was elected national education vice-president of the Australian Union of Students in 1983, then became the union's national president. She worked as a solicitor with the law firm Slater & Gordon and became a partner in 1990. In May 1996 she was appointed chief of staff to the then Victorian Opposition leader, John Brumby, and worked with Brumby until her election to Federal Parliament in 1998.

She served as a member of several committees before entering Labor's shadow ministry in 2001, serving in portfolios such as Population and Immigration, Reconciliation and Indigenous Affairs, Health, Employment and Industrial Relations, and Social Inclusion. Gillard was Labor's manager of Opposition business for three years before being elected deputy ALP leader in December 2006.

Gillard's social conscience developed in an environment where her parents struggled to make ends meet. John Gillard worked as a psychiatric nurse, often volunteering for extra shifts and sometimes working around the clock. At times he also worked in a second job in a nursing home. So Gillard went into politics wanting to change things in the area of employment, industrial relations, education and women's issues. She has also said she looks forward to a time when a mother is Prime Minister of Australia.

'She looks forward to a time when a mother is Prime Minister of Australia.'

Postscript

Despite her Labor credentials and performance as Deputy Prime Minister, some members of the media mocked Gillard's relationship with Mathieson. Referred to as 'the Acting First Bloke', he became the butt of 'handbag' jokes. Some commentators also criticised his appointment by Health Minister Nicola Roxon as one of the government's six honorary men's-health ambassadors. Mathieson's task in this role was to consult with men in ordinary settings—including pubs—around the country, find out why men in general are reluctant to seek medical

A Woman's Place is in Parliament

It had been a long struggle for women since Catherine Spence and her colleagues first won the vote for women in South Australia in 1894 through to 2007 when Julia Gillard became the first woman to become Deputy Prime Minister. Gillard was a self-made woman who climbed up through the ranks in true working class style. The daughter of poor manual workers who migrated from Wales to Australia to better their lives and who believed in education, Julia Gillard studied hard and excelled at school and university. She worked her way up through appropriate professions then won a seat for the Labor Party, performing well and positioning herself to stand for election on a shared ticket, with Kevin Rudd, as Deputy Prime Minister. No woman had dared to put herself forward for such a top position, but she won office, then served as Deputy Prime Minister—a role Catherine Spence could only have dreamed of. Next step for women: a female Prime Minister of Australia.

help, and urge them to get prostate checks. He then had to report to a group developing a national men's-health policy for the Federal Government. Mathieson said he could do this because of his rural background and thirty years as a hairdresser listening to men talking more freely than they do to doctors, but critics said he had no formal health qualifications nor any connection with men's lobby groups. Roxon stood by her appointment, saying his high profile would help him bring an important message to a wider community.

2008
PRIME MINISTER SAYS 'SORRY' TO ABORIGINES

'What would you like me to say, Nanna Fejo, when I say "sorry" in the Parliament in a few days?' the new Prime Minister, Kevin Rudd, asked the clan elder when he called to see her while preparing for his speech. 'What would you have me say about *your* story?'

Eighty-year-old Nanna Nungala Fejo thought for a few moments. 'What you should say is that all mothers are important,' she said, looking the earnest Prime Minister in the eye.

'All right, Nanna Fejo, I will,' Rudd said, as an aide jotted down her words.

'Families—keeping them together is very important,' she said.

'I couldn't agree more,' said the Prime Minister, a family man himself.

'It's a good thing that you are surrounded by love and that love is passed down the generations,' Fejo explained further.

'That's a lovely way to look at love—being passed down the generations,' Rudd said.

'That's what gives you happiness,' Fejo concluded, with a look of wisdom that impressed the young Prime Minister, who now had a real basis for his landmark speech.

Inspired by the Aboriginal woman who had given him the soulful foundation for his 'Sorry' speech, Rudd stood in Federal Parliament a few days later, on 13 February 2008, and, in front of a hushed audience of MPs and citizens in the public gallery, said: 'I move that today we honour the indigenous peoples of this land, the oldest continuing cultures in human history.'

He continued: 'We reflect on their past mistreatment. We reflect in particular on the mistreatment of those who were Stolen Generations—this blemished chapter in our nation's history.' The Prime Minister told Fejo's story, recounting how as a child she had been taken away from her mother and put in a series of institutions. 'She never saw her mum again.'

Rudd told Australians:

'There comes a time in the history of nations when their peoples must become fully reconciled to their past if they are to go forward with confidence to embrace their future.'

The time has now come for the nation to turn a new page in Australia's history by righting the wrongs of the past and so moving forward with confidence to the future. We apologise for the laws and policies of successive parliaments and governments that have inflicted profound grief, suffering and loss on these our fellow Australians. We apologise especially for the removal of Aboriginal and Torres Strait Islander children from their families, their communities and their country. For the pain, suffering and hurt of these stolen generations, their descendants and for their families left behind, we say sorry.

To the mothers and the fathers, the brothers and the sisters, for the breaking up of families and communities, we say sorry. And for the indignity and degradation thus inflicted on a proud people and a proud culture, we say sorry. We, the Parliament of Australia, respectfully request that this apology be received in the spirit in which it is offered as part of the healing of the nation.

For the future we take heart; resolving that this new page in the history of our great continent can now be written. We today take this first step by acknowledging the past and laying claim to a future that embraces all Australians. A future where this Parliament resolves that the injustices of the past must never, never happen again. A future where we harness the determination of all Australians, indigenous and non-indigenous, to close the gap that lies between us in life expectancy, educational achievement and economic opportunity. A future where we embrace the possibility of new solutions to enduring problems where old approaches have failed. A future based on mutual respect, mutual resolve and mutual responsibility. A future where all Australians, whatever their origins, are truly equal partners, with equal opportunities and with an equal stake in shaping the next chapter in the history of this great country, Australia. There comes a time in the history of nations when their peoples must become fully reconciled to their past if they are to go forward with confidence to embrace their future.

IT WAS A GREAT MOMENT because the Prime Minister of Australia had just apologised to the Aboriginal people for the way Europeans had mistreated them and their ancestors since 1788. Such a thing would have been unheard of during the days of the First Fleet settlement, when the British were taking Aboriginal land by force; it would have been unheard of during the colonial era, when European explorers and settlers spread relentlessly across the country, using force where necessary; and it would have been unheard of during the period of the Stolen Generations as the governments and churches attempted a policy of 'assimilation'. The fact that the leader of the white nation apologised to the Aborigines 220 years after the first European settlement represented a real political, social and cultural crossroad for the descendants of those who had talked about *terra nullius*.

Two hundred and twenty years after British settlers on the First Fleet displaced the original occupants of the land, Prime Minister Kevin Rudd said he was sorry for the subsequent mistreatment of Aborigines—especially members of the Stolen Generations, such as Nanna Nungala Fejo, who were forcibly removed from their outback families to be brought up in white society.

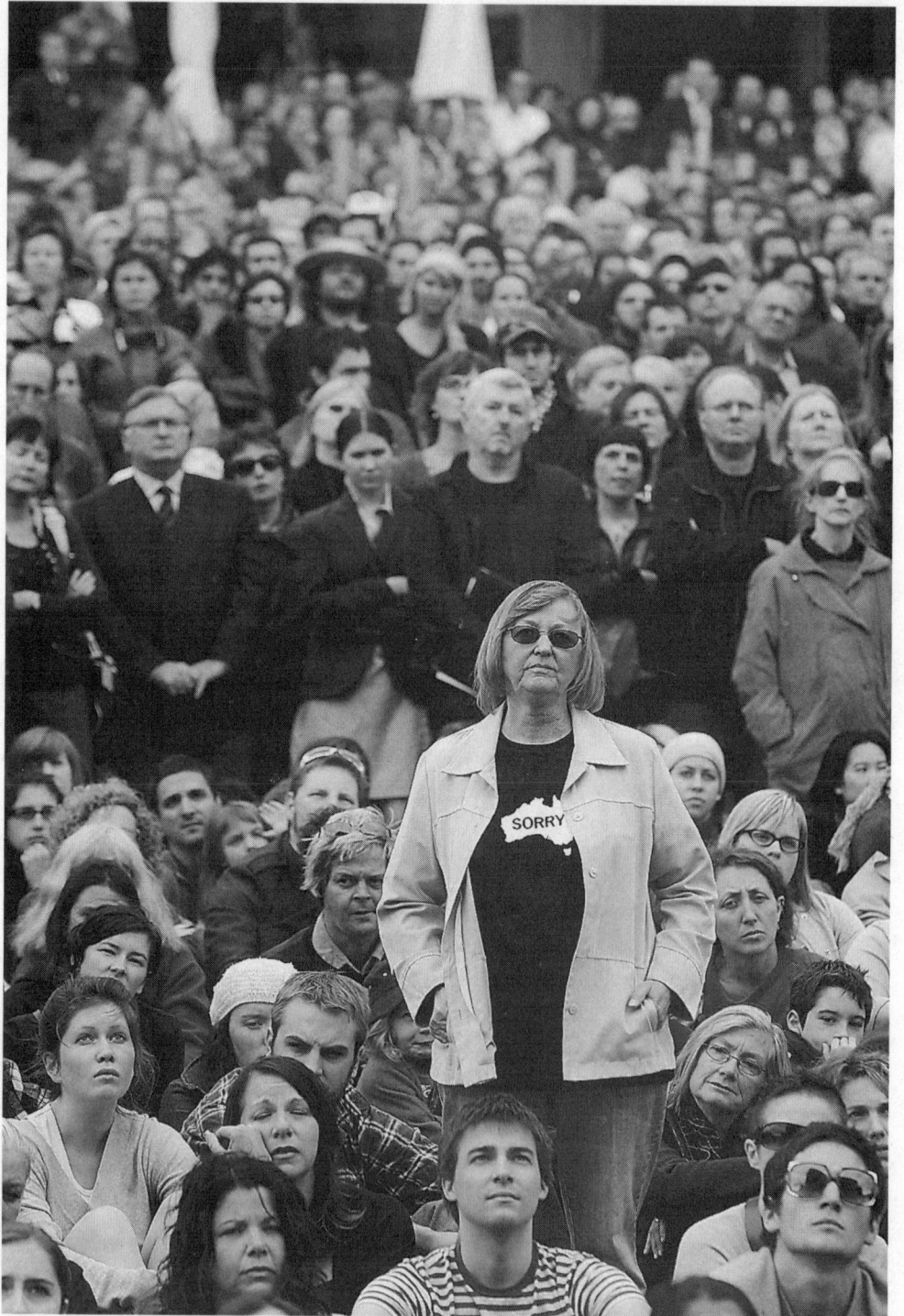

Prime Minister Kevin Rudd's apology for the mistreatment of Aborigines brought many Australians to tears as they watched his moving speech on television screens around the nation, confirming most voters had indeed wanted to say 'sorry'.

Historical background

Nanna Nungala Fejo—whose story was selected by the Prime Minister as representative of the Stolen Generations—was born in a bush camp near Tennant Creek. In 1932, at the age of four, she was kidnapped by welfare officers and an Aboriginal stockman and was taken by truck with her sister and brother to Alice Springs, where she lived for some time until she and her sister were taken to a Methodist mission on Goulburn Island, then moved to Croker Island. At sixteen she was allowed to leave the mission for an arranged job as a domestic servant in Darwin.

Kevin Rudd, who was born in 1957, developed a social conscience and respect for battlers while growing up in Eumundi, Queensland, where his father, a poor dairy farmer, died in a car crash when Kevin was eleven. An outstanding student, he attended Australian National University where he majored in Chinese language and history. Rudd met his wife, Therese Rein, at a Christian students' club. He joined the Department of Foreign Affairs, which posted him to Sweden and China, then worked for Queensland Labor Premier Wayne Goss before entering politics himself. He won the Federal seat of Griffith at his second attempt in 1998. After becoming party leader in 2006, he led Labor to power a year later on a reformist platform that included a better deal for indigenous Australians, to whom Rudd promised an apology should Labor win government.

Although government apologies were a new thing in Australia, Germany had earlier apologised for the Holocaust, and Canada had apologised for placing their children in residential schools as part of an assimilation effort.

An Australian apology was recommended by the 1997 report on 'the separation of Aboriginal and Torres Strait Islander children from their families', but John Howard's Coalition Government had refused, offering as one reason the risk of huge compensation claims. The Rudd Government's apology marked a milestone in the journey of the Australian nation.

Postscript

Although the Opposition had agreed with Rudd to establish a 'War Cabinet' to develop indigenous policies that would 'right the wrongs', the then leader of the Liberal Party, Brendan Nelson, delivered an ambivalent, half-hearted response to Rudd's speech—nothing like an unqualified apology. Those listening in the Parliament and in the grounds outside began shouting Nelson down not long after he started, then booed him. Many Aboriginal people stood and turned their backs on him.

The Prime Minister promised to provide every indigenous four-year-old in a remote community with early childhood education; to halve the gaps between white and black Australians in literacy, numeracy and employment within a decade; to halve indigenous infant-mortality rates within a generation; and to close the life-expectancy gap between Aboriginal and other Australians. There has been little progress on these aims. Indigenous people remain disadvantaged, especially in the Outback, where many are unemployed and on welfare and where alcoholism and petrol-sniffing continue, along with the associated domestic violence and child abuse. The Prime Minister did say: 'None of this will be easy, most of it will be hard, very hard—but none of it will be impossible.'

There have been many impressive advances since 1788, but there is still a lot of work to be done to bridge the gap between indigenous and white Australia.

2008

HMAS SYDNEY FOUND AFTER SIXTY-SIX YEARS

'Today's the day,' exclaimed HMAS *Sydney* search director David Mearns excitedly, his American accent still noticeable despite his long residency in Britain.

Mearns sat down in front of a screen displaying sonar images from his ship *Geosounder*'s remotely operated vehicle, which was searching the ocean floor nearly 2.5 kilometres below. 'I know it in my bones.'

'How can you tell we'll find it today?' asked Glenys McDonald, a director of the Perth-based Finding Sydney Foundation. She had been thinking, talking and dreaming about finding Australia's missing flagship for decades.

'We are approaching the coordinates where the Germans claim the wreck should be, and their coordinates for the other sunken ship, *Kormoran*, were spot on. I've found so many wrecks I just know when we're hot on the trail,' Mearns said, staring at the screen.

'I hope you're right,' McDonald said apprehensively. 'Finding the wreck of HMAS *Sydney* after sixty-six years wouldn't just be the end of our quest, it would mean so much to the descendants of those 645 sailors who went down with her.'

They waited as Mearns stared silently at the screen, searching for the slightest speck of evidence.

'What's that? Look . . . there she is—2468 metres!' Mearns shouted like a boy whose footy team had just won the grand final. 'That's it! That's got to be *Sydney*!' Then, turning to the documentary cameraman, he made the historic statement Australians had been waiting to hear: 'We've just found *Sydney*! We've got it. It's absolutely clear—you can take it to the bank!'

'My God!' McDonald—a nurse—cried out, bursting into tears. 'That's going to mean so much to so many people,' she said, wiping her eyes with a handkerchief. 'Oh my God. Oh my God.'

'And you know what?' Mearns added. 'She is at the *exact* coordinates where Captain Detmers and his crew said she would be! Those Germans from *Kormoran* were telling the truth—the records they left in German and in secret code were accurate, as I always said they were. They were exactly right about *Kormoran*, which we found four days ago, and the position they estimated for Sydney was right too.'

'But look at that wreckage,' McDonald said, still wiping her eyes and peering at the images of *Sydney* on the ocean floor. 'Now I understand why there were no survivors,' she sighed. 'She's a total wreck. The lifeboats and rafts have all been shot to pieces and the bow has broken clean off, which would have sent her straight to the bottom.'

'Now we know what happened,' Mearns said, 'after all these years.'

IT WAS A GREAT MOMENT because the shipwreck hunter David Mearns had just solved one of Australia's greatest mysteries. He had found the light cruiser HMAS *Sydney*, which had been missing since 1941—and uncovered the longed-for hard evidence about the nation's biggest naval disaster, in which all hands had perished.

It was 16 March 2008, and the news was immediately phoned through to Prime Minister Kevin Rudd, who announced it to an enthralled nation. On 1 December 1941, another prime minister, John Curtin, had reluctantly reported the loss of HMAS *Sydney* in battle but had been unable to tell his people what had happened to the ship or its crew. Now the discovery of the ship was front-page news, with photographs of the twisted wreck lying on the sea floor. It did not bring back the dead, but it told their descendants what had happened and identified the watery resting place of their loved ones.

Historical background

HMAS *Sydney* was Australia's worst and most famous shipwreck. On 19 November 1941 the naval cruiser was sunk in the Indian Ocean after a fierce battle with the German raider *Kormoran*; all on board were lost. While *Sydney*'s guns also

Even though critics claimed it was 'like finding a needle in a haystack', Ted Graham, chairman of the Finding Sydney Foundation, right, raised funds to employ shipwreck hunter David Mearns, centre, who, helped by Lieutenant Perryman, set sail on the *Geosounder* and found HMAS *Sydney* at the bottom of the Indian Ocean—sixty-six years after it was sunk.

sank *Kormoran*, many of the German crew escaped on rafts and lifeboats, with 317 surviving. The authorities interned the *Kormoran* survivors and interviewed them about the loss of *Sydney*. Despite all the evidence they provided, no search found either ship. It became one of Australia's greatest unsolved mysteries.

David Mearns, an American born in 1958 but now living in the UK, had found *Kormoran* on March 12 so he knew he was hot on the heels of HMAS *Sydney*. 'That's the Kormoran,' Mearns had told the cameraman filming his every move. Pointing to the image on the screen, he said, 'You can see the shadow of the wreck, that's it, and now our chances of finding *Sydney* are much greater.'

Mearns had a track record of locating high-profile wrecks, ranging from *Esmeralda*, part of Vasco da Gama's fleet and lost in 1503, to the Second World War British battleship HMS *Hood*, sunk by the *Bismarck*. Mearns, perhaps the world's leading sonar specialist, had studied the evidence about *Sydney*'s sinking carefully and come up with a 'search box' in which he felt certain he would find the ship. After all, if he could find HMS *Hood* at a depth of 3000 metres in the North Atlantic in 2001, it was likely he could find HMAS *Sydney* at a lesser depth.

Mearns said the key had been careful confirmation of their likely coordinates. He had initially got these in 2003 from material he found at the British Naval Historical Branch in London, in a research box marked PG—meaning 'pinched from the Germans'. The box with 'Kormoran' on its side, which contained accounts of the battle by German survivors, had been deposited in 1947 and never properly examined; yet some of these little-known accounts gave the coordinates not only of the *Kormoran* when it sank, but also of the *Sydney* at its last sighting.

It was a great moment for Mearns. As he said: 'At that moment I thought, "My God, this is incredible"—it was a Eureka moment. These positions had never appeared in any of the books written about *Sydney*. I'm pre-ordained to find the *Sydney*.'

Mearns gained more insights in Hamburg, Germany, from a German dictionary owned by Captain Theodor Detmers, in which Detmers had secretly recorded the story of the battle and sinking of *Sydney* by spelling out his account in a

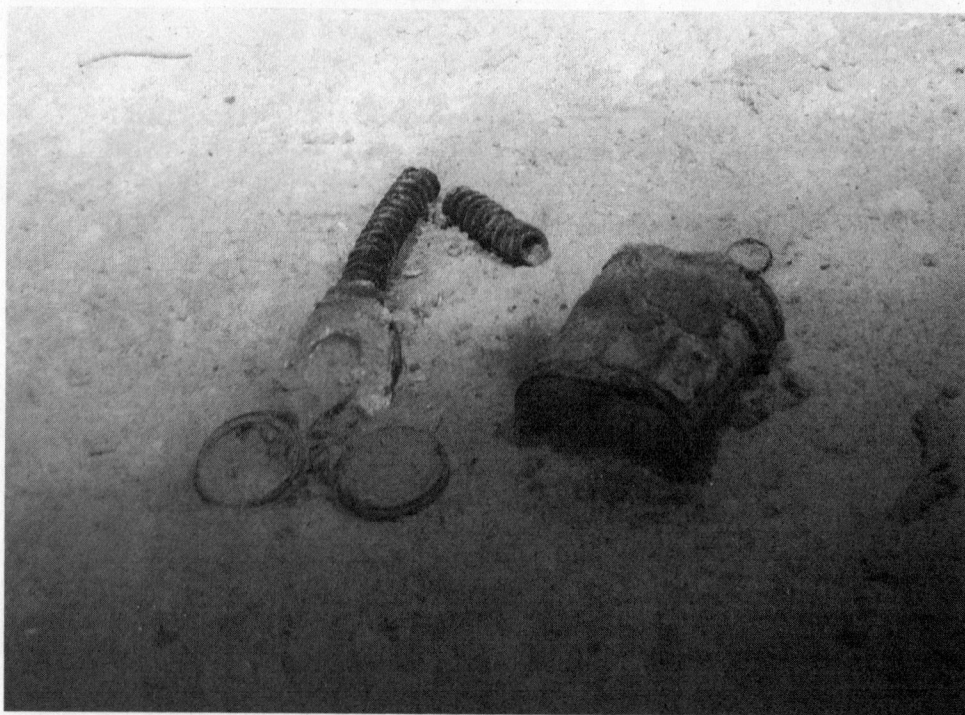

Using state-of-the-art equipment, the search party not only found, filmed and photographed HMAS *Sydney*, but also bits and pieces that had been on the doomed naval vessel, right down to gas masks found on the ocean floor where they had lain for sixty-six years.

code that used dots under key letters. This secret account also revealed the coordinates, giving Mearns further confirmation. Next, Mearns got hold of a copy of a notebook Detmers had with him when in prison in Australia which also had details of the battle in code, along with coordinates that confirmed the two earlier accounts. Now Mearns was ready to put to sea, though it would take the Finding Sydney Foundation and Ted Graham, the search leader, five more years to raise enough funds.

There were many theories and many people who claimed to have provided clues to the needle in the haystack task, but as Mearns said proudly: 'The bottom line is, I'm the one who went out and found the ships.'

Postscript

Despite all the conspiracy and other theories over the decades, after the wreck had been found and the Cole Inquiry had finished gathering evidence (from May 2008 to March 2009), the consensus was that the loss of HMAS *Sydney* was caused by human error.

After twenty-two days of evidence from sixty witnesses, 230 exhibits and 200,000 pages of archival material, it seemed that the camouflaged *Kormoran* had lured HMAS *Sydney* up close then removed its camouflage and fired the first shots. *Sydney* soon became a floating inferno, from which the crew was able to fire just enough shells to sink *Kormoran*. As the German fire had also destroyed *Sydney*'s lifeboats and floats, none of the surviving crew had a chance.

The discovery of the wreck gave the authorities the hard evidence it needed to establish the truth. As a result the Cole Inquiry was able to sort fact from fantasy, destroy the conspiracy theories and close the chapter on Australia's worst naval disaster.

'Mearns got hold of a copy of a notebook . . . which also had details of the battle in code, along with coordinates that confirmed the two earlier accounts.'

2009
RESIDENTS PIONEER 'GO' NOT 'STAY' IN NATION'S WORST BUSHFIRES

'That's a sight you won't see very often. It's called a bushfire sun.' Long-term St Andrews resident Gary Hughes stood beside his wife Janice and pointed up towards the orange orb glowing dimly through the massive plume of yellow smoke billowing overhead. Hughes tried to reassure himself that the Country Fire Authority was still publicly saying the fire at the base of the smoke column was at Kilmore, 35 kilometres away. What he and other local residents didn't know is that the fire, feeding off the unprecedented mix of fuel and weather conditions of 7 February 2009, had long ago overwhelmed firefighters and was racing towards them.

Black ash and burnt debris began to rain down. Then flames appeared about a kilometre to the north-west. 'I'm going to start hosing down the house,' said Hughes, a journalist with *The Australian*, putting into practice a well-prepared fire plan that had served the couple well each summer for the past twenty-five years. Fleeing under the CFA's 'stay or go' policy was never an option. Hughes and his wife had always planned to stay and fight, based on CFA advice. Besides, there was still no warning that what they now faced was anything more than a small spot fire.

'I'll try ringing triple zero again,' said Janice as she collected the family's pets in the bathroom, always considered a haven in the face of bushfires.

Rushing around the side of the house to start his petrol-powered fire pump, Hughes was unexpectedly confronted by a wall of flame racing towards him from the west, through the grass stubble of a freshly slashed paddock. In the seconds it took to fire up the pump, the fire was into a stand of trees just fifty

metres from the house. 'I'm in deep trouble here,' Hughes said to himself as heat and embers drove at him like an open blast furnace. 'If I stay here I'm dead.' Doubling back on his tracks, he ran inside to shelter 'until the fire front passes' like the authorities had advised him.

But inside he found the ember attack was like a fiery hailstorm from hell driving relentlessly at them with the wind, and the deadly embers, like the claws of a predator, were exploring every tiny gap in the house—blowing through the cracks around the closed doors and windows.

Frantically, he and Janice wiped at them with wet towels, fighting for all they owned, still hoping for the best. But then, despite their best efforts, the house began to fill with smoke, smoke alarms started to scream and the smoke got thicker. Hughes rushed outside to see if the front had passed yet. One of his two cars under the carport was burning; he rushed back inside to get the keys for the second car and reversed it to an open area in front of the house to save

Having survived Australia's worst bushfires, which claimed 173 lives, survivor Gary Hughes grieves with his family in the wreckage of their home and vows never to stay and fight bushfires now that climate change has arrived.

it—instinctive acts that would save their lives. Bolting around the side of the house, he saw that the plastic plant pots were on fire and turned on the garden hose—but nothing came out. The flames had melted it. He picked up a carefully positioned plastic bucket, but its metal handle just ripped out of the melting sides. Radiant heat drove him back inside. The smoke was now much thicker. There were now flames behind the louvres into the storage room. He opened the door and there was a fire burning fiercely inside the room.

Hughes finally registered, 'The house is gone—we are now fighting for our lives.'

Hughes and his wife Janice rushed into the last room in the house, furthest from where the firestorm hit, and slammed the door. But the room filled with black toxic smoke. He suddenly remembered CFA advice: 'When there is nothing else, a car might save you.' He rushed through a door onto the veranda, through the blast furnace to the remaining car to get it started. He wrenched open the car door, but there was no key in the ignition. Back up into the house he bolted, wondering in the chaos of thoughts, 'Where in hell did I put it?'

In the thick black toxic smoke, he couldn't even see Janice, whom he heard gasping and coughing. Groping desperately for the spare set in her handbag, which he couldn't see because of the smoke, he eventually felt the plastic spider chain attached to her keys. The crazy thought occurred to him that their lives would be saved by a plastic spider, which their daughter had given Janice as a joke.

'Time has run out—we have to get to the car!' he told his wife. They did, and with one last horrified glance back at their home, now blazing fiercely just metres away, he drove off—straight into fallen branches blocking the driveway. But he couldn't reverse because there were sheets of red-hot roofing metal blowing towards them. He put his foot down, ploughed through the branches and drove them safely into an open area. Here, trapped in the sanctuary of their car, they watched the fire destroying the houses of their neighbours all around them—and resolved never to stay and fight a fire again.

IT WAS A GREAT MOMENT because an ordinary citizen, Gary Hughes, with his wife Janice, had realised that this Black Saturday bushfire was a whole new kind of fire, and that no matter what the authorities said about staying to fight a fire, residents had to take matters into their own hands and go. Most of those who made the same decision and left rather than staying and fighting to the bitter end lived. Sadly, 173 people did not get out in time. But Gary Hughes left no doubt about the wisdom of his choice in his story, which was published in *The Australian* newspaper on 9 February 2009. Three days later, environmentalist Dr Tim Flannery wrote in the *Sydney Morning Herald* that 'This fire was different from anything seen before.' It was a fire fuelled by the unprecedented conditions of global warming, he said. These included a greenhouse-gas build-up, 'much of it from coal burning' in Victoria, 'which has the most polluting coal power plant on earth'; temperatures exceeding 46 degrees Celsius; twelve-year drought-dried bush, bone-dry plants and desiccated soil. 'And there is now no doubt that emissions pollution is laying the conditions necessary for more such fires,' Flannery added. The July 2008 edition of *National Geographic* had already claimed that because of permanent drought caused by global warming, 'these bad conditions could become routine and fires will return—bigger, hotter and more destructive than ever'.

Some residents realised this was the first of the unfightable future fires and got out—against the old advice to prepare well, stay and defend one's home. Their decision to go rather than stay marked a turning point, for these pioneers realised, well ahead of the government and fire-fighting organisations, that the age of global-warming fires had arrived. By taking an independent stand, they showed the way to save lives in the future. Others who chose to stay and fight died huddled in their burning homes.

Gary Hughes said that had he and Janice known what they know now, they would never have stayed and tried to fight the fire at all. The firefighting authorities were so disorganised, he said, that they soon lost control of the fires. Yet they did not admit this and warn residents to go. They did not know where the fires were, how big they would be, how many there would be, how fast they would travel, nor their ferocity. If the authorities had broadcast an adequate warning, Hughes said, nobody would have stayed.

The unprecedented words used by others who escaped the fires confirmed this new era had arrived: roller-coaster speed, skyscraper-high walls of fire, tsunami waves of fire, terrorist firebombs, explosions going off like atomic bombs, nuclear holocaust and so on.

Having learnt his lesson, Hughes said, he would never rebuild there. Asked where he and his wife would live in future, he replied, 'Wherever there is a whole lot of concrete.' As he concluded, speaking for many: 'It will change forever the way we look at bushfires.'

"'I'm in deep trouble here," Hughes said to himself as heat and embers drove at him like an open blast furnace. "If I stay here I'm dead.'"

Historical background

The Black Saturday bushfires were by far the nation's worst, claiming 173 lives and destroying at least 2000 homes in a large number of Victorian towns including Kinglake, Marysville, St Andrews and Flowerdale. The death toll was 100 more than that of the worst fires before these, the 1983 Ash Wednesday bushfires, which claimed seventy-three lives.

Sadly, many who obeyed instructions and stayed to fight died, including Lloyd Martin and his wife Mary, of Humevale. Their daughter Marisa Robbins told *The Age* on 12 February 2009 that 'the stay or go advice was nonsense' because 'in those extraordinary conditions you cannot defend your home, you have to go'. Said Robbins, 'Dad wasn't an idiot. Had he been given those instructions he would have left.' Robbins said her parents had everything needed to defend their house from an old-style fire. 'But with such high temperatures, forty-six degrees, and gale-force winds, to be putting out a message to people that implied they'd be able to beat the fire on a day like that—is just not on.'

Marysville was one of the worst-affected towns in the 'Black Saturday' bushfires; most of the houses were burnt to the ground, leaving an unprecedented scene of devastation— the picture was similar in Kinglake, Marysville, St Andrews and Flowerdale.

Postscript

Despite the terrible toll and the Victorian Government's long, exhaustive and expensive official Teague Royal Commission into the bushfires, it appeared as this book went to press that the responsible fire-fighting authorities still refused to admit their mistakes—and, worst of all, still refused to acknowledge that we had entered a new era that demanded a new policy of 'go' not 'stay'.

Unwilling to acknowledge the warnings, the government and fire-fighting authorities still seemed focused on more of the same, condemning future generations to impossible attempts to save their houses and their lives. They generously provided relief aid, helped people rebuild potential death-trap homes in dense bushland, offered residents more tips on saving their homes, but refused to increase the size of escape roads from fire-prone bushland, refused to commit to ordering mandatory evacuations in future fires, and refused to advise residents to move to 'wherever there is a whole lot of concrete'. Perhaps it takes a personal experience like Gary and Janice Hughes had to change one's thinking.

2009
CAPTAIN BLIGH'S DESCENDANT BECOMES FIRST ELECTED FEMALE PREMIER

'**Y**ou don't think these media articles about Captain Bligh will spoil my chances of winning the election, do you?' Premier Anna Bligh asked her husband, Greg Withers, as she pulled on her tracksuit at the back of their vehicle, parked among runners warming up for the start of the Gold Coast Half-Marathon.

'Why would it?' her husband asked, getting her gym shoes out of the family sports bag. 'The public has known ever since that 2006 *Gold Coast Bulletin* article that you are the great-great-great-great-granddaughter of William Bligh.'

'Yes, but I don't want any newspapers predicting I will drive my ministers so hard they will mutiny like Fletcher Christian did in 1789 against Bligh on the *Bounty*!' she said, lacing up her shoes.

'Yeah, but Bligh survived,' Withers said reassuringly.

'But then the troops also mutinied against him later when he was Governor of New South Wales—not a very good staff management track record,' she said with a laugh.

'But again he survived, and the British Government cleared him of all blame . . . you'll be right, the voters will see you as a great survivor,' he said, packing away her clothes. 'And don't forget, that article which also said your great-great-great-grandfather, Richard Bligh, was a barrister who served in the House of Lords—that'll attract the right-wing votes, anyway.'

'Well, I've tried to be bipartisan in my response to the disasters that have dominated this election, especially the floods in the north-west, that cyclone threat and the huge oil spill along the coast,' she said, picking up a water bottle.

It may have taken over 150 years for the first female to be elected Premier after the individual colonies (which later became states) won self-government from Britain, but when Anna Bligh took her place among the dark-suited prime minister and premiers she certainly made an impact.

'And you've won some right-wing farmers' hearts with your promises over the drought,' Withers said, throwing the kitbag into the back of the vehicle. 'And you've promised to create 100,000 new jobs,' so the left-wing workers will vote for you—and with your platform of social reforms I reckon you've got it covered.'

'But Greg, I believe in all these reforms—it's my mission to help across the board,' Bligh said, taking off her tracksuit bottom and shaking her calf muscles to loosen up before the run.

'You'll shoo it in—all Lawrence Springborg has done with his new Liberal National Party opposition is sing songs for the media!' Withers said, picking up her walking shoes and tossing them in the back of the vehicle. 'You'll be Australia's first elected female Premier.'

'Even though both the other women premiers, Carmen Lawrence from Western Australia and Joan Kirner from Victoria, lost their elections?' she persisted as she started warming up.

'But the people love you. Stop worrying about it and get on with this race,' he said, closing the back of the vehicle.

'I did get a text message from Therese Rein saying "Go Girl!" so that was encouraging,' she said, taking off her tracksuit top and throwing it to Withers as she moved off to join the runners.

'Enjoy the run—but save some energy for the main race,' Withers called after her, getting in and driving off.

Anna Bligh did go on to win the main event after this half-marathon. Not only did she chalk up a personal best in that race—despite blisters that forced her to finish in her socks—she also won the Queensland election 'by a country mile' on 21 March 2009.

'I did get a text message from Therese Rein saying "Go Girl!" so that was encouraging.'

IT WAS A GREAT MOMENT because Anna Bligh became the first woman in Australia to lead her party to a state election victory. Although two other women had served as premier, they took over after the resignations of their predecessors when their parties were already in power. Carmen Lawrence (Western Australia, 1990–93) and Joan Kirner (Victoria 1990–92) were also both defeated at the state elections following their appointment. Bligh had raised the bar in Australian politics, leaving only one political hurdle yet to be cleared by a woman: that of becoming Prime Minister.

Historical background

Anna Maria Bligh, who was born in 1960, grew up on the Gold Coast. After her parents divorced, she helped her mother run the household and look after the younger children. Initially she considered becoming a nun like one of her aunts, but was alienated by the Catholic Church's refusal to let her mother, as a divorcee, take communion. Bligh studied social sciences at the University of Queensland, where her social conscience was outraged after watching police beating protesters over the head at a right-to-march rally in King George Square, Brisbane. She then joined student protests against the Vice-Chancellor Brian Wilson's unpopular administrative restructuring within the university; helped the Women's Rights Collective, which campaigned against the anti-abortion policies of the Bjelke-Petersen Government; and campaigned against the distribution of *Playboy* on campus. She was elected women's vice-president of the student union.

After university Bligh moved to Sydney and worked for a child protection service in Redfern as well as the union that represented her fellow welfare workers.

She became secretary of the Labor Party's Fairfield branch in 1987 and met her husband, Greg Withers, a senior public servant, when he was handing out how-to-vote cards for the Nuclear Disarmament Party. They moved back to Queensland and Bligh was first elected to Parliament in 1995 in the safe Labor seat of South Brisbane. In 1998 she became Minister for Families, Youth and Community Care and Disability Services; she later assumed the Education and Arts portfolios. In July 2005, after Deputy Premier and Treasurer Terry Mackenroth retired, she was promoted to Deputy Premier and Minister for Finance, State Development, Trade and Innovation. The following year she became State Treasurer.

Beattie endorsed her as his replacement after announcing his retirement from politics in September 2007 and she was elected as leader unopposed. She went on to win the state election in 2009 by a comfortable majority.

Although she was the first to be elected Premier, Bligh was not Australia's first popularly elected female head of government: Rosemary Follett and Kate Carnell were both popularly elected Chief Minister of the Australian Capital Territory (in minority governments) and Clare Martin was elected Chief Minister of the Northern Territory (in a majority government).

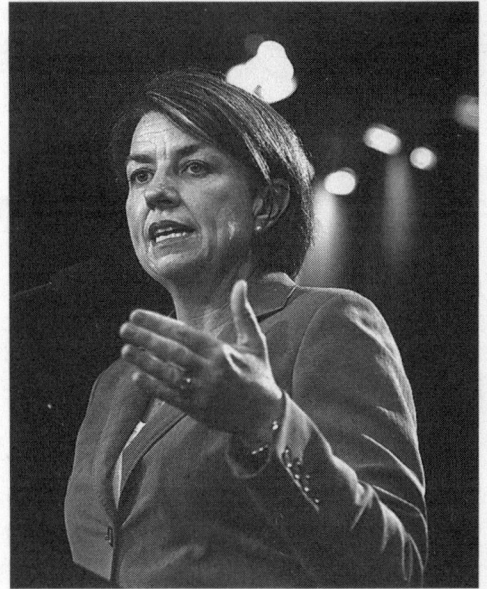

Two centuries after her ancestor the controversial Captain Bligh had been deposed as Governor of New South Wales, Anna Bligh won the first state election as a female Premier on a platform of political and social reforms that would have horrified the old tyrant, so feared for his dictatorial style of government.

Postscript

Anna Bligh, who of course was under heavy media scrutiny, could hardly have taken over the government of Queensland at a worse time. At the time of her election, this large state was faced with droughts, floods, oil slicks, the global financial crisis and the world environmental crisis. As Bligh said not long after becoming Premier, 'It's daunting in the sense that we are coming into a three-year period that is going to be very tough around the world.' Her first response was to launch a $17 billion public works program to stimulate the economy: the largest of its kind in postwar Australia.

Despite her popularity and impeccable behaviour in office, Bligh was criticised for appointing Withers as the head of the State's new Office of Climate Change, even though his experience as a senior public servant gave Bligh a first-class department head for the greatest issue of all—the environmental crisis.

ACKNOWLEDGEMENTS

The author thanks his wife, Jane King, who helped with the book from start to finish. He would also like to thank the following people, who gave freely of their time and knowledge: John Hampshire, who sub-edited the book at break-neck speed and with great spirit as only a high-powered, fact-checking newspaper sub-editor with great general knowledge can sub-edit; historical scholar Charlotte King, who wrote the Tent Embassy story and advised on content and assisted with research, inspiration and political balance; Professor Bain Attwood (Monash University), who provided advice for the Aboriginal Prelude; Professor Margaret Sankey (University of Sydney), who helped with Flinders; Professor Geoffrey Blainey for writing the foreword, historical advice and decades of encouragement; and senior *Australian* journalist Gary Hughes and his wife Janice, who so generously helped write the story about the 2009 bushfires.

The author thanks academic reader Nicole McGregor (Macquarie University); historical scholar Angela Lind, who checked early copy and who has participated in the author's historical projects from the 1988 First Fleet Re-enactment onwards; fellow scholar Anthony (Ace) Bourke, who helped with early colonial stories; Bill Fairbanks and Ken Gold, who helped with Flinders; Mark Robertson, who helped with Kokoda; The Royal Society of Victoria and also David Dodd, who suggested an Antarctica story; Malcolm Brown (*The Sydney Morning Herald*) who checked the 1941 HMAS *Sydney* story; Ted Graham (Chairman, Finding Sydney Foundation), who helped with the story of the wreck of HMAS *Sydney*, which he helped find in 2008; Sydney history teacher Helen Cooper, who read and corrected the page proofs; university lecturer and former secondary school department head Andrew Webster of Melbourne, who read and corrected the page proofs; and former secondary school head Ruth Forster, who helped with story selection, as did Belinda King, Philip and Katie Brown, Chris Nash,

Marilyn McGee, Bryony and Harry Lancaster, Mollie King, Alex Stafford, Stuart Walsh and Phil Maclean. The author also wishes to thank those who provided much-needed emotional support on this long haul: Kevin, Lowanna, Tallara, Edan and Juniper Doye along with Olive Lancaster.

The author also thanks the Authors Association of Australia; Susan Bridge; Jeremy Fisher; the Allen & Unwin team—Stuart Neal who conceived the project, senior editor Angela Handley who shaped the book so skilfully and Liz Keenan, the copy editor; Corinna Clarke of Photosonic, Avalon, and Courtney Raper for professional, high-quality painstaking scanning services; my old employer *Sydney Morning Herald* and Fairfax Photos, especially the fast, friendly and efficient Aimee Majurinen; News Limited and my old newspaper *The Australian*, which provided photographs so quickly, especially the 2009 bushfire photos; the National Archives of Australia, particularly Australia's fastest picture retriever, Pat Kuhn; the Australian War Memorial, especially my old friend and colleague Steve Gower, who has been so helpful with all my books and films; and the librarians at the wonderful library of Stroud, country NSW.

The author also thanks those historical characters whose stories are to be published and those still living who entered into the spirit of the fictionalised storytelling—especially those he sent copy to, including the Prime Minister, the Deputy Prime Minister, the Premier of Queensland and so forth. And, finally, the late Burnum Burnum (Harry Penrith), a treasured friend of the author (and his family), whose book—*Burnum Burnum's Aboriginal Australia*—was so helpful.

PICTURE CREDITS

The images in this book have come from many sources. The author has made every effort to trace and credit creators of the pictures and their sources; where he has been unable to do that he apologises and would be grateful if readers could contact him via the publishers to add any missing credits to later editions of the book.

Most pictures came from historical paintings, historical photographs, newspaper photo libraries, old copies of the *Women's Weekly*, private collections, and a wide range of secondary sources, including some of the author's previous books. He has also used photographs from private collectors who have provided these.

The author wants to thank the following institutions for the use of pictures throughout the book: the National Archives of Australia <www.naa.gov.au>; the Australian War Memorial <www.awm.gov.au>; The State Library of Victoria and La Trobe Collection <www.slv.vic.gov.au>; the State Library of New South Wales (Mitchell Library) <www.slnsw.gov.au>; The Finding Sydney Foundation <www.findingsydneyfoundation.com.au>; the Australian Olympics Committee; AP/Wide World Photos; Journal-Bulletin; the Tasmanian Wilderness Society; and the Greens Party of Australia.

Newspaper Libraries: The author is grateful for the special consideration he received at his former employer Fairfax, especially from Fairfax Photos which is a comprehensive image library and photo syndication service hosting award-winning photography from Fairfax Media publications, including *The Sydney Morning Herald*, *The Age*, *The Sun-Herald* and *The Australian Financial Review*. Updated daily, the site showcases a comprehensive collection of features, news, sport, business and lifestyle photography, as well as a range of creative and historical images from the more than 20 million images in the collection. Selected images from their extensive library are available as high-resolution downloads for home display and professional licensing. For orders and more information, readers can contact <fairfaxphotos@fairfaxmedia.com.au> or visit <www.fairfaxphotos.com>.

The author is also grateful for the generous assistance he received from his former employer News Limited, publishers of *The Australian* newspaper, who provided photos from their extensive photo library, where a wide range of photographs are available for readers. For orders and more information readers can contact <newspix@newsltd.com.au> and readers can also look at the photos at <www.newsphotos.com.au>. The author especially wants to thank *The Australian* for the photos of the 2009 Black Saturday bushfires to accompany the story written by bushfire survivor Gary Hughes, senior writer for *The Australian*.

Comics, cartoons and drawings: The author made every effort to trace the artists, especially the great comic artist John Curtis, whose wonderful drawings the author enjoyed in *The Silver Jacket* boys' magazine in the 1950s; the author thanks Curtis for the selected images used, but was unable to trace him through the Australian Publishers Association or North York Publishing Company and New Century Press Pty Ltd (both of which no longer exist) and who originally published these Curtis images.

Pictures were credited in the captions where the artist or photographer was known; however, in many cases these artists or photographers were not known. The author wishes to especially thank deceased Aboriginal artists for the use of their work; for Bill Fairbanks for permission to publish the map by Matthew Flinders; and the Historical Records of New South Wales for the picture of William Bligh.